GALATIANS
Liberated for Christian Living

By

DR. HARRY E. STANLEY II

PUBLISHING

A division of Squire Publishers, Inc.
4500 College Blvd.
Leawood, KS 66211
Phone: 1 (888) 888-7696

ISBN: 1-58597-038-7

Library of Congress Catalog Card No. 00 133110

A division of Squire Publishers, Inc.
4500 College Blvd.
Leawood, KS 66211
Phone: 1 (888) 888-7696

Before you read this book,

"Are you 100% sure if you died today that you would go to Heaven?"

If you are 100% for sure that you are going to heaven, GREAT! If not let me tell you how you can be.

The Bible clearly states that all men will die and face judgment one day. *Hebrews 9:27 states, "It is appointed unto men once to die, but after this the judgment."* This includes you. This judgment that is mentioned concerns what we have done with Jesus Christ while physically alive on this planet. If you will, from your heart, acknowledge and turn from your sin, placing your faith in God's only begotten son, God the Son, Jesus Christ as your personal Savior you can be saved from your sins for all eternity.

I mentioned earlier that all will face the judgment. In order to be ready to face this judgment a person must believe and act upon the following truth from Scripture.

1. Turn from your sin.

a. Admit you are a sinner.

The Bible says in Romans 3:10, *"There is none righteous, no, not one."* Again in Romans 3:23, *"For all have sinned, and come short of the glory of God."* Have you ever humbly admitted your faults to someone? The most important person in the universe to humble yourself before for your sin (All the bad things you have done — lying, stealing, cheating, immorality, murder, cursing, etc.) is God. God has already declared that you, along with every other human being born into this world, is a sinner with a heart that has a bent toward sinning. You must simply humble yourself before Him and agree with Him that He is righteous, holy, and perfect and you are a sinner. *"Behold, the LORD's hand is not shortened, that it cannot*

save; neither His ear heavy, that it cannot hear: but your iniq-
uities have separated between you and your God, and your sins
have hid His face from you, that He will not hear." (Isaiah
59:1-2)

 b. Acknowledge there is a penalty for your sin.

 The Bible states in Romans 6:23, *"For the wages (penalty,*
what we earn) of sin is death; but the gift of God is eternal life
through Jesus Christ our Lord." If you'll notice all of this verse
is one complete sentence or thought. God is comparing what
we earn (wages of sin) with what He freely offers (gift of God).
Notice we have earned death (eternal, not physical, separation from God eternally in hell). The contrast is eternal death
with eternal life. Because all men have sinned, therefore, all
deserve to die and spend eternity in hell separated from God
forever. Yet God offers to all men this gift of eternal life which
is received when a person turns from their sin to trust Christ
as their Savior. John 3:16 states, *"For God so loved the world,*
that He gave His only begotten Son, that whosoever believeth
in Him should not perish but have everlasting life." If you have
never accepted Jesus Christ, God's Son, as your only way to
heaven and you decided to stop reading this now, and you died
today, you would drop into an everlasting place of torment
called hell. "Why?" you ask. *"He that believeth on Him is not*
condemned: but he that believeth not is condemned already,
because he hath not believed in the name of the only begotten
Son of God." (John 3:18) Spiritually, right now, you are condemned to an eternity without God in everlasting punishment
because you are a sinner. However, you do not have to go on
another moment in this predicament.

2. Trust Jesus Christ as your Savior.
 a. Acknowledge the payment of the penalty for your sin by
  Jesus Christ.

 How did Jesus Christ, God's only begotten Son, pay the
penalty for your sins already? *"But God commendeth (showed)*
His love toward us, in that, while we were yet sinners, Christ

died for us." (Romans 5:8) About 2,000 years ago Jesus Christ, God's Son, was supernaturally born of a virgin. He lived a perfect life. He never sinned, not once. He lived a righteous, holy life. The Jewish religious leaders of his day talked about living a righteous life and hated Him because they had an outward, partial conformity to God's Law and He perfectly kept God's Law. With a jealous hatred toward Jesus Christ, they had Him crucified. Not realizing that they were fulfilling the prophetic Scripture about their Jewish messiah which states, *"He [God] shall see of the travail of His [Jesus Christ] soul, and shall be satisfied: by His knowledge shall my righteous servant justify many; for He [Jesus Christ] shall bear their iniquities."* (Isaiah 53:11)

So why did Jesus Christ have to die? He had to shed His holy, spotless blood as the payment for the sins of all mankind to redeem (buy back) us (who are sold under sin and condemned to hell) back to Himself. *"Neither by the blood of goats and calves, but by His own blood He . . . obtained eternal redemption for us."* (Hebrews 9:12) Christ gave His physical life to pay for our eternal life. However, He rose again three days later from the grave conquering sin, death, and hell once and for all. Sometime after His resurrection, while speaking to the Apostle John, Jesus Christ confirmed this when He said, *"I am he that liveth, and was dead; and, behold, I am alive for evermore, Amen; and have the keys [power, authority over] of hell and death."* (Revelation 1:18)

b. Accept Jesus Christ as your personal Savior.

If you personally accept and simply believe the above truth stated thus far, then in order for you to be 100% sure that you will go to heaven when you die, you must personally accept Christ as your Savior. *"That if thou shalt confess with thy mouth the Lord Jesus, and shalt believe in thine heart that God hath raised him from the dead, thou shalt be saved. For with the heart man believeth unto righteousness; and with the mouth confession is made unto salvation."* (Romans 10:9, 10)

God, according to His grace, is offering you the free gift of eternal life through Jesus Christ right now. It is purely a gift and you can do nothing to earn it. *"For by grace are ye saved through faith; and that not of yourselves: it is the gift of God: not of works, lest any man should boast."* (Ephesians 2:8, 9) All you have to do is simply reach out and take it, receive the gift! *"For whosoever shall call upon the name of the Lord shall be saved."* (Romans 10:13)

You can receive God's free gift of eternal life and be assured of a home in heaven forever, if, from your heart, you (while acknowledging the above truths) would pray a simple prayer to God like the following prayer:

"Dear Lord Jesus, I know that I am a sinner and I deserve to die and go to hell for all eternity to pay for my sins. Thank you for dying on the cross willingly to pay the penalty for my sins. I, here and now, on _____(date) accept your free gift of forgiveness of those sins. I ask you now to come into my heart and save me and give me eternal life. Amen."

If you just prayed the above prayer, you need to tell someone today. *"For the scripture saith, Whosoever believeth on him shall not be ashamed."* (Romans 10:11) Please take a moment and write me and let me know what you have done as a result of reading this today so that I can rejoice with you, pray for you, and send you some literature that will help you get grounded in your new faith in Christ. When I was 13 years old, I personally knelt by my bed at home and prayed a prayer similar to this one on a Sunday evening after church. The next day I told my parents about my decision to receive Christ and the following Sunday I went before my church and made my private decision public by telling others. May I encourage you to do this as well.

Although the enemy (the devil) will try to convince you later that this was not important or "You never really received Jesus

Christ as your Savior," remember what God's Word says, *"And this is the record, that God hath given to us eternal life, and this life is in his Son. He that hath the Son hath life; and he that hath not the Son of God hath not life. These things have I written unto you that believe on the name of the Son of God, that ye may know that ye have eternal life."* (1 John 5:11-13)

Your decision to accept Christ as your personal Savior is the most important decision you will ever make in your life. Accepting Jesus Christ as your Savior is only a one- time decision. Once you are confident you have accepted Christ as your Savior, you should start attending a local, Bible-believing church. You should start reading/studying your Bible daily (please contact me if you need one). You should start praying and talking with the Lord daily. These events, when they become a habit for you, will help you to grow spiritually and closer to God in your daily walk with Him. May God continue to bless you.

Dr. Harry E. Stanley II

PREFACE

Although it is not necessary to know the original languages to be an effective communicator of the gospel it is a tool that will definitely enhance the student's understanding and hewn his knowledge of the Scriptures. Not all believers have had the opportunity to study and obtain a working knowledge of the original languages in which the Scriptures are written. Therefore, this verse-by-verse commentary based upon the original Greek text, the *Textus Receptus*, that is both grammatical and practical is an essential tool of study.

Definition of Terms

All quoted definitions in this section are from *Webster's New World Dictionary*, Second College Edition, published by William Collins Publishers in 1980.

1. **Westcott and Hort type text**. This is the Greek text based primarily upon the Greek manuscripts Aleph (Codex Sinaiaticus) and B (Codex Vaticanus). This includes Westcott and Hort's Greek text and those based in some way or another upon their Greek text, especially the *Nestle/Aland*-United Bible Society Greek text (all editions).

2. **MSS**. The abbreviation *MSS.* stands for manuscripts.

3. **Extant**. The word *extant* implies actually existing or presently surviving.

4. **Parsing**. This term is for defining a word's distinctive features such as a verb, which has tense, voice, mood, person, and number.

5. **Active (Act) Voice**. "Denoting the voice or form of a verb whose subject is shown as performing the action of the verb."

6. **Aorist (Aor) Tense**. "A past tense of Greek verbs, denoting an action without indicating whether completed, continued, or repeated."

7. **Future (Fut) Tense**. "Indicating time to come."

8. **Genitive (Gen) Case**. "Designating, of, or in a relational case, as in Latin, shown by grammatical inflection or by an analytical construction and typically expressing possession, source, or a partitive concept."

9. **Imperative Mood**. "Designating or of the mood of a verb that expresses a command, strong request, or exhortation."

10. **Imperfect (Imp) Tense**. "Designating or of the tense of a verb that indicates a past action or state as incomplete, continuous, customary, or going on at the same time as another."

11. **Indicative Mood**. "Designating or of that mood of a verb used to express an act, state, or occurrence as actual, or to ask a question of fact: it is the usual form of the verb."

12. **Infinitive**. "The form of the verb which expresses existence or action without reference to person, number, or tense and can also function as a noun."

13. **Middle (Mid) Voice**. "Designating or of a voice of the verb, passive in form, in which the subject is represented as acting reflexively."

14. **M/P.** *M/P* stands for Middle/Passive.

15. **Optative Mood**. "Designating or of the grammatical mood, as in Greek, which expresses wish or desire."

16. **Participle**. "A verbal form basically having the qualities of both verb (Any of a class of words expressing action, existence, or occurrence, or used as an auxiliary or copula, and constituting usually the main element of a predicate) and adjective (any of a class of words used to limit or qualify a noun or other substantive).

17. **Passive (Pass) Voice**. "Denoting the voice or form of a verb whose subject is the receiver (object) of the action of the verb."

18. **Perfect (Perf) Tense**. "Expressing or showing a state or action completed at the time of speaking or at the time indicated."

19. **Pluperfect (Plpf) Tense**. "Designating a tense in any of certain languages corresponding to the past perfect in English."

20. **Plural (Plur)**. "Designating or of that category of number referring to more than one."

21. **Present (Pres) Tense**. "Indicating action as now taking place or state as now existing."

22. **Singular (Sing)**. "Designating or of that category of number referring to only one."

23. **Subjunctive**. "Designating or of that mood of a verb used to express supposition, desire, hypothesis, possibility, etc., rather than to state an actual fact."

24. **Exegesis**. To lead or draw out, specifically in explanation of a word or a literary passage.

TABLE OF CONTENTS

GALATIANS
LIBERATED FOR CHRISTIAN LIVING
Introductory Notes

Historical Background of the book of Galatians

Gal. 1:2 states that this book was written to "the churches of Galatia." Scholars have not questioned this fact; however, as to the location of the churches of Galatia much has been written. The debate of location has come about because of the question, "Was Paul writing to the region that included north central Asia Minor or to a specific Roman province?" This question has been answered in such a way to satisfy both views. This conflict is known as the North Galatia theory versus the South Galatia theory. Sir William Ramsey states the conflict as thus,

> It is, of course, not open to dispute that Paul founded churches in four cities of South Galatia, **viz.**, Antioch, Iconium, Derbe and Lystra. The only point in dispute is whether Paul founded also another set of churches in North Galatia. The South Galatian theory is that no churches were founded by Paul in North Galatia;
> and that when he speaks of the churches of Galatia, he means the four churches in the south of the Province Galatia. The North Galatian theory is that Paul also founded churches of North Galatia, and excludes the four South Galatian cities.[1]

North Galatia. The term *Galatia* first became associated with a group of Gauls that migrated from Europe into Asia about 277-278 B.C.[2] This north central area of Asia Minor was known as *Galatia* to the Greeks and *Galla* to the Romans.[3] This same area was a separate Roman state and became known as Galatia approximately 232 B.C.[4] In 25 B.C. the king of the area, King Amyntas, died. It was at this time that the area either lost its independent rule or endowed it to Rome and became known as the Roman province Galatia, located in the northern section of central Asia Minor. Kenneth Wuest discusses some distinguishing differences between this and South Galatia, which was located in the south central region of Asia Minor, when he states,

> There was a wide difference between North and South Galatia in respect to language, occupation, nationality, and social organization. The northern section was still mainly populated by the Gauls, and was pastoral, with comparatively little commerce and few roads.[5]

This area was known as *Galatia* according to its geographical location during the first century and some believe it may have been populated by the Gauls only; however, this was not so. According to Sir William Ramsey,

> The method usual among New Testament Scholars, treating Galatia as if it were simply a country peopled by the Gaulish tribes, is an erroneous one and leads to much misapprehension.[6]

This region is the area that scholars presently call North Galatia when dealing with this subject.

South Galatia. South Galatia was the area in the south central region of Asia Minor located between Ephesus and Syrian Antioch, which were the capitals of the Asiatic and Greek Monarchs.[7] This historical region points toward the trading route and highways that many travelers followed. This aforenamed region also distinguishes the differences between this area and North Galatia. Some of these differences are brought to light by Wuest when he states,

> This section was full of flourishing cities, and was

enriched by the constant flow of commerce across it. This was the natural result of its geographical position and political history.[8]

One way these cities were kept flourishing and the highways open was by repopulating the area with people under Roman rule. One such person who was responsible for repopulating was King Antiochus the Great. He repopulated the areas of Lydia and Phrygia with 2,000 Jewish families and was noted for doing so by Josephus who recorded the words of a letter sent from King Antiochus to Zeuxis, his father, which states,

> Having been informed that a sedition is arisen in Lydia and Phrygia, I thought that matter required great care; and upon advising with my friends what was fit to be done, it hath been thought proper to remove two thousand families of Jews, with their effects, out of Mesopotamia and Babylon, unto the castles and places that lie convenient.[9]

This repopulating was important because it was through this the Caesars of Rome could keep the roads open for their trade routes and for their military. The area known as South Galatia was very active and modern for that era, populated with Jews and Gentiles alike. Of course, there were more of the latter than former; nevertheless, the Jews were present.

Bible references to Galatia. The Bible refers to Galatia six times. The first two references are found in Acts 16:6 and 18:23. Luke, the author of Acts, in writing about Galatia in these two passages, dealt with the regions of "Phrygia and Galatia" according to the ethnographical areas. There is no question whether or not Paul had converts in this area since Acts 18:23 makes reference to Paul's "strengthening all the disciples" in the area. However, there are no references to churches being found in this area, instead only disciples.[10]

The next three times that the term *Galatia* is found in the New Testament the Apostle Paul uses it. These references are found in 1 Cor. 16:1, Gal. 1:2, and 2 Tim. 4:10. In both 1 Cor. 16:1 and Gal. 1:2, Paul makes reference to the churches of Galatia without specific references to any other geographical or provincial areas. *(See map in Appendix A.)* However, in 2 Tim. 4:10 Paul does refer to other provincial Roman districts than just the Galatian. From this, one can conclude that the only times Paul uses the term *Galatia* he is referring to provincial areas.[11]

The last time that the Bible uses the term *Galatia* is found in 1 Pet. 1:1. In this verse Peter refers to other provincial areas as well as to Galatia. Thiessen reveals this fact when he states, "Peter surely uses the term 'Galatia' in the political [provincial] sense, since he employs it in a list with four others, all of which designate provinces."[12] This statement leads us to believe that Peter also was aware of the churches in Galatia. In this verse, since he also refers to "strangers," he must also have been aware of the disciples that Luke mentioned in Acts 18:23.

North or South Galatia? The question that needs answered is, "Was Paul writing to North Galatia or South Galatia?" In coming to his conclusion on the matter, H. C. Thiessen asks some very pertinent questions:

1. Since Paul always uses the provincial names of the districts under Roman domination, never the territorial, except as the two were identical, is it likely that he would speak of Galatia in any other sense?

2. Would it not be strange for Luke to tell us so much about the founding of the Churches in South Galatia (Acts 13:14-14:23) and for Paul to say practically nothing about them?

3. Does it not seem strange, on the other hand, to think that Paul would write so weighty a letter as the Epistle to the Galatians to Churches whose founding is passed over in silence by Luke, as would be the case if the Epistle is addressed to North Galatia?

4. Would it not be strange also for the Judaizers from Palestine to pass by the most important cities of Iconium and Antioch in South Galatia, where there were a good many Jews and, no doubt, some Jewish Christians, and go to the remoter Galatian country in the North to do their mischievous work?[13]

These questions pose a very important argument in favor of the south Galatian theory. Even though there are scholars who claim this argument carries no weight, other Scripture backs up this argument in which both Paul and Luke use the names of the districts without making reference to the ethnographical areas. This can be seen often in these passages: Acts 2:10 (Romans), Acts 18:2 (Pontians), Acts 18:24 (Alexandrians), Acts 19:29 (Macedonians), 2 Cor. 6:11 (Corinthians), 2 Cor. 9:2, 4 (Macedonians), and Phil. 4:15 (Philippians). Both Paul and Luke name the people not by ethnographical background but by the name of the Roman province in which they are living. Hence, when Paul was writing to the churches in Galatia, he must have been writing to the churches of what is known as South Galatia.

Authorship

All evidence points conclusively to Paul the Apostle as the author of the Book of Galatians. He names himself twice in the book as the author in both Gal. 1:1 and 5:2. In Gal. 1:1 Paul declares himself to be the apostle called and sent by Christ Himself. In Gal. 5:2 Paul draws the attention of his readers back to who the writer of this epistle is when he states, "Behold, I Paul say unto you." He wanted the Galatian churches to keep in mind that the person writing this letter to them was the one that God used to begin them. The facts of the personal testimony that the Apostle shares with his readers in this book align themselves directly with Acts and other Epistles written by the Apostle Paul. The credibility of the authorship of Galatians is established both internally (what is written) and externally (all other aspects), so much so that even the most liberal scholars today believe, just as your most conservative, that Paul beyond a shadow of a doubt wrote the Book of Galatians.

Destination

Paul mentions right from the beginning in Gal. 1:2 that he wrote the book to the churches in Galatia. There has never been a question about that; however, the question has arisen as to whether or not Paul was writing to churches in the north central region of Asia Minor, to people whose forefathers were Gauls who migrated there about 278-277 B.C., or to the churches that he had founded in the south central region of Asia Minor, which were located in the Roman province of Galatia. As to the former, the only Biblical evidence of believers that we have is found in Acts 18:23 where it says that they went there to strengthen the disciples or converts. However, there cannot be found any Biblical references to churches in that locale.

When our attention is focused on the south central section of Asia Minor, the Roman province of Galatia, scripturally we find four different cities (Antioch of Pisidia, Iconium, Lystra, and Derbe) in which the apostle won "many" to the Lord, ordained elders, and started churches (Acts 14:21-23). These churches fell directly into the trading routes of that day which would have provided easy access to them for the Judaizers, not to mention that there were Jews already in the area stirring up the people against Paul on his first missionary journey. Some of the very people that Paul wrote to may have been there casting stones at him in Lystra on his first time through the city. Scriptural context and author can help determine to whom the letter was written. In Acts 16:6 and 18:23 Luke makes reference to the regions of "Phrygia and Galatia." Phrygia is not a Roman province but it is a geographical region; therefore, this reference to Galatia must be too. Also note that in Acts 18:23 there are disciples or converts mentioned but not churches. When Paul uses the term Galatia in 1 Cor. 16:1, Gal. 1:2, and 2 Tim. 4:10, he is not making reference to a region (north central section of Asia Minor) but rather to a Roman province (south central Asia Minor) just as Peter does in 1 Pet. 1:1. Neither Paul nor Luke ever called a people according to the name of their ethnographical background, but they did according to their Roman provincial name. With all of this Scriptural evidence, it is conclusive that the Galatian churches were in the south central portion of Asia Minor, the same churches that Paul began on his first missionary journey.

Date and Place

Paul most likely wrote this Letter to the Galatians between his first missionary journey and his second one. Scholars believe that Paul finished his first missionary journey in approximately A.D. 47-48. This would put the time of this writing about A.D. 49. He probably wrote it from Antioch of Syria since this is where he was believed to be located at that time.

Purpose

The Apostle Paul had a threefold purpose in mind when he wrote the Book of Galatians. First, he wrote to defend his apostolic authority in the Church of Christ. Since the Judaizers had attacked Paul's apostleship, he reminded the Galatians that he was just as much an apostle of Christ as the others in Jerusalem. Second, he wrote to divide the truth from the error concerning the mixing of the obedience to the law of Moses with simple faith in Jesus Christ as being necessary for salvation. The Judaizers had been adding circumcision as a necessity for salvation along with trusting in Christ's finished work on the cross. Third, he wrote the Book of Galatians to define the practical aspects of a mature believer in Christ who is living according to the Spirit. From the opening statement to the closing benediction Paul wrote the Book of Galatians with the emotional intensity of a marathon runner who is neck to neck with a strong opponent entering the last sprint of the race. He poured his very heart and soul into every aspect of this Letter to the Galatians.

OUTLINE OF GALATIANS

2. The Galatians' forgotten faith—3:1-5
   a. Paul's question concerning their betrayer—3:1
   b. Paul's question concerning the Spirit—3:2
   c. Paul's question concerning their maturity—3:3
   d. Paul's question concerning their suffering—3:4
   e. Paul's question concerning the miracles—3:5
3. The example of Abraham's faith—3:6-9
   a. Abraham's belief in God—3:6
   b. Abraham's children of faith—3:7
   c. Abraham's blessing to all—3:8
   d. Abraham's companions by faith—3:9
4. The curse of the law without faith—3:10-13
   a. A curse for those under the law—3:10
   b. The just live by faith-3:11
   c. Christ's redemption from the curse—3:12-13
5. The reception of the promise by faith—3:14-18
   a. The Gentiles receive it—3:14
   b. The example is of a man's covenant—3:15
   c. The promise is made to Christ—3:16
   d. The law does not disannul the promise—3:17
   e. The inheritance is received by the promise—3:18

B. The change in position from being a servant to a son—4:1-20
1. Christ has redeemed the servant and made him a son—4:1-7
2. The son must not turn back to the world as its servant—4:8-11
3. Paul chastises the Galatians for their following the false brethren—4:12-20

C. The challenge given in the allegory of Ishmael and Isaac—4:21-31
1. Bondage due to the flesh—4:21-25
2. Freedom results from faith—4:26-28
3. The flesh and faith and their children contrasted—4:29-31

IV. Liberation in loving action—5:1-6:10
A. Circumcision or Christ—5:1-6
B. Circumcision or the cross—5:7-12
C. Called or consumed—5:13-16
D. Contrary or crucified—5:17-26
E. Condemning or considerate—6:1-6
F. Corruption or crown—6:7-10

V. A benediction for the brethren—6:11-18
A. Paul's large letter—6:11
B. The Judaizer's glorying in circumcision—6:12-13

C. The Christian's glorying in the cross of Christ—6:14
D. The creature that avails in Christ—6:15
E. Peace and mercy upon the Israel of God—6:16
F. The marks of Christ—6:17
G. Grace with your spirit—6:18

[1] William M. Ramsey, *A Historical Commentary on St. Paul's Epistle to the Galatians* (Grand Rapids, MI: Baker Book House, 1979), 128.
[2] H. C. Thiessen, *Introduction to the New Testament* (Grand Rapids, MI: Wm B. Eerdmans Publishing Co., 1943), 214.
[3] Gromacki, 227.
[4] Kenneth S. Wuest, *Galatians in the Greek New Testament* (Grand Rapids, MI: Wm. B. Eerdmans Publishing Co., 1944), 11.
[5] Ibid.
[6] Ramsey, 18.
[7] Wuest, 12.
[8] Ibid.
[9] Flavius Josephus, *The Works of Josephus: New Updated Edition* (Peabody, MA: Hendrickson Publishers, 1991), 317.
[10] Thiessen, *Introduction*, 214-15.
[11] Ibid.
[12] Ibid.
[13] Ibid.

I. Salutation from a servant—Gal. 1:1-10
A. A gracious greeting—Gal. 1:1-5
1. Paul's calling—Gal. 1:1

1:1 Παῦλος ἀπόστολος (οὐκ ἀπ'
    Paul,   an apostle, (not from
ἀνθρώπων, οὐδὲ δι' ἀνθρώπου, ἀλλὰ
    men, neither by   man,   but
διά 'Ιησοῦ Κριστοῦ, καὶ Θεοῦ
by Jesus Christ, and God
    πατρὸς   τοῦ   ἐγείραντος
the Father the one who raised
αὐτὸν ἐκ νεκρῶν),
him   from [the] dead),

Paul, an apostle, (not of men, neither by man, but by Jesus Christ, and God the Father, who raised him from the dead;)

ἐγείραντος Aor. Act. Participle Masc.
    Gen. Sing. ἐγείρω Meaning =
    raised up, raised from sleep or death

Grammatical Remarks
    The word ἀπόστολος (comes from the two Greek words ἀπό "from" and στέλλω "to send." These two words together

describe the apostle as one who is sent from someone.

The word ἀπο, "from," is a preposition that can show direction, relation, agency and cause.[1] Here in this verse ἀπο is used specifically to show direction. Paul states that he was sent as an apostle from the direction of Jesus Christ and God the Father rather than from men.

The word διά is an important prepositional phrase that can be used to express direction, relation, agency, means, cause or purpose.[2] In this verse, the word διά is used to express agency. Not only does Paul give the direction from which he is sent as an Apostle, but he also gives us the agent sending him. He shows this when he states, "neither by man, but by Jesus Christ, and God the Father."

Paul begins his Letter to the Galatians, under the power and in the inspiration (God's unique "in-breathing" of His words into the human writers of Scripture[3]) of the Holy Spirit, by reacquainting the Galatians with himself. He states that he is an apostle, or an ambassador (one who is chosen and sent with a message with the full authority as a representative of the sender). An apostle in the Church was one who had been hand-picked and personally taught by the resurrected Lord Jesus Christ. After this brief introduction, Paul then delves into the specifics of an apostle and especially his own apostleship.

Paul states next who is his Master. How does he do this? He points out that his Master and the One who sent him are the same person. He first states who is not his master when he says, "not from men, neither by man." He states that there was not a group of men who got together and decided that they would send Paul out preaching the message that he preached. As far as Paul's apostleship was concerned, no group of men had sent him out from them in order to fulfill their purposes. Paul did not receive his commission, authority, or ordination from God through a mediation of men. In fact, he says that there was no mere human involved in his being thrust out as an apostle. He says that it was neither by man (singular), which refers to mankind as a whole. Paul then states that his Master is Jesus Christ. He tells the churches at Galatia that he has been commissioned by Jesus Christ Himself as one of His apostles. "He had been called by Him, and commissioned by Him, and sent by Him, to engage in the work of the gospel."[4]

Paul, concerned with the specific details of his apostleship, adds another person as his commissioner, God the Father. It is possible that Paul makes a distinction here at the beginning of his letter, so that both the true believers and the false teachers would note that Jesus is the Son of God. This fact would be relevant in his message later when dealing with the heretical teaching of the false teachers. They believed that placing their faith in the finished work of Christ on the cross would not be enough to save them. They also believed that they needed to keep the law to get to heaven.

Once these specific pillars of truth are settled, Paul then points to the centralmost truth of the gospel: Jesus Christ has risen from the dead. Paul points to this truth as the message that he has been commissioned to carry to the world as an Apostle of Jesus Christ. He includes both God the Father and Jesus Christ together to help the understanding of these Galatian Christians. They needed to have the facts restated to them. Jesus Christ is God the Son.

Illustration

Paul's appointment to be an apostle by Jesus Christ was very similar to the appointment of a Supreme Court justice here in America. Only the President has the privilege of choosing or appointing an individual to that position. The individual must then meet the approval of, and be passed by, the Senate. It is almost as if the Apostle Paul, here in verse 1, is saying that Jesus chose or appointed Paul, and God the Father had approved of it.

Illustration

There is a sense, of course, in which every Christian has an apostleship. We are all of us to be witnesses, no matter

what our other calling, profession or labor. A generation ago there was a wealthy man in the Midwest who was an outstanding Christian layman. People used to ask him what he did. He would reply, "I am a witness for Jesus Christ, but I pack pork to pay expenses." Your apostleship differs in degree but not in kind from the apostleship that was given by God to Paul.
— *Donald Grey Barnhouse*[5]

Applications
1. Paul states his purpose for life. Do you have a life purpose? Are you focused on accomplishing that purpose?
2. From whom have you received your life purpose — your friends, your family, or your Lord?
3. Are you sharing with others the message that Jesus Christ is the Son of God and has risen from the dead?
4. Is Jesus Christ your Master?
5. Has God placed a call on your life to full-time Christian service?
   Has God called you to preach?

2. Paul's companions-Gal. 1:2

1:2 καὶ   οἱ   σὺν   ἐμοὶ   πάντες
And the   with   me   all
ἀδελφοί,   ταῖς   ἐκκλησίαις
brothers, to the   churches
τῆς Γαλατίας·
of   Galatia:

And all the brethren which are with me, unto the churches of Galatia:

Commentary Remarks
     Paul goes on to substantiate this letter that he is writing to the churches of Galatia by showing that he is with other Christian "brethren." He does not give the names of the brethren with him. However, the fact that there are other Chris-

tians who are saluting these churches in this letter shows that they are placing their approval on the content of it as well.

Since Paul addressed this letter to the churches of Galatia, we must ask ourselves, "To which churches did the Apostle write?" If the churches that he wrote to were in the north section of Galatia, we have no record as to how many churches there were or to their locations. The only Scriptural references to converts in the north section of Galatia are to disciples. If he wrote this letter to the churches in south Galatia we would understand these churches to be located at Iconium, Lystra, and Derbe. This, of course, would seem to be the more probable, since these cities were close to the more traveled ancient trade routes of the day. Just as churches that are located fairly close together today associate with each other, and have the same character, so too these churches were very similar since Paul and Barnabas started them. Paul, knowing how close these churches were to each other on the map as well as the type of people in them, realized that if one were being infected with false doctrine, that it would be very likely for them all to be in the same situation.

3. Paul's compassion-Gal. 1:3-5

1:3 χάρις ὑμῖν καὶ εἰρήνη ἀπὸ
Grace to you and peace from
Θεοῦ πατρός, καὶ Κυρίου ἡμῶν
God [the] Father, and Lord of us
'Ιησοῦ Χριστοῦ,
Jesus Christ,

Grace *be* to you and peace from God the Father, and *from* our Lord Jesus Christ,

Grammatical Remarks

In the *Textus Receptus* this verse reads as is seen above, however, following is the reading found in some MSS: πατρός ἡμῶν καὶ Κυρίου 'Ιησοῦ Χριστοῦ. This reading differs in that the possessive pronoun ἡμῶν instead of being placed directly behind Κυρίου, the word that it is directly related to (which is a normal reading and placement found in New Testament Greek), has been disjointedly placed in front of Κυρίου, and separated by the conjunction καὶ. If this were the actual reading of the verse, then the complete statement "and our Lord Jesus Christ" would be separated and would place the genetive possessive pronoun ἡμῶν directly after the nominative noun πατρός which would not flow with the overall euphony of the verse. About the structure of the sentence, A. T. Robertson writes, "In general the words go together that make sense."[6]

Word Study

The Apostle Paul, probably more than any other of the New Testament writers, had become aware of God's grace in his life. Why would the Apostle Paul use this word *grace* (χάρις) at least four out of every five times that it is found in the New Testament if he had not understood what it meant?[7] Many times I have heard the grace of God referred to as "unmerited favor." This is mostly true according to its use in Scripture, except for the fact that it does not point out the originator of the favor, benevolence, or blessing. According to its use in many places in Scripture, it would be defined best as unmerited divine favor or benevolence. Anyone coming to God with an ounce of pride left in himself would be offended by this one aspect of God. In Scripture, this word is found to mean joy, . . . favor, acceptance, . . . a kindness granted or desired, a benefit, thanks, gratitude. A favor done without expectation of return; the absolutely free expression of the loving kindness of God to men finding its only motive in the bounty and benevolence of the Giver; unearned and unmerited favor.[8]

A difference exists between saving grace and living grace. An individual who accepts Jesus Christ as his personal Savior has experienced God's saving grace. However, he must continue growing in grace which goes beyond the salvation experience. This grace is seen in the life of the Apostle Paul when he was given a thorn in the flesh. When Paul asked God to remove it, Christ responded, "My grace is sufficient for thee"

(2 Cor. 12:9). This grace is also seen in Rom. 6:1, which states, "What shall we say then? Shall we continue in sin, that grace may abound?" This grace is the same power that we are saved by (Eph. 2:8), and it is the same power that we are to live according to, not in sin, but rather step-by-step in obedience to God and His Word. Just as the Christian has bowed the knee before God for salvation, so must he humble himself before God daily. As he makes this decision, he will receive more grace (James 4:6). In humbling ourselves, we too, as believers, can experience just what the apostle was hoping these Galatian believers would experience: God's wonderful outpouring of His benevolent favor in their lives.

Commentary Remarks

The apostle's customary way of saluting those to whom he wrote a letter was not kept out of this letter, even though he was about to upbraid them with the most stern words. Paul was quite aware of the make-up of the congregations of these churches so he addressed both Jews and Gentiles in his salutation. "Grace" was the Greek salutation and "Peace" was the Hebrew salutation. Paul greeted the Galatian churches with both the Grecian and the Hebrew greetings because of their multicultural backgrounds.

It is interesting to follow Paul's continuation of placing emphasis upon both God the Father and Jesus Christ. He desired grace and peace from both while at the same time, once again, he acknowledged the two on the same level of equality. By doing so, he displayed the deity of Christ again.

Applications

1. The Apostle Paul wishes both grace and peace upon the readers of this letter, even though he is about to scold them emphatically. He sets an excellent example for us by being kind to those who disagree with him; do you show this same Christlikeness in your life?

2. If you haven't accepted the Grace that God offers to all,

you never will experience the Peace that He has to give.

1:4 τοῦ   δόντος   ἑαυτὸν
The one who   having offered   himself
ὑπὲρ   τῶν ἁμαρτιῶν ἡμῶν,
on behalf of the   sins   of us,
ὅπως   ἐξέληται   ἡμᾶς ἐκ
so that   he might rescue   us   out of
τοῦ   ἐνεστῶτος   αἰῶνος
the[this]   present   age[period of time]
πονηροῦ,   κατὰ   τὸ θέληται τοῦ
evil,   according to the   will   of the
Θεοῦ καὶ   πατρὸς   ἡμῶν·
God   and   Father   of us:

Who gave himself for our sins, that he might deliver us from this present evil world, according to the will of God and our Father:

δόντος Aor. Act. Participle Masc.
    Gen. Sing. δίδωμι Meaning = gave, offered
ἐξέληται   Aor. Subj. Middle 3rd. Sing.
    ἐξαιρέω Meaning = delivered,
    rescued, plucked out
ἐνεστῶτος Perf. Act. Participle
    Masc. Gen. Sing. ἐνίστημι
    Meaning = present, impending, to be instant

Grammatical Remarks
    An added article in some MSS in this verse places too much emphasis on the wrong aspect of the verse. Compared to the above reading of the *Textus Receptus*, τοῦ ἐνεστῶτος αἰῶνος, which renders a literal interpretation of "this present period of time (age)," another text reads τοῦ αἰῶνοςτοῦ ἐνεστῶτος, which renders a literal interpretation of "the age — namely the present one."[9] It then becomes obvious that there is over-

emphasis added to the wrong portion of the verse. Which part of the verse is more important: that Christ offered Himself on behalf of our sins that He might rescue us, which is the positive centerpiece of the complete sentence, or that the present age is evil, the negative aspect? Is the wickedness of the age so much more important that it should receive added emphasis above what Christ has done for us? No. It detracts from the beauty of Christ's great rescue of us, His Church, according to the will of God.

The Greek word δόντος comes from δίδωμι which means "to give, offer, sacrifice, consecrate, or yield." Δόντος followed by the preposition ὑπέρ tends to speak of sacrifice or consecration of oneself in place of or on behalf of another. This definition is clearly focused on by the apostle in his choice of prepositions. The word order shows the relation of Christ to our sins. He sacrificed Himself in place of them. Christ exchanged Himself with us. He took our sins and placed upon us His righteousness.

The word ἐξέληται comes from ἐξαιρέω which means "to take out of affliction or danger, to deliver, followed by the accusative and ἐκ, out of."[10] It is followed by ἡμᾶς which is an accusative (object of a transitive verb). Since the believer is the direct object of the verb, Christ is delivering, rescuing, or taking him out. But the thought does not end here. The preposition ἐκ signifies the direction of the action when it is translated "out of." Christ gave Himself for our sins so that He might rescue us out of this present evil world.

Ἐνεστῶτος is a perfect participle which shows the state of the evil age (world). A. T. Robertson states, "The perfect participle either represents a state (intensive) or a completed act (extensive)."[11] Paul says that the state of the age is present with us now, or that it is impending upon us.

Commentary Remarks

Paul continues the opening sentence of this letter begun in verse 1 by focusing on the finished work of Christ. Why? Because this finished or completed work of Christ is the start-

ing point of the Galatian believer's faith in God. It is the starting point of the Christian faith. He knew that the Galatians
had lost sight of this truth and that it had been made obscure
in their eyes by the false brethren or Judaizers. He states
that Christ voluntarily yielded Himself as the sacrifice on behalf of their sins. In this first sentence, Paul has placed Jesus
Christ and God the Father on equal ground with each other
and then he reiterates what God the Son has done for the
Galatians. Each beautiful aspect of this picture must be
painted in the minds of these believers if they are to see just
how much the heretical doctrine of the false brethren has
marred their understanding of this truth.

As Paul further describes what Christ has done for those
whom He has saved, he reminds the Galatians of what Christ
has rescued them from. He describes the world and all that is
included in it. He describes this present age and the result it
produces in a person's life who has not been taken out of it by
Christ. "This age is evil, corrupt and corrupting, deceived and
deceiving. The word *evil* (Gr. πονηρός) means not only evil in
its nature but actively and viciously evil in its influence."[12]
Paul reminds these Galatian Christians how a distinct, 180
degree turnaround occurred in their lives once they were saved,
snatched out of this present evil world (age), and placed into
God's eternal family. Rather than having their lives affected
with the evil of this world, which would have caused them sor-
row over their spiritual position in this world, they had been
placed into God's family by the Holy Spirit. They had been
influenced by Him for good since they were saved. It is almost as if Paul is trying to help them see how different they
became since Christ had saved them by giving them the best
lifelike portrait possible, the world around them.

Why had they been snatched out of this present world? It
was the will of God the Father. Christ voluntarily yielded His
right to stay in heaven and limited His glory in order to take
on the form of a human and come to this world to fulfill His
Father's will: to die on the cross. Jesus Christ yielded 100 percent of His rights to His glory in heaven to come to earth and

die on the cross. Nothing caught Christ off guard or altered
His focus on fulfilling the Father's will while He was on the
earth, nothing.

Applications
1. So far, we have seen that Paul is committed to completing
    the will of God for his life. Christ was focused on fulfilling
    His Father's will; are you?
2. Have you even taken the time to discover what that will
    is, or are you still working out your own will?

> **1:5**   ᾧ   ἡ   δόξα   εἰς   τοὺς
> To whom [be] the   glory   unto the
> αἰῶνας   τῶν   αἰώνων.
> ages   of the ages
>   ἀμήν.
> [or (for ever and ever)]. Amen.

To whom *be* glory for ever and ever. Amen.

Commentary Remarks
    Just as Paul made reference to this present evil age (world),
he concludes his opening sentence focusing on the opposite age.
He glorifies God for all eternity for His will and what it has
meant to him. "It is not uncommon for Paul to introduce an
ascription of praise in the midst of an argument. . . It results
from the strong desire which he had that all the glory should
be given to God, and showed that he believed that all blessings
had their origin in him, and that he should be always acknowledged."13 It is just as if Paul gets blessed by the truth that he
is writing and gives all praise and glory to God for His mercy
and grace. Just as he recognized that God is an eternal Being,
so he desires his praise to God to be throughout all eternity.

Application
1. The Apostle Paul gives God the glory and praises Him for
    all eternity with his pen. Do you praise God daily and

glorify Him with your life?

2. With what areas of your life could you praise Him more?

B. A Shocking Scolding-Gal. 1:6-10

1. The Perversion of the Gospel of Christ-Gal. 1:6-7

1:6 Θαυμάζω   ὅτι   οὕτω   ταχέως
I am astonished that   so   quickly
    μετατίθεσθε   ἀπὸ   τοῦ
you are removing from   the [one]
    καλέσαντος ὑμᾶς ἐν   χάριτι
having called   you   into   [the] grace
    Χρστοῦ εἰς   ἕτερον
of Christ to another [of a different kind]
    εὐαγγέλιον·
     gospel:

I marvel that ye are so soon removed from him that called you into the grace of Christ unto another gospel:

Θαυμάζω Pres. Act. Indicative 1st.
     Pers. Sing. Θαυμάζω Meaning =
     marvel, wonder, be astonished
μετατίθεσθε Pres. Pass. Indicative
     2nd. Pers. Plur. μετατίθημι Meaning
     = carried over, removed, changed sides, turned from
καλέσαντος Aor. Act. Participle Masc.
     Gen. Sing. καλέω Meaning = bid, called (forth)
ἕτερον Adjective (Anarthrous) ἕτερος
     Meaning = altered, another, different

Word Study

One word that should be noted a little more in depth is θαυμάζω. Since this word is in the present tense, it is obvious that Paul has just received this news concerning these churches in Galatia. Luther, in his commentary, states that this word is as mild a word as possibly could have been chosen by Paul to express his amazement concerning the change in the Galatians.[14] Luther was right. In the Greek language, to express this same idea, there are approximately five other words that Paul could have chosen, they are θαμβέω, ἐκθαμβέω, ἐκπλήσσω, ἐξίστημι, and φρίσσω. The first word θαμβέω carries a very similar meaning to the word that Paul chose. However, the next four words all tend to indicate greater depths of marvel or astonishment. The next word, ἐκθαμβέω, bears the connotation of being greatly amazed or astonished. Ἐκπλήσσω is the next greater level of astonishment with the meaning "to be struck with astonishment, admiration or amazement."[15] The other word that Paul could have written was φρίσσω which has the idea of "to shudder or quake, to tremble." This appears to have been the word that Paul would have chosen if he were wanting to express the deepest shocking concern for the Galatians that he could. However, God the Holy Spirit did not choose for Paul to write this word since His condemnation for the Galatian churches, although condemning, reflected His gentleness. If the news would have caused him to be "worried" about them, he would have expressed it this way. However, Paul does not go to this extreme when dealing with the Galatians. Rather he scolds them mildly, showing them the true concern that they not only see they are wrong, but that they see God's care for them as he can best express it.

Grammatical Remarks

The reading, οὕτω ταχέως, in the *Textus Receptus* differs from that, οὕτως ταχέως, suggested by some other MSS by one letter, the movable ς. The use of the movable ς and the movable ν are very similar in that neither can be reduced to any clear rule.[16] However, Robertson does point out the historical use of both of these final movable consonants in the Attic and the Greek. In the older Attic (before 403 B.C.), these consonants were rarely used. The main MSS supporting another prominent Greek text employ the movable consonants at the end of words before both vowels and consonants with few ex-

ceptions.[17] Blass points out, however, that the Byzantine gram-
marians employed the rule that these movable consonants
should be used before vowels and not before consonants.[18]
From these facts it is obvious that the backgrounds of these
two Greek texts are from different regions. The Byzantine MSS
(which support the *Textus Receptus*) follow certain rules concerning these final movable consonants which would also reflect the findings in the older Attic, while the other texts seem
to have no guiding rule at all. The same can be said for our
later editions of the New Testament. Since Erasmus steered
away of Alexandrian type manuscripts and used mainly Byzantine, his use of these final movable consonants reflected his
findings in those manuscripts. The exact opposite was true of
Westcott and Hort. "The early New Testament editors used to
print οὕτω before consonants and οὕτως before vowels, but
Westcott and Hort print οὕτως 196 times before consonants
and vowels and only 10 times οὕτω (all before consonants).[19]
This principle being stated now will be displayed more throughout this commentary by the simple notations of the uses of
these final movable consonants. Its significance is that it shows
the unity between the Attic and the Greek as well as the ho-
mogeneity of the history of the *Textus Receptus* with the region from which the New Testament Autographs originated,
supporting all the more strongly that the *Textus Receptus* was
not only the "Received Text" by the Church in Erasmus' day
but also dating back to the oldest Byzantine manuscripts "received" by the early Church.

    Another difference between the *Textus Receptus* and an-
other leading Greek text found in this verse is in the phrase
ἐν χάριτι Χριστοῦ. In the other Greek text the word Χριστοῦ
is in brackets signifying a lesser importance on Christ than
on grace, ἐν χάριτι [Χριστοῦ]. One of the major flaws with an
Alexandrian type text is that many times when Christ should
be lifted up and exalted in the Scriptures (as He is in the *Textus
Receptus*), He is lowered to a less significant position than the
context within which He is found. Such is the case here. When
the person responsible for the grace has less significance than

the grace itself, the question is raised, "Which is truly being worshipped-grace or the One (God) who provides it?" The *Textus Receptus* keeps Christ in the right position emphasizing Him as the God of grace, the provider of it without demeaning His name.

As Paul is writing this letter to the Galatian churches, he conveys to them that he is presently astonished at the message that he has received concerning them. To do this he uses the progressive present tense to denote the continuation of existing results. Paul knows that for this message to have come to him, the situation had to have already taken place. When he received the message, he was probably awestruck to hear it, because he had invested so much truth into the churches in Galatia. He again emphasizes his amazement at them as a present reality, that is, the existing result of receiving such a message when he writes, "I am astonished."

Commentary Remarks

Paul shows his amazement at the hearing of the news concerning these Galatian churches. He says that he is amazed that they have changed sides from Him (God) who called them into the grace of Christ. His amazement is not that of utter horror or complete disbelief, which would lead him to harsh criticism. Neither, however, is it the type of compassion that is deeply emotional but lacks communication of the truth. No, rather Paul is showing his compassion for the Galatian believers by writing this letter to them to lead them back to the One who has called them into the grace of Christ. In other words, Paul received the news and it broke his heart to hear how the Galatians were doing. He chose his words carefully to direct their focus purely to the grace of Christ and the deep compassionate concern that Christ has for these believers. This does not mean that there is not a sting in the reprimand that he gives to the Galatians, but that it is accompanied with what drew them to Christ in the first place, His grace. Paul was simply surprised to hear what had been happening to these Galatian believers.

Who was the one that had called them? Scholars are divided about who this individual is. Some say that it was Paul since he was the one who started these churches in Galatia. Some say that it was Christ, their Messiah. I must agree with those who say that it is God. Just as Christ obeyed the will of God by dying on the cross, so these Galatians have obeyed the will of God in trusting Christ for their personal salvation. God must be the person to whom Paul is referring as being the One who has called them to the grace of Christ, because when Paul uses the word καλέω in reference to God, he uses it to express the blessings of salvation. Zodhiates writes, "In the epistles, particularly Paul's, there is found a more definite meaning of the word καλέω as the call of God to the blessings of salvation."[20]

Perhaps one of the most direct choices of words is found in the word ἕτερον, which is translated "another." This word does not speak of another of the same kind, such as when you have one banana and you get another one to eat. Rather, the illustration would be when you have a banana and you get an apple. Both of these are a type of fruit, but they are both distinctly different types of fruit. One is a banana and the other is an apple. So it is with this word here that Paul is using to describe the gospel. There is only one gospel that speaks of grace through faith in Jesus Christ. If there is anything different about it, then it is a "gospel" of a different kind.

You might ask what other types of gospels are there. I only know of one which is the one that Paul will go on to deal with, and that is adding anything (such as works) to the grace of Christ for salvation.

Application
1. Have you changed sides from the One who called you into the grace of Christ?
2. Have you fallen for another gospel of a different kind since you trusted Christ as your personal Savior?

1:7 ὅ   οὐκ ἔστιν   ἄλλο,
Which not   is   another
       εἰ   μή
[of the same kind],if not [except, but]
τινές   εἰσιν   οἱ   ταράσσοντες
some there are ones [that] troubling
ὑμᾶς καὶ θέλοντες μεταστρέψαι
you and intending to pervert [corrupt]
τὸ εὐαγγέλιον   τοῦ   Χριστοῦ.
the   gospel   [the] of Christ.

Which is not another; but there be some that trouble you, and
would pervert the gospel of Christ.

> ἔστιν Pres. Act. Indicative 3rd. Pers.
>   Sing. εἴμι Meaning = is
> ἄλλο Adjective (Anarthrous) ἄλλος
>   Meaning = another, unaltered
> εἰσιν Pres. Act. Indicative 3rd. Pers.
>   Plur. εἴμι Meaning = are, be
> ταράσσοντες Pres. Act. Participle
>   Masc. Nom. Plur. ταράσσω
>   Meaning = stir, agitate (roll water), trouble
> θέλοντες Pres. Act. Participle Masc.
>   Nom. Plur. θέλω Meaning = will, desire, determine,
>   intend
> μεταστρέψαι Aor. Act. Infinitive μεταστρέφω
>   Meaning = to turn across, transmute, turn,
>   corrupt, pervert

Grammatical Notes

The word ἄλλο which is translated "another" in this verse
means another of the same kind without any changes. It
means that the other has not been altered from the original
in any way.

Ταράσσοντες is an adjectival participial used restrictively.
This means that it "denotes an affirmation that distinguishes

the noun which it qualifies as in some way specially defined, or marked out in its particular identity."

The short combination of εἰ μή used here by the apostle has various meanings such as "if not, unless, except, and only."[21] In this passage it means "only." As Paul is writing about this other gospel, he limits its proclamation to only those people who are troubling the Galatians and who are perverting the one and only true gospel of Christ.

Commentary Notes

As Paul continues his discussion of the Galatians' being led astray to a different gospel, he gives a brief but clear description of this other gospel. He states, "which is not another." The Greek word ἄλλο is important because Paul clarifies what kind of a gospel the Galatians have fallen prey to. This word ἄλλο carries the idea of being in an unaltered state or being of the same kind. Paul states that this is not another gospel of the same type as the grace of Christ. It is a gospel that has been altered. It has been altered by human hands.

It was different and therefore no gospel at all. A message of salvation by works is not good news to lost sinners. The message of the legalists was diametrically opposed to the gospel of God's grace. When the works of the law are added to grace, you no longer have grace.[22]

Paul uses a restrictive adjectival participle to mark the ones who are troubling the Galatians. He describes them as the ones who are stirring things up in the Galatian churches. In his wording he uses the graphic picture as the ones who are "rolling water" or stirring it to cause it to move. He says they are agitating the believers in these churches similar to the agitator in a washing machine mixing the water, clothes, and soap together. These people are mixing up the grace of Christ and the law in these Galatian churches.

Paul next points out why these people are agitating the churches. He says that their intention is to pervert or to corrupt the purity of the truth of the grace of Christ. Anytime that anything is added to grace (such as works) then grace loses its purity. If a child has to do anything to receive his gift either at Christmas time or on his birthday, it is no longer a gift but a payment, a reward, a wage, or an earning. Paul is trying to tell these believers that if they are trying to keep their salvation that Christ has given to them by doing any-thing, it is no longer purely the grace of Christ.

Applications
1. Have you perverted the gospel of Christ by adding any-thing to it for salvation?
2. Is the gospel that your church preaches and teaches purely grace?

2. The passion of the curse on a preacher-Gal. 1:8,9

1:8 ἀλλὰ καὶ ἐὰν ἡμεῖς ἢ ἄγγελος
    But even if   we or an angel
ἐξ οὐρανοῦ   εὐαγγελίζηται
from heaven should preach a gospel
ὑμῖν   παρ'   ὅ
to you other than that which
εὐηγγελισάμεθα   ὑμῖν,
we have preached to you,
    ἀνάθεμα   ἔστω.
eternally condemned   let him be.

But though we, or an angel from heaven, preach any other gos-pel unto you than that which we have preached unto you, let him be accursed.

εὐαγγελίζηται Pres. Midd.Pass.
    Subjunct. 3rd. Sing. εὐαγγελίζω
    Meaning = declare, bring glad tidings, preach (the gospel)
εὐηγγελισάμεθα Aor. Mid. Indicative
    1st. Pers. Plur. εὐαγγελίζω

Meaning = declare, bring glad tidings, preach (the gospel)

ἀνάθεμα Noun (Anarthrous) ἀνάθεμα

Meaning = a (religious) ban or (concretely) excommunicated (thing or person),accursed, curse

ἔστω Pres. Act. Indicative 3rd.

Pers. Sing. εἰμι Meaning = be, is

Word Study

The word ἀνάθεμα has a very strong meaning. This word does not mean some kind of discipline that would come after disobedience. It has the meaning of a great condemnation. "Eternally condemned" is a good understanding. It basically means "a gift given by vow or in fulfillment of a promise, and given up or devoted to destruction for God's sake . . . therefore, given up to the curse and destruction, accursed."[23] Vine's defines the verb form of the word as "to declare anathema, i.e., devoted to destruction, accursed, to curse, or to bind by a curse."[24] Ἀνάθεμα is very much like the Hebrew word חֵרֶם which means "a doomed object, an accursed thing, dedicated thing, things which should have been utterly destroyed." Just as when God commanded Saul to "utterly destroy" all that the Amalekites had and spare them not in 1 Sam. 15:3. God meant for Saul to annihilate the people and their belongings both children and animal. Saul disobeyed and the Bible says in 1 Sam. 15:9 that he "spared Agag, king of the Amalekites, and the best of the sheep, and of the oxen, and of the fatlings, and the lambs, and all that was good, and would not utterly destroy them." Ἀνάθεμα not only means eternally condemned but facing the punishment too of being utterly destroyed.

Grammatical Remarks

Paul is writing a personal letter to the churches at Galatia and directs his statement on the preaching of the gospel to them in particular. He wrote "to you" specifically emphasizing the importance of the gospel in their life. This emphasis of the pronoun is clear from our *Textus Receptus* and it follows

a grammatical truth that G. B. Winer brings up about the use
of personal pronouns when he states,

> In the use of the pronouns the language of the N. T.
> agrees in most respects with the older Greek prose, and
> with Greek usage in general. The only peculiarity is
> (1) The more frequent use of personal and
> demonstrative pronouns, for the sake of greater
> clearness (or emphasis). . .[25]

This same genitive pronoun signifying clearly to whom the
gospel would be preached is in brackets in another Greek text.
It is treated as if it were not in the original autographs and is
simply an afterthought. This goes directly opposite of what
normal findings are in the Greek New Testament, yet the
Textus Receptus states clearly and precisely to whom Paul was
directing this statement.

Wuest makes a very helpful comment when he writes, "*But*
is from ἀλλά, the stronger of the two Greek adversatives. This
strong language shows how serious Paul considered the differences to be between his gospel and the message of the
Judaizers."[26]

Paul begins this verse with a concessive clause. "Concessive clauses are, in their essential nature, conditional clauses,
but differ from the latter in that with the condition the apodosis
attains reality by reason of the protasis, while in the concessive clause realization is secured in spite of the protasis."[27] A
protasis is the statement that contains the supposition and
essentially means "if." An apodosis is the statement that is
based on the supposition of the protasis and essentially is the
then clause. Paul was saying whoever, if anyone, preaches another gospel, will be accursed not because they preached it but
rather because they believed it. This concessive statement is
an emphatic concession which means that the supposed assumption has no likelihood of fulfillment.[28] Paul was saying
with added emphasis that there is absolutely no possibility of
Paul or an angel from heaven preaching any other gospel than
that which he had preached to them. Of course, not very many

men could make this statement so boldly as Paul could. Since not many men were taught personally by Jesus Christ and especially not one-on-one like the Apostle Paul for the duration of time that he was taught. Paul also had the confidence that no angel would preach any other gospel than that which he had preached since he had received it from their "Commander-in-chief."

Commentary Remarks

This verse shows the intensity with which the Apostle Paul is concerned about the gospel of Christ. "His own strong sense of the serious difference between the two messages is responsible for the vehemence of his feelings in the premises."[29] He pronounces a curse on either himself, those with him, or any angel that "preaches" **any other** gospel than that which he has already preached. This truth is significant even today because there are cults such as the Mormons that have other gospels. They advertise that they have the other "testament" of Christ (Book of Mormon) different from the Bible. Of course, they claim divine origin through the angel who delivered it to them. However, the Book of Mormon does not line up with Scripture, especially the gospel of the grace of Christ. Under divine inspiration the apostle pronounces a curse that would fall upon the fallen angels if they preached any other gospel (such as that in the Book of Mormon). They are bound by this curse given by God Himself to eternal destruction. "Another gospel" would also apply very much to the gospel that the Judaizers were teaching and accusing Paul as now preaching, that of adding observance of the Mosaic law along with trusting in Christ as being necessary to salvation. Paul proclaims directly that if he and the other apostles or even an angel would preach any "other gospel" than that which he first preached to them, then judgment would come upon them. Paul is very bold indeed when he includes himself in this pronouncement.

1:9 ὡς   προειρήκαμεν,
Just as we have previously mentioned,

κὰι ἄρτι πάλιν λέγω, εἴ τις
even now again I say, if any
ὑμᾶς εὐαγγελίζεται παρ᾽
to you preach a gospel contrary [to]
ὅ παρελάβετε,
which ye received,
ἀνάθεμα ἔστω.
eternally condemned let him be.

As we said before, so say I now again, If any *man* preach any other gospel unto you than that ye have received, let him be accursed.

προειρήκαμεν Perf. Act. Indicative
    1st. Pers. Plur. προεῖπον Meaning
    = foretold, said or spake before, previously mention
λέγω Pres. Act. Indicative 1st. Pers.
    Sing. λέγω Meaning = say, speak, utter
εὐαγγελίζεται Pres. Pass. Indicative
    3rd. Pers. Sing. εὐαγγελίζω
    Meaning = have preached, declared
παρελάβετε Aor. Act. Indicative
    2nd. Pers. Plur. παραλαμβάνω
    Meaning = received, taken
ἀνάθεμα Noun (Anarthrous) ἀνάθεμα
    Meaning = accursed
ἔστω Pres. Act. Imperative 3rd. Pers.
    Sing. εἴμι Meaning = be, is

Grammatical Notes
    The adverb of time, ἄρτι, is used in this verse as Paul reminds the Galatians that at some previous time (probably the first time that he preached the gospel to them) he made this strong statement to them. He tells them once again that he still stands by it when he says, "so say I **now** again."

Commentary Notes

Paul pronounces the powerful words of God by restating them. This time he includes all men when he states, "if any man." In other words, any man that preaches any other gospel than that which has been preached by Paul and others, that man will be eternally condemned. Paul tells us that he was not the only one who had preached the gospel of the grace of Christ to the Galatians because he states once again, "we."

Illustration

The penetrating words of the German Reformer Martin Luther flash through my mind concerning the preaching of the true gospel today:

If you preach the Gospel in all aspects with the exception of the issues which deal specifically with your time — you are not preaching all the Gospel.[30]

Application

1. Many times today we do not have to worry about whether or not the people in our churches are preaching the wrong gospel; we would just like to know that they are preaching the gospel.

3. The persuasion of men or of God?-Gal. 1:10

1:10 ἄρτι γὰρ ἀνθρώπους
     now For   men
    πείθω   ἢ τὸν Θεόν; ἢ
do I strive to please or [the] God? or
    ζητῶ   ἀνθρώποις ἀρέσκειν;
do I aim   men   to please (serve)?
εἰ γὰρ ἔτι ἀνθρώποις ἤρεσκον,
if for still   men I pleased (served),
Χριστοῦ δοῦλος οὐκ ἂν ἤμην.
of Christ a servant not I would be.

For do I now persuade men, or God? or do I seek to please men? for if I yet pleased men, I should not be the servant of Christ.

πείθω Pres. Act. Indicative 1st. Pers.
    Sing. πείθω Meaning = assure, convince, trust,
    believe, persuade, win over, strive to please,
ζητῶ Pres. Act. Indicative 1st. Pers.
    Sing. ζητέω Meaning = desire,
    require, endeavor, seek after, aim
ἀρέσκειν Pres. Act. Infinitive ἀρέσκω
    Meaning = please (through the idea of exciting
    emotion)
ἤρεσκον Imp. Act. Indicative 1st. Pers.
    Sing. ἀρέσκω Meaning = please
    (through that of exciting emotion)
ἤμην Imp. Act. Indicative 1st. Pers.
    Sing. εἰμί Meaning = should be

Grammatical Notes

Paul uses the word γὰρ, a causal conjunction meaning "for," in the illative sense introducing a ground or reason.[31] This is a normal use of this word and is expected here in this sentence as is found in the *Textus Receptus*; however, some MSS leave out the word resulting in a deemphasis of what the Apostle Paul is emphasizing!

Once again Paul makes use of this word ἄρτι. He is now reminding the Galatians of his purpose in life. He reminds them of Who sent him. It was not men who sent him so he is not striving to please men. Before he was saved, however, that was his purpose for what he was doing. Since, according to the Jewish religious leaders of the day Christianity was wrong, Paul's actions were pleasing to them (jailing believers in Christ). Paul says, "now" by way of contrast, that his actions are not to please men but God.

Commentary Notes

In the first rhetorical question that Paul asks he uses the word πείθω which means "to persuade or affect by kind words and motives." Paul is showing these Galatian believers that his goal is to please God not men. His goal is to please the One by whom he has been sent. He used to strive to please men as a Pharisee, but now he is striving to please the God of the universe. His goal now is to please the One who saved him and taught him personally the truth of the gospel.

Paul's second rhetorical question is stronger in its direction of where he is going than the first. He then asks, "Do I aim to please men?" One can sense the emotion in the statement because he uses the word ἀρέσκω, which means to please not only by way of relationship but by actions. Paul is saying that he is not living his life now for the approval of men, because if he were he would not be able to please Christ. Paul's life's goal had changed from trying to please the religious leaders on this earth to pleasing the God of this earth. The best way that Paul knew how to do this is revealed through his next choice of words. He says, "For if I still served (or aimed to please by way of actions) men, I should not be the servant of Christ." He uses the word ἀρέσκω again in describing his actions, but he shows what the motivation for his actions are when he says that striving to please men would render null his δοῦλος, or his bondservanthood to Christ. Paul had surrendered himself by choice as a bondservant to Christ, not men. Because of this, he now had one master, not many.

Applications
1. Christian, what are you living your life for? Are you striving to please men?
2. Are you a man pleaser or a God pleaser? You cannot be both.
3. Have you recognized just how great God's gift of eternal life in Christ is? Have you surrendered your life to Christ as His bondservant or slave? Why not do it now?

II. Attestation to Paul's apostleship-1:11-2:17
A. The certification of apostleship-1:11-12

1:11 Γνωρίζω   δὲ   ὑμῖν,   ἀδελφοί,
   I declare But   to you, brethren,
τὸ εὐαγγέλιον τὸ   εὐαγγελισθὲν ὑπ'
the   gospel   which was preached by
ἐμοῦ, ὅτι οὐκ ἔστι   κατὰ   ἄνθρωπον.
me, that not it is   according to man.

But I certify you, brethren, that the gospel which was preached of me is not after man.

Γνωρίζω Pres. Act. Indicative 1st. Pers.
   Sing. γνωρίζω Meaning = certify,
   declare, make known, give to understand
εὐαγγελισθὲν Aor. Pass. Participle
   Nom. Neut. Sing. εὐαγγελίζω
   Meaning = preach
ἔστι Pres. Act. Indicative 3rd. Pers.
   Sing. εἴμι Meaning = be, is

Grammatical Notes
   Paul begins a new paragraph here with the adversative particle δὲ, which in this use is translatable as "but." Some manuscripts offer a different conjunction, γὰρ, here in place of δὲ. However, Paul is not expressing a ground or reason, an explanation, or a confirmation or assurance, which are the many uses of γὰρ.[32] He is redirecting the attention of his readers in an adversely opposite direction of the previous focus, from man to God (Christ). It only makes sense grammatically, knowing that this is the primary function of the word δὲ, for him to use it in this manner in this verse.[33]
   When Paul says, "But, I make known to you brethren. . ." he is not saying that he was making it known at the very moment that he penned the words. Instead, he was expressing the fact of what he had done in the past with a present tense. This is called the aoristic present and it sets forth an event

that has happened in the past as now occurring.

Paul ends this verse with an aoristic present when he says, "The gospel . . . is not according to man." Paul wants to express a present fact without making reference to the progress of the fact or reference to past time. He does so with the aoristic present because it sets forth an event as now occurring. The fact that he seems to be reminding the Galatians is that the gospel that he preached to them is not simply that which has originated with man, nor would it follow that of a man's logic.

Commentary Notes

Paul begins a new paragraph with the word γνωρίζω, which is used to introduce matters of great importance. He used this word when writing to the Corinthians three times. The first time, found in 1 Cor. 12:3, deals with spiritual gifts and, specifically, the subject of their unknown tongues. Some were cursing Christ "in an unknown tongue" and attributing it the Holy Spirit. The second time is found in 1 Cor. 15:1, where Paul gives the greatest treatise on the gospel of Jesus Christ found in Scripture. The third time is found in 2 Cor. 8:1, where Paul begins to stir up the Corinthian believers to contribute to the saints. Each one of these statements that Paul has introduced by this word γνωρίζω have been close to the apostle's heart, since he had experienced the result of them. Now, as he writes to the Galatians, he leaves the introduction of the letter with the statement of who he is and what he is writing for, and turns down the first street of his letter, the one on which he lives, his personal testimony.

Paul not only states that he is an apostle of Christ at the beginning of this letter, just as he does in others, but he also gives his full testimony from before experiencing Christ's saving grace up to his one negative encounter with Peter, which had positive results. It is as if his apostleship has been attacked or challenged by the Judaizers, so Paul restates his own personal testimony to these Galatians. Many scholars believe his apostleship to have been attacked, and, with such a strong response from the apostle, they are probably correct. The Judaizers proposed, as evidenced by Paul's response, that Paul was just teaching what he had been taught by the apostles in Jerusalem, and that he was not truly an apostle as Peter was. Almost every point in Paul's response seems to negate an accusation of these Judaizers, beginning with the fact that the gospel which Paul had preached unto them had not come from man.

1:12 οὐδὲ   γὰρ ἐγὼ   παρὰ ἀνθρώπου
  neither For I   from   man
παρέλαβον αὐτό, οὔτε ἐδιδάχθην,
  received   it,   nor was I taught [it],
ἀλλὰ   δι'   ἀποκαλύψεως
but through [the] unveiling
'Ιησοῦ   Χριστοῦ.
of Jesus   Christ.

For I neither received it of man, neither was I taught *it,* but by the revelation of Jesus Christ.

παρέλαβον Aor. Act. Indicative 1st.
    Pers. Sing. παραλαμβάνω Meaning = receive, take
    along
ἐδιδάχθην Aor. Pass. Indicative 1st.
    Pers. Sing. διδάσκω Meaning = teach
ἀποκαλύψεως Noun ἀποκάλυψις
    Meaning = unveiling, uncovering, disclosure, revelation

Grammatical Notes
    The preposition παρὰ, translated "from," indicates and emphasizes the idea of transmission of the message from one person to another. Paul uses this word to show that the gospel that he preached or gave away was not received from man. The giver and receiver relationship that Paul did share was with Jesus Christ.
    Paul emphasizes himself here by expressly using the pronoun ἐγω with the verb and not simply the verb. Supporting this, Wuest writes,

The word *I* is not here from the person of the verb, but from the word *ego* which is the Greek pronoun meaning *I*. In the Greek language, the verb itself indicates the person doing the acting or representing the state mentioned in the verb, and therefore a pronoun is not needed as in English. That means that when a pronoun is used in connection with a verb, special emphasis is stressed.[34]

Commentary Notes

Paul was a very scholarly individual. He had sat at the feet of many learned individuals among whom was Gamaliel. Paul understood Judaism from the inside out. He lived it to its fullest degree of potential. Yet, when it came to the gospel, he was not taught it in its entirety by any mere human. He received it from the risen Son of God. In fact, Paul says that the gospel was veiled to his mind until Jesus Christ himself, in a way that only Christ could, unveiled it to him. Whether Paul was referring specifically to his experience on the road to Damascus or his secluded time in Arabia with Christ is not known. But what is known is that on both occasions Jesus Christ, the risen Lord, appeared to Paul and communicated with him in the unique one-on-one manner that He did with the other disciples. As He called them specifically at personal encounters with them, so He did with Paul also. He taught them personally the gospel, and so He did with Paul also. Paul had come by his knowledge of the gospel just as the other apostles had, at the feet of Jesus Christ himself. In this was Paul indebted to Christ and Christ alone. No other man was responsible for his knowledge of the gospel because he had acquired it entirely from the Savior.

B. The Conversion of Paul-1:13-17
1. Paul's Persecution of the Church-1:13
1:13 ἠκούσατε   γὰρ   τὴν   ἐμὴν
ye have heard For of the of me [my]

ἀναστροφήν ποτε   ἐν τῷ ’Ιουδάσμῷ,
way of life previous in   Judaism,
ὅτι καθ’   ὑπερβολὴν
that how exceedingly beyond measure
ἐδίωκον τὴν ἐκκλησίαν   τοῦ Θεοῦ,
I persecuted the   church   of God,
καὶ ἐπόρθουν αὐτήν·
and ravaged   it:

For ye have heard of my conversation in time past in the Jews'
religion, how that beyond measure I persecuted the church of
God, and wasted it:

ἠκούσατε Aor. Act. Indicative 2nd.
    Pers. Plur. ἤκουω Meaning = give
    audience, hear, understand
ἀναστροφήν Noun ἀναστροφήν
    Meaning = behavior, conversation
ἐδίωκον Imperfect Act. Ind. 1st. Pers.
    Sing. διώκω Meaning = persecute, ensue
ἐπόρθουν Imperfect Act. Ind. 1st. Pers.
    Sing. πορθέω Meaning = destroy,
    waste, ravage (figuratively)

Commentary Notes
    As Paul continues to build his case for the authenticity of
his apostleship, he reminds the Galatian believers of his
lifestyle and testimony before his conversion. He had already
shared this at other times with these churches when he
founded them (cf. Acts 22 and 26). Paul describes here in verse
13 his lifestyle. First of all, he reminds them that he was a
Jew both in belief and conduct. He followed all of the laws of
Moses, as well as all of the traditions that had become a part
of Judaism. It must be remembered that the Judaism that
Paul was brought up in was not the same that had been given
to Moses by God. In that religion there was salvation by faith
in God, believing that He would send a Messiah to pay the

price for sin. However, by the time of Paul, the Jewish people were longing not for a Messiah to free them from spiritual bondage but rather for a Messiah to free them from the political bondage of the Roman Empire and Caesar. It was this same religion that rejected and murdered Jesus Christ, the Jew's Messiah, rather than accepting and trusting in Him. The Judaism that Paul had been trained in was an apostate Judaism focusing only on the physical without considering the spiritual. Although by name and action it was the same Judaistic religious system established by God through Moses, it had turned into an ethical, unspiritual faction with human traditions superimposed upon it. This Judaism did not believe in salvation by grace through faith plus nothing; it believed in works. Until the apostle came face to face with Jesus Christ on the road to Damascus, he was trusting his works to get him to heaven, and he had some works to trust in.

It was in this religion without measure that Paul exceedingly persecuted the church of God. In fact, the phrase that Paul employs here, καθ' ὑπερβολὴν, he also employs other places when he wishes to denote something that is immeasurable or too excessive to be verbalized in ordinary language.

Application
1. When Saul the Persecutor became Paul the Apostle, there was a decided difference in his life. Christian, is there any difference in your life since you trusted Christ as your Savior?
2. Have you allowed Him to become your Shepherd, too?

2. Paul's profiting in his religion-1:14
1:14 καὶ προέκοπτον ἐν   τῷ 'Ιουδαϊσμῷ
    And I advanced in   Judaism
ὑπὲρ πολλοὺς συνηλικιώτας ἐν τῷ
above many   my own age   in the

γένει μου, περισσοτέρως
nation of me, more abundantly
ζηλωτὴς ὑπάρχων τῶν
zealous　being　of the
　πατρικῶν　　μου παραδόσεων.
fathers [ancestry] of my　traditions.

And profited in the Jews' religion above many my equals in mine own nation, being more exceedingly zealous of the traditions of my fathers.

προέκοπτον Imperfect Act. Ind. 1st.
　　Pers. Sing. προκόπτω Meaning = increase, profit, proceed, be far spent, to drive forward, advance
περισσοτέρως Adverb περισσοτέρος
　　Meaning = more frequent, more abundantly, exceedingly

Commentary Notes

In verse 13 the apostle tells us that he persecuted the Church of God and ravaged it. Why did he do this? Was it due to all of his years of training that he spent with the Law, the Writings, and the Prophets. No. Although Paul had much training in God's Word, he had just as much training, if not possibly more, in the traditions of men. Here in verse 14 he says that he advanced well beyond many his own age in his nation in his religion. Paul was a very zealous individual, and if you and I had known him at the time we would likely have said that he had wisdom beyond his years.

Paul received more teaching than from the Scriptures themselves. He learned much about the traditions that had been passed down from his fathers. At the time that Paul was going through his training to become a Pharisee, the traditions of the fathers were not recorded on paper for them to study. They were passed down from one generation of Pharisees to another by word of mouth. Today we could find these traditions recorded for us in the *Mishna*. When Paul says that he was more exceedingly zealous, he is saying that he made sure to pay close attention to every detail that was given. Certainly Paul should be praised for such zeal; however, it is this same strong degree of zeal focused on the wrong subject, the traditions of men rather than the Scriptures, that drove him to persecute the Church of God and which troubled his conscience later. By putting such strong effort into studying the traditions of man, Paul nearly nullified all of the right training that he had received when studying the Scriptures. Hence, murder meant nothing to him as a Jew, even if under Roman rule he had no right to murder those of other religious beliefs. Jesus Christ points out that the study of man's traditions will cause the Word of God to be of none effect (Matt. 15:1-6; Mark 7:3-13). It is very possible that Paul was trying to help the Galatian believers see through the zeal of the Judaizers as they pushed them toward practicing the law as part of their means of salvation. By showing them how vehement he was before he was saved, he would help them to see how wrong he was and how little his vehemence (and these Judaizers) meant.

Illustration

Some hill people in India called the Kurkue have a strange religion which demands that they should be filled with demons! When this supreme desire has been satisfied, they believe their lives will be immune to outward attacks from the Devil. While they recognize that a "good spirit" has created the world and brought them into existence, they disregard him because they feel he is too benevolent to harm them. A missionary who visited this tribe of approximately 100,000 declared, "If the same number of God's people had as their ultimate aim in life the desire to be filled with the Holy Spirit, I believe such a blessed surrender would cause a tremendous awakening. The evangelistic results would reach to all corners of the globe!"35

Application

1. Paul was just as zealous for Christ after he got saved as

he was against Him before. How about you, Christian: are you zealous for Christ in witnessing to others?

2. What is hindering you from being zealous for Christ in witnessing to others?

3. Christ's petitioning of Paul—1:15

1:15 ὅτε   δὲ   εὐδόκησεν   ὁ
     when   But   it pleased   the [one]
Θεός,   ὁ   ἀφορίσας με   ἐκ
God, who   appointed   me   from
    κοιλίας   μητρός μου καὶ καλέσας
[the] womb   mother   my   and   called
διὰ   τῆς   χάριτος αὐτοῦ,
by   the   grace   of Him,

But when it pleased God, who separated me from my mother's womb, and called *me* by his grace,

εὐδόκησεν Aor. Act. Indicative 3rd.
    Pers. Sing. εὐδοκέω Meaning = to think well of,
    approve, be well pleased, (have, take) pleasure
ἀφορίσας Aor. Act. Participle Nom.
    Masc. Sing. ἀφορίζω Meaning = to set off by
    boundary,   limit, exclude, appoint, divide, separate,
    sever
καλέσας Aor. Act. Participle Nom.
    Masc. Sing. καλέω Meaning = bid, call, name

Grammatical Notes
    Paul used the article with the proper name of the individual that was pleased to appoint Paul, God, with the phrase ὁ Θεός. In another prominent Greek text this phrase is considered as disputed and not important to the verse. This phrase consisting of an article and a proper name is used here to draw specific attention to the individual Paul desires to be the fo·

cus of his readers' attention. Dana and Mantey write,
Frequently the article is used with the name of some person
whose identity is made clear by the context, or assumed as
well known by the reader. Thus in the New Testament, which
was written for those already acquainted with the historical
facts of the Christian religion, when we find ὁ Ἰησοῦς, we know
immediately that it is the particular Jesus who was the Messiah and Savior.[36]

When the proper name of God becomes considered unim-
portant to a verse of Scripture, what can be of more significance? The name of God is of utmost importance and grammatically should be in the text. God is not just simply meant
to be an understood individual without even a pronoun reference in this verse.

Commentary Notes

Paul shows the glaring contrast here between his previous actions and what truly did please God. He begins with δέ
(but). In the middle of walking down life's path, doing what
he thought was pleasing to God (his works), he recognized what
actually pleased God and what it was that truly changed his
life, God's grace. Paul directs all attention to the One who can
make a difference in a person's life, God. All of the good that
ever happened to Paul from the time that he was in his
mother's womb he attributes to God. Paul recognized that
God's destiny and purpose for his life was to be a preacher of
the gospel as well as an apostle. Paul focuses the thoughts of
his readers toward the sovereignty of God in his own personal
life. God, in his own way, timing, and desire had separated
Paul not to be a Pharisee, but a preacher of the gospel. God
had so directed the path of the Apostle Paul so that Paul could
look back at the grace with which God had so directed his life
and say, "I am what I am only by God's sovereign grace." The
Pharisees were separatists in the physical realm, holding themselves off from people, not eating with sinners and publicans
like Zacchaeus. Jesus saw through their outward facade, and,
since his conversion, so had the Apostle Paul. After he was

saved, Paul still considered himself to be a separatist, but not by his own actions and definitely not in the physical realm. He considered himself to be separated in the spiritual realm from the darkness of cold religion to be a preacher of the gospel (Rom. 1:1), specifically to the Gentiles (Acts 9:15 and Gal. 2:9). Paul would have come to this understanding just as Jeremiah points out in Jer. 1:5, that he was known of God before conception and he was ordained of God to be a prophet unto the nations before he was born.

Paul continues the sentence speaking of what simply pleases God the most, His grace. Paul recognized that the only reason he was a preacher of the gospel and not an agonistic Pharisee was simply because of God's grace.

4. Christ' purpose for Paul's conversion-1:16-17

1:16 ἀποκαλύψαι τὸν υἱὸν αὐτοῦ   ἐν
       To reveal   the son of Him   in
ἐμοί,   ἵνα   εὐαγγελίζωμαι αὐτὸν
me, in order that I might preach Him
ἐν   τοῖς ἔθνεσιν, εὐθέως   οὐ
among   the Gentiles, immediately not
προσανεθέμην σαρκὶ   καὶ αἵματι·
I conferred with flesh and   blood:

To reveal his Son in me, that I might preach him among the heathen; immediately I conferred not with flesh and blood:

ἀποκαλύψαι Aor. Act. Infinitive
ἀποκαλύπτω Meaning = to take off the cover, disclose, reveal
εὐαγγελίζωμαι Pres. M/P Subjunctive
    1st. Pers. Sing. εὐαγγελίζω
    Meaning = declare, preach
προσανεθέμην Aor. Mid. Indicative
    1st. Pers. Sing. προσανατίθημι
    Meaning = to consult, in conference, confer

Grammatical Notes

Paul uses the word εὐαγγελίζωμαι (to preach) in the present tense signifying that this is to be a continuous action. Paul had the Son of God revealed in him so that he might go on revealing Him to others. The word αὐτόν (Him) is in the accusative signifying who or what is to be preached. Paul shows here his purpose for being saved is to lead others to Christ by preaching Christ and Him crucified.

Commentary Notes

Paul goes on to state why God called him, as well as every other person that God calls: to reveal His Son in them. When Christ is revealed in an individual's life, it will result in that person doing just exactly what God wants him to do. For Paul, his specific task was to preach Christ among the Gentiles. God's specific task for a believer might be different from the apostle's specific calling, but all of us are called to witness or share the gospel with others in our world. Too many Christians today believe that God's purpose for saving them is for them to have a life of ease from then on. The Apostle Paul did not believe that and neither should we. If we consider that sharing the gospel with every person we come into contact with is a life of ease, then so be it. This evangelistic fervor was the heartbeat of the apostle, and should be ours as well.

Paul continues to establish his dependence upon God and not on man as he describes his "immediate" reaction to God's call. He did not take time to ask those around him what they thought he should or should not do. He did not care what the head Pharisee thought back in Jerusalem. Immediately, Christ appeared to him and, immediately, he believed. He decided to follow Jesus, no turning back and without any questions. He did not confer with any human for any reason, he made up his mind on the spot. He was a decided individual. He decided for Christ, and to follow Christ. He did not need to ask anyone else for advice. There was no need for him to have a conference with someone else. He did not need to lay the matter before anyone else. Christ called, he answered.

1:17 οὐδὲ   ἀνῆλθον εἰς Ἱεροσόλυμα
    Nor   did I go up to Jerusalem
πρὸς τοὺς πρὸ ἐμοῦ ἀποστόλους, ἀλλ'
    to   the before me   apostles;   but
ἀπῆλθον   εἰς Ἀραβίαν, καὶ πάλιν
I went apart to Arabia, and again
ὑπέστρεψα εἰς Δαμασκόν.
I returned to Damascus.

Neither went I up to Jerusalem to them which were apostles before me; but I went into Arabia, and returned again unto Damascus.

ἀνῆλθον Aor. Act. Indicative 1st.
    Pers. Sing. ἀνέρχομαι
    Meaning = to ascend, go up
ἀπῆλθον Aor. Act. Indicative
    1st. Pers. Sing. ἀπέρχομαι
    Meaning = to go off, aside, go
    (aside, away, back), pass away
ὑπέστρεψα Aor. Act. Indicative
    1st. Pers. Sing. ὑποστρέφω Meaning
    = come again, turn back, return

Commentary Notes

The apostle points out here specifically that just after his conversion he did not go back to Jerusalem. This is where the other apostles were. At this time Jerusalem represented a place of authority in the church because all of the other apostles were working in, as well as out of, Jerusalem. The apostle is quick to point out that he did not go back to Jerusalem to receive any instructions from, or to have any conferences with, the other apostles. He recognizes them to have been apostles before him and, thereby, recognizing their seniority; however, he does continue to keep them on the same level as himself, an apostle.

He went down into the Arabian desert and then back to Damascus. How much time he spent in either place is unknown. We do know that Luke does not mention this time in the Book of Acts, so it probably was not of as great significance as the rest of Paul's life. Paul himself only makes reference to it and does not go into any great detail either.

Although we do not know how much time he spent in the Arabian desert, and how much in Damascus during these three years, we do know that it was a time that he had separated out for the Lord to work on him. Other men in the Bible had times of separation for learning too. Moses had received the finest education of his day and, yet, God took him to a desert to tend sheep for forty years because he had to add the finishing touches and smooth out the rough edges in Moses' life. This time would prepare him to work with the approximately two million faithless Israelites coming out of Egypt. David learned at a young age while tending his father's sheep to commune with the Lord. It was this close relationship with Yahweh that kept him strong during the years Saul was trying to kill him. Imagine knowing that you have been anointed to be the next President and the one still in office is hunting you down and trying to kill you during his whole term, practically. This was the proving time for David to see just how important it was for him to stay under his authority and to honor his authority. By doing so, he kept the blessing of God on his life. Paul undoubtedly had some special one-on-one teaching sessions with the Lord while out in the desert, but that was not all. Just as the other apostles had many opportunities to help Christ and to go out and preach and heal, so the Apostle Paul had these opportunities back in Damascus. Although he does not say specifically what he did while in Damascus, I am sure he did what all preachers do when they have a captive audience, he preached! Although Paul had been trained to be a Pharisee, he still had to hone his oratory skills just like the rest of us. So, why not start in the city to which he had been going to kill Christians, by spreading the wonderful good news of how Jesus Christ had saved him?

C. The churches of Judea-1:18-24

1:18 Ἔπειτα μετὰ ἔτη τρία
     Then after years three
ἀνῆλθον εἰς Ἱεροσόλυμα ἱστορῆσαι
I went up to Jerusalem   to visit
Πέτρον, καὶ ἐπέμεινα πρὸς αὐτὸν ἡμέρας δεκαπέντε.
Peter, and stayed with him days fifteen

Then after three years I went up to Jerusalem to see Peter, and abode with him fifteen days.

ἀνῆλθον Aor. Act. Indicative 1st. Pers.
     Sing. ἀνέρχομαι Meaning = go up, to ascend
ἱστορῆσαι Aor. Act. Infinitive
ἱστορέω Meaning = see, to visit for information, interview
ἐπέμεινα Aor. Act. Indicative
     1st. Pers. Sing. ἐπιμένω Meaning
     = to stay over, remain, abide, continue, tarry

Word Study

Paul employs the use of the word ἱστορῆσαι, which comes from the root word ἱστορέω and is rendered "to see" or "to visit" in the English. If Paul were simply wanting to record the fact that he saw and became acquainted with Peter, this would not have been the word to use, but rather the word ὁράω which means to see with the idea of becoming acquainted and obtaining a mutual understanding. This is the only place in the New Testament that the word ἱστορέω is found. Paul uses the word to describe his visit with Peter there in Jerusalem, for the express purpose of explaining what his visit was concerning. He did not visit Peter to give a report as a subordinate does to a superior. He did not visit Peter to gain official recognition from the other apostles as one too. He visited Peter for the exact purposes that this word suggests, to spend time with him and to get to know one another.

This word ἱστορέω is the same Greek word from which we get our English word *history*. It carries the idea of learning

facts from personal inquiry or examination as well as to narrate the facts as a historian would do. Peter and Paul were
likely asking each other questions and telling what God was
doing in their lives.

Commentary Notes

The Apostle Paul went to visit Peter for a personal time of
getting to know one another. Paul calls Peter here by his Aramaic name, Cephas. Peter and Paul got to enjoy sharing with
one another all that the Lord had been doing in Damascus
and in Jerusalem. Their visit was a personal, intimate, and
friendly one. Paul abode with Peter for fifteen days. When
someone comes to visit and stay with us for two weeks, usually that person is either family or a close friend. I am sure
that their strong bond with Christ drew them altogether closer
to each other as apostles and friends.

The visit ended after fifteen days for one of two reasons.
Either the two apostles were finished communing with each
other, or (what some scholars believe to be the case) the Grecians (Hellenistic Jews) had plotted to kill Paul (Acts 9:29) and
the Lord appeared to him while he was praying in the Temple
and told him to leave quickly (Acts 22:17-18).[37] At any case,
God ended the visit.

> **1:19** ἕτερον δὲ τῶν ἀποστόλων οὐκ
>   other But the apostles   not
> εἶδον, εἰ   μὴ   Ἰάκωβον τὸν
> I saw, if only [except] James the
> ἀδελφὸν τοῦ Κυρίου.
> brother of the Lord.

But other of the apostles saw I none, save James the Lord's
brother.

> εἶδον 2nd Aor. Act. Indicative
>   1st. Pers. Sing. ὁράω
>   Meaning = see

Commentary Notes

Paul says that he saw no other apostles (other than Peter) except for James, the half-brother of Christ. This would distinguish him from James, the son of Zebedee, and James the Less. The James that Paul met is the same James that he later calls a pillar in the church at Jerusalem. This James is also the James that wrote the Book of James in the Bible.

1:20 ἃ   δὲ   γράφω ὑμῖν,
the things that Now   I write to you,
ἰδοὺ   ἐνώπιον   τοῦ Θεοῦ, ὅτι
behold, in the presence of God,   that
οὐ ψεύδομαι.
not   I lie.

Now the things which I write unto you, behold, before God, I lie not.

γράφω Pres. Act. Indicative 1st. Pers.
    Sing. γράφω Meaning = write, describe
ἰδοὺ Aor. Mid. Imperative 2nd. Pers.
    Sing. εἶδον Meaning = behold, lo, see
ψεύδομαι Pres. Mid. Indicative
    1st. Pers. Sing. ψεύδομαι Meaning = falsely, lie

Commentary Notes

The Apostle Paul confirms everything that he has written so far, and that he is about to write with a solemn oath. It is as if he were standing before a judge on the witness stand in our country today and were pledging to tell "the truth, the whole truth, and nothing but the truth so help me God." Only, in this case instead of having his hand on a Bible, he is being used to write part of it! The purpose of Paul's statement is to prevent all suspicion of falsehood. Paul knows that since he had no personal eyewitnesses for the Galatians to check his story with, that the only one he could use to affirm all of his writing would be God. Since Paul's true knowledge of the gospel came from no man but from God Himself, the only one who could confirm exactly what he was writing was God. Paul had to focus the Galatians' attention back to God to support everything he had written.

Illustration

"Four high school boys were late to their morning classes one day. They entered the classroom and solemnly told their teacher they were detained due to a flat tire. The sympathetic teacher smiled and told them it was too bad they were late because they had missed a test that morning. But she was willing to let them make it up. She gave them each a piece of paper and a pencil and sent them to four corners of the room. Then she told them they would pass if they could answer just one question:

Which tire was flat???"

— Paul Harvey[38]

It is obvious that these young men had been caught in a lie. How about yours and my conscience? Does it bear witness for us or against us? The Apostle Paul's bore witness for him.

Application

1. Paul could say in this verse that he did not lie before God. Christian, do you have a problem with lying, or have you just learned how to try not to get caught if you do?

> **1:21** ἔπειτα ἦλθον εἰς τὰ κλίματα
>   Later I came into the regions
> τῆς Συρίας καὶ τῆς Κιλικίας.
> of [the] Syria and of [the] Cilicia.
> Afterwards I came into the regions of Syria and Cilicia;

> ἦλθον Aor. Act. Indicative 1st. Pers.
>   Sing. ἔρχομαι Meaning = come, enter, go

Commentary Notes

Since it was not necessary to describe his encounter with the Grecians in Jerusalem (Acts 9:29), Paul skims over it to discuss where he went next. When Paul left Jerusalem and the region of Judea, he went north to the region of Syria of which Antioch was its capitol. Paul spent a considerable amount of time here witnessing for Christ. Paul says that he also went to the region of Cilicia. This was a province of Asia Minor, of which the capitol was Tarsus, Paul's home town. Syria was between Jerusalem and Cilicia.

Paul recognized that God had guided him to take the gospel specifically to the Gentiles. He did not need to spend much time in Jerusalem, which was the center of the Jewish community. Paul does not state why he went to these regions, but most probably because it was the closest concentrated area of Gentiles. Another reason that the apostle might have gone to these regions was to witness to his relatives (Acts 11:25). He was just as concerned about his relatives and wanting to see his mother and father in heaven as any person today would be. With the zeal that he had, I am sure he went back to his home, where he had lived as a Pharisee, and told the people he grew up with and had gone to school with what had taken place in his life. In fact, the next few verses would lead in this direction also, because the churches in Judea heard of the testimony of Saul, the persecutor of Christians, becoming Paul, the preacher of the gospel! Once he started telling people, the news spread fast.

1:22 ἤμην δὲ ἀγνοούμενος τῷ
I was And   unknown   by
προσώπῳ   ταῖς ἐκκλησίαις
appearance to the churches
τῆς   Ἰουδαίς   ταῖς
of [the ones of] Judea that [the ones]
ἐν Χριστῷ·
in Christ.

And was unknown by face unto the churches of Judaea which were in Christ:

ἤμην Imperfect Act. Indicative
    1st. Pers. Sing. εἰμι Meaning = was
ἀγνοούμενος Pres. M/P. Participle
    Nom. Masc. Sing. ἀγνοέω Meaning = not know,
    ignorant, not understand
Commentary Notes

Paul did not have any personal relations with any of the churches in Jerusalem. He did not visit them to see what they were doing or what they were teaching. When in their region, he visited only with Peter and James to narrate to them what God was doing in his life, and, naturally, it probably was reciprocated. Paul was indebted neither to the apostles nor to the churches in Judea for his message or his knowledge of Christianity.

1:23 μόνον δὲ ἀκούοντες ἦσαν ὅτι
    only But heard they, that
ʽΟ διώκων ἡμᾶς ποτέ,
he who persecuted us previously,
νῦν εὐαγγελίζεται τὴν πίστιν ἥν
now preaches the faith which
  ποτε ἐπόρθει.
formerly he ravaged.

But they had heard only, That he which persecuted us in times past now preacheth the faith which once he destroyed.

ἀκούοντες Pres. Act. Participle Nom.
    Masc. Plur. ἀκούω Meaning = give audience, come, be
    noised, hear, understand
διώκων Pres. Act. Participle Nom.
    Masc. Sing. διώκω Meaning = ensue, given to,
    persecute, press forward, follow

εὐαγγελίζεται Pres. Mid. Indicative
   3rd. Pers. Sing εὐαγγελίζομαι
   Meaning = preach, bring glad tidings, proclaim,
   declare
ἐπόρθει Imp. Act. Indicative
   3rd. Pers. Sing. πορθέω Meaning = to ravage
   (figuratively), waste, destroy

Grammatical Notes

The word ἀκούοντες translated "heard" is in the present tense, which implies continuous action. The churches in Judea did not just hear this message once. They continued to hear it over and over as the Gentile believers would come to their area.

Commentary Notes

The message that was transmitted from the Gentile world to the Jewish over and over again was that Saul, the persecutor, was now Paul, the preacher. Paul, the man whose one passion in life was to weed out Christianity, now proclaimed it everywhere, planting the seed of its faith in any way possible.

1:24 καὶ   ἐδόξαζον   ἐν ἐμοὶ τὸν   Θεόν.
         And they glorified in   me [the]   God.

And they glorified God in me.

ἐδόξαζον Imp. Act. Indicative
   3rd. Pers. Plur. δοξάζω Meaning = glorify, honor,
   magnify

Commentary Notes

These believers back in Judea praised God for His handiwork in the apostle's life (Eph. 2:10). Paul tells the Galatians this testimony to help them see that the true Hebrew believers were glorifying God and praising Him for turning Paul's

1 H. E. Dana and Julius R. Mantey, *A Manual Grammar of the Greek New Testament* (New York, NY: MacMillan Co., 1927), 114.

2 Ibid.

3 Michael C. Bere, *Bible Doctrines for Today*, Book 1 (Pensacola, FL: A Beka Book, 1987), 78.

4 Albert Barnes, *Barnes' Notes on the New Testament* (Grand Rapids, MI: Kregel Publications, 1994), 917.

5 Parsons Technology, *Bible Illustrator* [computer file]. Cedar Rapids, IA: Parsons, 1991.

6 A. T. Robertson, *A Grammar of the Greek New Testament in the Light of Historical Research* (Nashville, TN: Broadman Press, 1934), 419.

7 Craig Rairdin and Parsons Technology, Inc., QuickVerse for Windows, Version 3.0j, Computer Program, Hiawatha, IA: 1992-1994.

8 Spiros Zodhiates, *Lexical Aids to the New Testament.* (Chattanooga, TN: AMG Publishers, 1992), 1469.

9 J. Gresham Machen, *New Testament Greek for Beginners* (New York, NY: Macmillan Publishing House, 1923), 36.

10 Ibid., 598.

11 Robertson, 909.

12 Edward E. Hindson and Woodrow Michael Kroll, ed. *The KJV Parallel Bible Commentary* (Nashville, TN: Thomas Nelson Publishers, 1994), 2371.

13 Barnes, 918.

14 Martin Luther, *A Commentary on St. Paul's Epistle to the Galatians* (London: J. Clark Publishing, 1953), 60.

15 Spiros Zodhiates, *The Complete Word Study Dictionary: New Testament* (Chattanooga, TN: AMG Publishers, 1993), 552.

16 Robertson, 219.

17 Ibid., 220.

18 F. Blass, *Grammar of New Testament Greek* (2. Aufl., Germany, 1902), 19.

19 Robertson, 221.

20 Zodhiates, 812.

21 Dana and Mantey, 247.

22 Hindson and Kroll, 2372.

23 Zodhiates, *The Complete Word Study Dictionary: New Testament,* 148.

24 W. E. Vine, Merrill F. Unger, and William White, Jr., *Vine's Complete Expository Dictionary of Old and New Testament Words* (Nashville, TN: Thomas Nelson Publishers, 1985), 141.

25 G. B. Winer, *A Treatise on the Grammar of New Testament Greek* (Edinburgh, Germany: T. & T. Clark, 1882), 176.

26 Kenneth S. Wuest. *Galatians in the Greek New Testament* (Grand Rapids, MI: Wm. B. Eerdmans Publishing Co., 1944), 39.

27 Dana and Mantey, 291.

28 Ibid., 292.

29 Wuest, 39.

30 Parsons, *Bible Illustrator.*

31 Dana and Mantey, 242-43.

32 Ibid.

33 Ibid., 244.

34 Wuest, 44.

35 Yoho, Walter Allen. Pneumatology class notes, Pensacola Christian College, 1995.

36 Dana and Mantey, 142.

37 Wuest, 53.

38 Parsons, *Bible Illustrator.*

39 Wuest, 56.

D. The consenting of apostles-2:1-10
1. Confirmation of the gospel-2:1, 2

2:1 Ἔπειτα διὰ δεκατεσσάρων ἐτῶν
after Then fourteen years
πάλιν ἀνέβην εἰς Ἱεροσόλυμα
again I went up to Jerusalem
μετὰ Βαρνάβα, συμπαραλαβὼν
with Barnabas, [and] took along with
καὶ Τίτον.
[me] also Titus.

Then fourteen years after I went up again to Jerusalem with Barnabas, and took Titus with *me* also.

ἀνέβην Aor. Act. Indicative 1st. Pers.
Sing. ἀναβαίνω Meaning = arise,
ascend, come up, go up
συμπαραλαβὼν Aor. Act. Part. Nom.
Masc. Sing. συμπαραλαμβάνω
Meaning = take with, to take along in company

Commentary Notes
Paul states that he went back to Jerusalem fourteen years later. Some believe that this was fourteen years after his conversion. However, the logical conclusion from the grammar

would indicate that it was fourteen years after his previously mentioned visit with Peter. This timing does not affect the content of the book so much as it does the determining of the date of it. However, the content of the trip and the reason for it are of consequential importance to the understanding of the apostle's argument. The situation that is described in Acts 15:2 by Luke seems to be pointing to the same incident that Paul is about to set forth here in Galatians. In Acts 15 it is noted that the church sent Paul and Barnabas to Jerusalem along with certain others, probably men representing both sides of the question as to whether or not a Christian would have to be circumcised to be saved. Titus is not mentioned probably because he was not considered a leader in the church at that time. Others mentioned in Acts 15 are not named specifically because Paul and Barnabas were leaders there at the time.

Here in Galatians, however, to support his argumentation as evidence, Paul mentions Titus specifically because Titus was completely of Gentile descent. In the Book of Acts, Titus is not mentioned specifically by name; however, both he and Timothy were students of Christ at the feet of Paul. Paul had such close relations with them that in his letters to them he addresses each as "my son." Paul probably mentions Titus specifically here because the Galatians were familiar with him. As Paul describes the events at Jerusalem concerning Titus, he writes of him as if the Galatians were already familiar with him, not as though they had no idea who he was.

2:2 ἀνέβην δὲ κατὰ ἀποκάλυψιν,
　　I went up And　by　　revelation,
καὶ　ἀνεθέμην　αὐτοῖς　τὸ
and made known　to them　that
εὐαγγέλιον　ὅ　　κηρύσσω　ἐν
　　gospel　which　I preach　among
τοῖς　ἔθνεσι, κατ᾽ ἰδίαν　δὲ
the　Gentiles, [to] privately　but
　　　τοῖς
to those [the ones] who

δοκοῦσι,   μή   πως
were of reputation, lest somehow
εἰς κενὸν   τρέχω   ἢ ἔδραμον.
in   vain I should run, or had run.

And I went up by revelation, and communicated unto them that gospel which I preach among the Gentiles, but privately to them which were of reputation, lest by any means I should run, or had run, in vain.

> ἀνέβην Aor. Act. Indicative 1st. Pers.
>   Sing. ἀναβαίνω Meaning = arise,
>   ascend, come up, go up
> ἀνεθέμην Aor. Mid. Indicative
>   1st. Pers. Sing. ἀνατίθημι Meaning
>   = communicate, declare, to set forth,
>   place before, propose, make known
> κηρύσσω Pres. Act. Indicative 1st. Pers.
>   Sing. κηρύσσω Meaning = preach,
>   proclaim, publish
> δοκοῦσι Pres. Act. Participle Dat. Masc.
>   Plur. δοκέω Meaning = be accounted,
>   of reputation, seem, think, suppose
> τρέχω Pres. Act. Subjunctive 1st. Pers.
>   Sing. τρέχω
>   Meaning = have course, run

Grammatical Note
   The *Textus Receptus* differs from the Alexandrian type text in this verse by two movable final consonants "ν" before words that begin with consonants. The *Textus Receptus* follows its regular pattern of no final consonants before words that begin with consonants while the *Another Greek text*, which does not have a set pattern, places them on the ends of the words ἔθνεσι and δοκοῦσι, which precede words that begin with consonants. The consistency of the *Textus Receptus* is only reassured by these letters.

Commentary Notes

The apostle boldly proclaims once again that he acts not on what man thinks or determines he should do, but out of obedience to direct revelation from God. This identification of his authority is important as the apostle is showing to these Galatian believers that he is on the same level as the other apostles. He determines that the subject is not one that is to be taken lightly or should be handled only here in Antioch of Syria. What helps him to determine this truth is that it is direct revelation from the Holy Spirit. Paul obeys the Holy Spirit and not simply what men determined he should do. Paul gives this personal account to help the Galatians see that he is fulfilling the gift of the apostle and is in accordance with the Spirit of God, who is guiding the other apostles as well. Paul acts not on his own accord but rather according to the express charge of God.

When we study the account of this incident in Acts 15, it appears that the church sent the apostle and Barnabas to Jerusalem. If this be true, it would seem to contradict what Paul has written here. When the two accounts are brought together, however, they complement each other rather than contradict. Luke was recording the event as it occurred in the church at Antioch, which shows that God was in control of and working through mature believers there at Antioch. The same revelation that God had given directly to Paul (that is, to go to Jerusalem and settle the dispute about obedience to the law of Moses for salvation) had been the same conclusion that the church had come to. They readily approved of Paul and Barnabas's going to Jerusalem to clear up the water that had been muddied over salvation purely by grace. There is no question why the believers were first called Christians at Antioch. They were mature believers. Imagine having the team of Paul and Barnabas as ministers to this body of believers growing in number (in a city of approximately 500,000) and in depth, spiritually. Paul and Barnabas had not been there long when they were separated out to be missionaries, but their influence on the church had had a very intense impact. The church had probably been hearing this mixed doctrine coming from Jewish believers for a little while and wished to have the question settled completely, so that all of the people could continue in unity in the church, both Jew and Gentile alike.

Paul traveled to Jerusalem as directed by God to make known to the Jews there the same gospel that he had been proclaiming to the Gentiles. The apostle presented the same gospel, in all of its entirety (its doctrines, its principles, and its nature), to the church in Jerusalem. He presented the very same gospel that Christ had made known to him by revelation. According to Acts 15 there were some from a sect of the Pharisees who maintained that it was needful for saved Gentiles to be circumcised and to keep the law of Moses. Then, Paul had another conference with only those of reputation in private. He did not want to go and accomplish nothing when he went to Jerusalem so he presented the gospel to the churches' leadership and the other apostles, so that they could interact with him on it. He went with them alone so that their conference would be without the interference or misunderstanding by those less mature believers who might have "selective hearing." Paul knew that since they were mature they would listen to him completely as he made known to them everything he was teaching. Paul had no doubt as to whether or not he was in the right. Remember, his gospel had come expressly by revelation of Jesus Christ. He did not want it to be a source of contention in the church and cause any greater of a schism. He did not do it in secrecy so that no one would know however. He understood that sometimes some people are not supposed to know everything that happens in the relationships of the leadership, so that they can form a unified front and a unified group. This is sort of what the founders and framers of the United States Constitution did when they met in Philadelphia in 1787 to form a new Constitution of the United States. Those fifty-five delegates, with George Washington presiding over the Philadelphia Convention, decided that any part of their conversations were not to be rehearsed outside of the doors of that room for thirty years. They did this because they knew that the unity of this brand new nation rested upon their unity and unified front. With this being the case, they left the meeting in August of that year and within four short years all thirteen colonies had ratified the new Constitution, thus allowing us to be called the United States of America.

Paul knew how important time is. He did not want to waste the precious time that God had given him to help unify the church by causing more of a division than was already present. He knew in his heart that he proclaimed the truth and wanted the rest of the church to know that both he and the apostles in Jerusalem were in 100 percent agreement on salvation by grace, plus nothing. If any more division occurred, it could only hurt the spreading of the gospel and not help.

2. Compelled not to be circumcised-2:3

2:3 ἀλλ’   οὐδὲ   Τίτος
Indeed not even Titus
    ὁ   σὺν ἐμοί,
the one who [was] with me,
Ἕλλην ὢν,   ἠναγκάσθη
a Greek being , was compelled
    περιτμηθῆναι·
to be circumcised:

But neither Titus, who was with me, being a Greek, was compelled to be circumcised:

    ὢν Pres. Act. Participle Nom. Masc.
        Sing. εἰμι Meaning = be, come, have
    ἠναγκάσθη Aor. Pass. Indicative
        3rd. Pers. Sing. ἀναγκάζω Meaning
        = compel, constrain
    περιτμηθῆναι Aor. Pass. Infinitive
    περιτέμνω Meaning = circumcise

Commentary Notes

Paul acted boldly to take with him an uncircumcised Greek to the conference at Jerusalem. Titus, who evidently had two Greek parents, was not compelled to be circumcised. Titus could be a Greek to the Greeks (1 Cor. 9). It is possible that Titus had this question in his mind and went with Paul to Jerusalem to receive an answer directly from the apostles there. "Paul introduces this case of Titus undoubtedly to show that circumcision was not necessary to salvation."[1] The end result, as Paul was stressing here, was that obligation to the Mosaic law was not necessary to the Gentile converts.

Titus could have gone with Paul for any number of reasons. He could have gone with Paul because he was seriously considering circumcision in his own life and wondered whether or not it was necessary for him as a believer in Christ. Another reason that he might have gone was to be an example for Paul to display that Titus was a mature believer in Christ even though he was not circumcised.

So why on one occasion did Paul take part in the circumcision of Timothy, and, yet, would not even dare impose the act on Titus? Although Timothy's father was a Gentile, his mother was a Jew. According to his Jewish heritage, Timothy should have been circumcised, but not for salvation purposes. The purpose for Timothy being circumcised was his voluntary compliance with the normal custom of the Jews (Acts 16:3). In his case, it was not pushed as being obligatory for salvation, but, rather, might even help to harmonize Timothy with the favor of the Jews, and he submitted to it. Circumcision was the sign that God gave to Abraham to set his descendants apart from all others of the human race. Circumcision in the physical realm had no other specific purpose. However, circumcision of the heart in the spiritual realm was what God had wanted from Israel all the time from Abraham until Paul's day. The Judaizers were not circumcised in their hearts and did not want to be, but wanted to make sure that all of the same outward things that they had been practicing as Jews would still be practiced by Christians and would not be done away with.

They wanted to reduce Christianity to what they had been practicing all this time, abject slavery. Not that Moses' Law was abject slavery in and of itself, but without the right heart attitude (a circumcised heart) that was what it had been reduced to. Titus possessed the right heart attitude, a circumcised heart; hence, he went on to be used of the Lord to plant churches for him!

3. Contradiction of the truth-2:4-6

2:4 διὰ   δὲ   τοὺς
    due to   And   that [the]
    παρεισάκτους   ψευδαδέλφους,
stealthily brought in   false brethren,
    οἵτινες   παρεισῆλθον
    who   came in by secrecy
κατασκοπῆσαι τὴν ἐλευθερίαν ἡμῶν
    to spy out   the   liberty   of us
    ἣν   ἔχομεν   ἐν Χριστῷ ᾽Ιησοῦ,
which   we have   in   Christ   Jesus,
    ἵνα   ἡμᾶς
in order that   us
      καταδουλώσωνται·
they might bring into bondage:

And that because of false brethren unawares brought in, who came in privily to spy out our liberty which we have in Christ Jesus, that they might bring us into bondage:

    παρεισάκτους Adjective παρεισάκτος
      Meaning = smuggled in, unawares brought in,
      secretly brought in, stealthily brought in
    παρεισῆλθον Aor. Act. Indicative
      3rd. Pers. Plur. παρεισέρχομαι
      Meaning = enter, come in privily, come in stealthily
    κατασκοπῆσαι Aor. Act. Infinitive
    κατασκοπέω Meaning = spy out

ἔχομεν Pres. Act. Indicative 1st. Pers.
    Plur. ἔχω Meaning = have
καταδουλώσωνται Aor. Mid.
    Subjunctive 3rd. Pers. Plur.
καταδουλόω Meaning = bring
    into bondage

Grammatical Notes

In this verse, above all others, the apostle reveals to the Galatian churches the motives of the false brethren, the teachers of damnable heresy, to bring true believers into bondage. This bondage was not from Jesus Christ because He came to set the captive free. So who was it from? Satan. He brings bondage, Christ brings liberty. The apostle was guided specifically by the Holy Spirit not to write καταδουλώσουσιν, which is found in another Greek text, but καταδουλώσωνται, which is found in the *Textus Receptus.* What is the difference between these two words which are the same Greek root word with different endings? The impacting difference is that with the one (*The other Greek text* word), bondage will or already has occurred with certainty, and with the other (*Textus Receptus* word), it is only a probability and not a reality.

If the Apostle Paul had written καταδουλώσουσιν, then he would have had to admit that he had been in bondage to the false doctrine of the Judaizers. This word is a future active indicative third person plural. The significance of the verb form is that the indicative mood is the mood of certainty.[2] If this form had been used by the Apostle Paul, he would have been displaying a strong possibility that he and the Galatian believers along with him could not withstand against this false doctrine and would eventually be brought into bondage by it.

However, the Spirit's guidance was not to a future active indicative but rather to an aorist middle subjunctive in the word καταδουλώσωνται. The subjunctive mood is the mood of probability.[3] "While the indicative assumes reality, the subjunctive assumes unreality. It is the first step away from that which is actual in the direction of that which is only conceivable."[4] As Paul penned these words, he knew with a certainty in his heart that he had not fallen prey to their false doctrine and never would. He also truly believed the same about the Galatian churches. He knew that bondage and not liberty was the true goal of the false brethren. He knew that they were not there to help the purpose of Christ but to thwart it; hence, he brings to light before the Galatians the intents of the hearts of these false brethren, to bring them into bondage. He reminds the Galatians that although that might be the goal of the false brethren, the Galatians do not have to succumb to bondage.

Commentary Notes

There was a group of people that seemed to work their way into some of the churches that Paul had been in, and these people were Christian in name only. They had not experienced the saving grace of God, and were concerned only with the works of themselves and other believers. They are marked by the apostle who uses the article τοὺς, which specifies exactly who he is talking about in these churches. He calls them false brethren (ψευδαδέλφους), which is found only here and in 2 Cor. 11:26. They made their way into the Christian church and enjoyed the outward fellowship, yet did not possess Christ internally. They missed the depth and true kinship bonding that takes place in a body of true believers. These same people made it into the meeting here in Jerusalem and were demanding that Titus be circumcised to be considered a part of the church. Paul explains that if Titus were to be circumcised, that would show that these false brethren were right in their thinking and that salvation not only included grace but also circumcision and Moses' law. The false brethren came in alongside the true Christians of the Jerusalem church, demanding of the leadership and apostles that Titus be circumcised. Paul, rather than making it an open debate in front of the Jerusalem church, decided to have a private meeting with the church leadership and other apostles only, and that he did.

Paul unveiled the reason the false brethren were there.

These false brethren had come in to spy out the Christian's
(Gentile's, especially) liberty (which means freedom with responsibility) from the Mosaic law. No longer did the Jew who
had placed his faith in Christ have to submit himself to the
ceremonial law, as was spelled out to Moses by God in the
Pentateuch. That was gone. Paul, especially, considered it
bondage in his day since the Judaism of his day was an apostate Judaism. This Judaism lacked the heart belief in Christ
as the Messiah as evidenced by its rejection of Him. Paul recognized that any time any kind of works are added to grace it
becomes bondage. The Judaizers were trying to require the
Gentile believers to practice the Mosaic law in order to call
themselves Christians.

> **2:5** οἷς   οὐδὲ πρὸς   ὥραν
> To whom not   for   an hour
> εἴξαμεν τῇ ὑποταγῇ, ἵνα ἡ
> we did yield by subjection, that the
> ἀλήθεια τοῦ εὐαγγελίου
> truth of the gospel
> διαμείνῃ   πρὸς ὑμᾶς.
> [it] might remain   with you.

To whom we gave place by subjection, no, not for an hour; that
the truth of the gospel might continue with you.

> εἴξαμεν Aor. Act. Indicative 1st. Pers.
>   Plur. εἴχω Meaning = give place
> διαμείνῃ Aor. Act. Subjunctive
>   3rd. Pers. Sing. διαμένω Meaning =
>   continue, remain, endure,
>   not to change

Grammatical Notes
     In this verse as it is stated here in the *Textus Receptus*, we
have purity in the text, as well as harmony with the staunch
and sober stand taken by the apostle throughout the rest of

the Book of Galatians. However, there are extant manuscripts which have been corrupted (changed) to weaken the strong, firm stand taken by Paul. The words οἷς οὐδε (to whom, not) are missing in these manuscripts making it say that Paul did of his own free volition yield to these false brethren, either for, or after a little while, so that the overall permanent concerns of the gospel might be better negotiated at this meeting. Another Greek New Testament makes allowance for, and gives the names of the manuscripts that support this reading, thus allowing for Paul to have compromised the foundational truth of justification by faith alone for a short while. Concerning this problem, Barnes writes,

> This opinion has been gaining ground for the last century, that the passage here has been corrupted; but it is by no means confirmed. The ancient versions, the Syriac, the Vulgate, and the Arabic, accord with the usual reading of the text. So also do by far the largest portion of MSS.; and such, it seems to me, is the sense demanded by the connexion.[5]

Commentary Notes

Paul declared to the Galatians that he and Barnabas did not yield themselves by way of self-subjection for even the briefest moment of time. But rather they held fast to their position and were unmoved, unbudged by the Judaizers at all. The laws of Moses were not to be imposed upon the Gentile believers as part of their obligation to salvation in any way.

The reason the apostle would not, or could not, give in for an hour was so that the full truth of the gospel could remain with the Gentile believers. Paul remained firm so that the gospel would remain firmly held by the Gentiles. The word διαμείνῃ is used by the apostle here and means to remain permanently or to continue in the same place, remain the same, endure, not to change. Why would the apostle write with such firmness concerning the gospel and, yet, not take such a firm stand on it in person? He did take a firm stand and, yes, en-

dured a little persecution for it. Yet, all of Christianity was on
trial at this point. Either it would be the truth of justification
by faith in Christ plus nothing, or it would be a modified form
of legalistic Judaism. Anything being added to it would change
it from truth to error, even such a thing as circumcision. Not
only would the Gentile Christians be affected by the outcome
of the decision, but the Jews would be also. Christianity was
supposed to be a spiritual religion, just as the true Judaism.
True Judaism, in the past, and, now, Christianity were both to
be comprised of the true children of Abraham, those of spiritual faith and not just the physical seed.

2:6 ἀπὸ δὲ   τῶν
    of But   those who
    δοκούντων   εἶναί   τι
[the ones] seemed to be of reputation,
    (ὁποῖοί   ποτε   ἦσαν   οὐδέν
(of what sort once they were, no
    μοι   διαφέρει·
to me it is of value:
    πρόσωπον   Θεὸς
the outward appearance God
    ἀνθρώπου οὐ λαμβάνει)– ἐμοὶ γὰρ
    of man   no He receives:) to me for
    οἱ
those who
        δοκοῦντες
seemed to be of good reputation
    οὐδὲν   προσανέθεντο·
nothing   imparted:

But of these who seemed to be somewhat, (whatsoever they
were, it maketh no matter to me: God accepteth no man's person:) for they who seemed *to be somewhat* in conference added
nothing to me:

δοκούντων   Pres. Act. Participle Gen.
Masc. Plur. δοκέω Meaning = seem,
please, be accounted, think, be of reputation
εἶναι Pres. Act. Infinitive εἴμι
Meaning = to be
ἦσαν Imp. Act. Indicative 3rd. Pers.
Plur. εἰμί Meaning = they were
διαφέρει Pres. Act. Indicative 3rd.
Pers. Sing. διαφέρω Meaning = make matter, differ
from, be better, carry
λαμβάνει Pres. Act. Indicative 3rd.
Pers. Sing. λαμβάνω Meaning =
accept, have, obtain, hold, receive, take
δοκοῦντες Pres. Act. Participle Nom.
Masc. Plur. δοκέω Meaning =
seem, please, suppose, think
προσανέθεντο Aor. Mid. Indicative
3rd. Pers. Plur. προσανατίθημι
Meaning = confer, in conference add

Grammatical Notes

The *Textus Receptus* in the middle portion of this verse reads πρόσωπον Θεὸς ἀνθρώπου οὐ λαμβάνει. As is obvious, the word Θεὸς has no article, neither has need of one. When Θεὸς is written and there is no article present, it signifies divine essence.[6] However, another Greek text reads πρόσωπον ὁ Θεὸς ἀνθρώπου οὐ λαμβάνει, which includes the article. The article is not necessary in this case since God is in contrast with humanity. Dana and Mantey quote Webster who stated on page 29 in *Syntax and Synon. of the Greek* in 1864, "Θεὸς occurs without the article where the Deity is contrasted with what is human."[7] Such is the case in this verse.

Commentary Notes

At first glance, the apostle seems to be using some strong language to identify the other apostles that he met with at Jerusalem; however, he was not. He was simply stating the facts. He said that these apostles seemed to be of reputation, and that is what he meant. When he went to Jerusalem to meet with the other apostles, he did not go seeking their approval for the gospel he was preaching. He went so that it would be established before all types of believers that he had been preaching and would continue to preach the same gospel that the other apostles were preaching, justification by faith alone. Paul is not placing the other apostles in a negative light, he is simply stating that they were on the same level that he was, an apostle of Christ. However, the Judaizers did not see it this way. They thought that the apostles at Jerusalem were more authoritative than Paul since they had walked with Christ during His earthly ministry. So, Paul simply states that God does not accept the outward appearance of someone over the inward state of being. Both Paul and the other apostles had been appointed by God and knew it in their hearts. It was time that others such as the Judaizers simply acknowledged that. Paul simply stated that the other apostles did not add anything to his authority as an apostle or to the authenticity of the gospel that he preached. Both Paul and the other apostles were the same before he went to Jerusalem, while he was at Jerusalem, and after he left Jerusalem. They neither added to nor took away from him.

Application
1. God does not receive the outward appearances of men; do you, Christian?

4. Commitment of the gospel-2:7-8
   a. To Peter-2:7
   2:7 ἀλλὰ   τοὐναντίον,
      But on the contrary, when
   ἰδόντες   ὅτι
   they saw   that
      πεπίστευμαι   τὸ
   [it] had been entrusted to me   the

εὐαγγέλιον τῆς   ἀκροβυστίας,
  gospel   for the uncircumcised ,
καθὼς Πέτρος τῆς   περιτομῆς
just as Peter for the circumcised;

But contrariwise, when they saw that the gospel of the uncircumcision was committed unto me, as *the gospel* of the circumcision *was* unto Peter;

ἰδόντες 2nd. Aor. Act. Participle Nom.
  Masc. Plur. ὁράω Meaning = see,
    know, perceive, understand, consider
πεπίστευμαι Perf. Pass. Indicative
  1st. Pers. Sing. πιστεύω Meaning =
    believe, commit, put in trust with

Commentary Notes

  The apostles recognized that Paul's gift had made room for him just as Peter's gift had made room for him. This verse does not mean that Paul was not supposed to preach to Jews, and Peter was not supposed to preach to Gentiles. It simply means that the apostles recognized how God had been blessing both Peter and Paul. Remember, Peter was the first one to preach to Gentiles who received the Holy Ghost. This practice was not the norm for Peter, however, but simply God's leading in a specific instance to help him understand that the liberty of the gospel was for all men and not just the Jews. God placed different desires in Peter's heart and Paul's heart and then fulfilled them by blessing their ministries. All that the other apostles did was simply recognize this.

b. To Paul-2:8
  2:8 (ὁ   γὰρ ἐνεργήσας Πέτρῳ
  (He who For was mighty in Peter
  εἰς ἀποστολὴν τῆς   περιτομῆς,
  to the apostleship of the circumcision,

ἐνήργησε   καὶ   ἐμοὶ
worked effectively   the same   in me
εἰς   τὰ   ἔθνη),
toward   the   Gentiles:)

(For he that wrought effectually in Peter to the apostleship of the circumcision, the same was mighty in me toward the Gentiles:)

ἐνεργήσας Aor. Act. Participle Nom.
      Masc. Sing. ἐνεργέω Meaning = do, make effectual,
      be mighty in, work, show forthself
ἐνήργησε Aor. Act. Indicative
      3rd. Pers. Sing. ἐνεργέω
      Meaning = do, make effectual, be mighty in,
      work, show forthself

Commentary Notes

Paul states it simply: God is the One who has done the work. It was God's power that worked mightily and effectively, using Peter to win many of the Jews to the Lord, just as it was God's power that worked mightily and was very effective in using Paul to win many of the Gentiles to the Lord. At any rate, it was God's Holy Spirit who did the work, not Peter and not Paul. Paul did not want the Galatians to get caught up with all outward appearances and forget Who was the force behind it all.

Why did Paul mention the Apostle Peter? Peter had been the spokesman for the rest of the apostles. When he said, "I go afishing," they went also. When he jumped into the water and swam toward Christ on shore, they followed. Peter was the apostle that the others looked up to. Peter was also the oldest of the other apostles and the most influential (or so it seemed). He preached the message at Pentecost and seemed to be the leader of the group after Christ ascended. Just as Peter was successful in proclaiming the gospel to the Jews, so Paul was successful in proclaiming the gospel to the Gentiles.

Application

1. Paul said that he was dedicated to taking the gospel to the Gentiles, just as Peter was to the Jews. Are you dedicated to taking the gospel to the people where you live—your neighborhood, your workplace, your grocery store?

5. The comradeship of the circumcision with the uncircumcision-2:9-10

2:9 καὶ   γνόντες   τὴν
And when [they] understood the
χάριν τὴν   δοθεῖσάν   μοι,
grace that had been granted [to] me,
Ἰάκωβος καὶ Κηφᾶς καὶ Ἰωάννης,
James,   and Cephas, and   John,
οἱ δοκοῦντες στύλοι εἶναι,
who seemed   pillars to be,
δεξιὰς   ἔδωκαν   ἐμοὶ
the right hands they gave to me
καὶ Βαράβᾳ   κοινωνίας, ἵνα
and Barnabas of fellowship, that
ἡμεῖς εἰς τὰ   ἔθνη,
we   to   the Gentiles
αὐτοὶ δὲ εἰς τὴν   περιτομήν·
they and to   the ones circumcised.

And when James, Cephas, and John, who seemed to be pillars, perceived the grace that was given unto me, they gave to me and Barnabas the right hands of fellowship; that we *should go* unto the heathen, and they unto the circumcision.

γνόντες Aor. Act. Participle Nom.
    Masc. Plur. γινώσκω Meaning =
    allow, know, perceive, understand
δοθεῖσάν Aor. Pass. Participle Nom.
    Fem. Sing. δίδωμι Meaning = give, grant, deliver

δοκοῦντες Pres. Act. Participle Gen.
    Nom. Plur. δοκέω Meaning =
    please, seem, suppose, think, be of reputation
εἶναι Pres. Act. Infinitive εἴμι
    Meaning = be, is
ἔδωκαν Aor. Act. Indicative 3rd. Pers.
    Plur. δίδωμι Meaning = give

Grammatical Notes

Paul continues his description of Peter, James, and John with a word picture that he paints with the word στῦλοι. This word, στῦλοι, comes from the Greek word στῦλος and means a pillar or column which stands by itself or supports a building. This word can also be used figuratively to mean any firm support or persons of authority and influence in the church. Paul, who had just previously written about the other apostles and himself being on the same level, now writes about these three and how they affected the church in Jerusalem. He likens them to pillars or columns which stand by themselves and, yet, in many cases are used to support different structures in a building. Paul says here that Peter, James, and John were the undergirding, or so it seemed, of the church. They were its firm supports as well as the ones who influenced the church greatly. They had a sturdy impact upon the church and were used greatly of God as the unmoving pieces upon which He built the rest of His Church.

Commentary Notes

When Peter, James, and John recognized the same hand of God blessing Paul's endeavors as had been upon their lives, they understood what God was doing through Paul. They noticed that God was blessing him and them both in equal amounts. Just as only the Spirit of God can do, He bound the hearts of these three apostles with Paul's heart in his ministry to the Gentiles. They rejoiced with him and extended the right hand of fellowship to both him and Barnabas. This spirit of cooperation is probably stated best by Hindson and Kroll who wrote,

Fellowship speaks of cooperation and joint participation. The right hand of fellowship was given to equals and indicated a token of approval and a pledge of fidelity and agreement to work in their respective fields, so that all men would be evangelized by the same gospel.This was the dramatic conclusion of the pact for cooperation in independent spheres of evangelism. The legalists were brushed aside when these five men shook hands as equals in the work of Christ.[8]

2:10 μόνον τῶν πτωχῶν ἵνα
     Only   the   poor   that
        μνημονεύωμεν,   ὅ
we should keep in remembrance; the
καὶ   ἐσπούδασα   αὐτὸ
also   I made every effort   same
τοῦτο   ποιῆσαι.
which   to do.

Only *they would* that we should remember the poor; the same which I also was forward to do.

μνημονεύωμεν Pres. Act. Subjunctive
     1st. Pers. Plur. μνάομαι Meaning =
     be mindful, remember, have in remembrance
ἐσπούδασα Aor. Act. Indicative
     1st. Pers. Sing. σπουδάζω Meaning
     = do diligence, endeavor, make effort, be prompt
ποιῆσαι Aor. Act. Infinitive ποιέω
     Meaning = do, make, perform

Commentary Notes
    Paul recalls the one stipulation that these three men placed on their parting: remember the poor. They were not simply asking Paul to remember the poor in the world, but rather those in Jerusalem. Judea had experienced famine and the

Christians there were poor as a result, as well as being ostra-
cized for their beliefs. Paul said that he was diligent to remember the poor. No one needed to prompt him to remember
the poor there in Judea as he ministered to the Gentiles. He
knew that the generosity of the Gentile believers toward the
Jews would only draw them closer together rather than alien-
ating them from each other.

Application
1. How do you treat the poor people? James tells us that the
   true test of our religion is how we treat the widows and the
   fatherless, those who are usually poor.
2. Do we keep the poor in remembrance as Paul did here?

E. The confronting of Peter-2:11-17
1. Peter's fellowship-2:11-12
2:11 Ὅτε δὲ   ἦλθε   Πέτρος
       when But [he]had come Peter
εἰς Ἀντιόχειαν, κατὰ πρόσωπον αὐτῷ
to   Antioch,   to the   face   of him
ἀντέστην,   ὅτι   κατεγνωσμένος
I resisted, because to be blamed
   ἦν.
he was.

But when Peter was come to Antioch, I withstood him to the
face, because he was to be blamed.

    ἦλθε Aor. Act. Indicative 3rd. Pers.
       Sing. ἔρχομαι Meaning = come
    ἀντέστην Aor. Act. Indicative
       1st. Pers. Sing. ἀνθίστημι Meaning
       = oppose, to stand against, resist, withstand
    κατεγνωσμένος Perf. Pass. Participle
       Nom. Masc. Sing. καταγινώσκω
       Meaning = blame, condemn, to note against, find
       fault with

ἦν Imp. Act. Indicative 3rd. Pers. Sing.

εἰμι Meaning = am, was, were

Commentary Notes

Paul continues here with a story that will support his apostleship beyond doubt, as being from God, and not from man. The apostle unfolds how Peter came to Antioch. When Peter came is not known, but it was probably not long after Paul's visit to Jerusalem. Paul goes on to write that the Apostle Peter, whom he had previously shaken hands with, he now had to resist and reprimand to his face because he had caused a rift between the Jewish believers and the Gentile believers and was to be blamed for it. Paul does not belittle Peter but rather points out to him how he is not living a consistent life with the gospel that he preaches. In the previous instance they are working together unified, but in this instance it is as if Peter causes a strife tearing down the work that Paul has done.

This story is the first introduction that we get to the differentiation of the ceremonial law and the moral law of the Old Testament. Wuest states,

In this verse Paul opens the question *as to whether the Jew himself is still bound by the Mosaic law.* In the Jerusalem council, the question was *as to whether the rite of circumcision should be required of the Gentiles.*

The particular Mosaic legislation to which Paul had reference here and which he presented as a test case before the Galatians, had to do with the Levitical legislation regarding the eating of certain foods. While one purpose of the giving of this legislation permitting the eating of certain foods and the prohibition regarding other foods, was a dietary one to promote the physical well-being of the Jews, yet another was that of keeping the Jews a separate people from the Gentiles, thus preserving clean the channel which God was using to bring salvation to the earth. The forbidden foods were found on the tables of the Gentiles. Hence a Jew could never accept a dinner invitation of a Gentile. This was one of the factors which kept the nation Israel apart from the Gentile world.

God had made clear to Peter that this legislation was set aside at the Cross, by the vision He gave him while he was on the housetop of Simon the tanner, with the result that Peter was willing to go to the home of Cornelius (Acts 10).[9]

When Christ paid the price of sin and salvation for all mankind on the cross, the ceremonial law was done away with just as quickly as John the Baptist had said, "Behold, the Lamb which taketh away the sin of the world." The curtain between the Holy Place and the Holy of Holies was rent in twain marking the open relationship that man would have with God the Father through Christ Jesus as our great High Priest forever. The ceremonial law will be instituted again during the Millennium when Christ shall rule with an iron rod, and the sacrifices will be maintained in the temple again.

What about the moral law and its fundamental representatives, the Ten Commandments? Were they done away with when Christ died on the cross and was resurrected three days later? No. The moral law is still in effect. Jesus Christ, Himself, restated every one of the Ten Commandments except the one about the Sabbath. The importance of this commandment now lies in the fact that in the New Covenant man rests and worships on the first day of the week and not on the seventh. This is so since the first day of the week was the day of Christ's resurrection. Man was still to be a mirror image of the moral character of God which is spelled out in practical terms in the Ten Commandments and the other Old Testament laws that deal with correct morality in human relations. Paul had to reprimand Peter to his face because Peter, who was a Jew, had separated himself from eating with Gentile believers (which was a ceremonial law dealing with uncleanness) and was leading others Jewish believers to do the same.

2:12 πρὸ   τοῦ   γὰρ ἐλθεῖν
    before those For   came
    τινὰς   ἀπὸ   Ἰακώβου, μετὰ τῶν
certain men from   James,   with the
    ἐθνῶν   συνήσθιεν· ὅτε   δὲ
Gentiles   he did eat: after but
    ἦλθον,   ὑπέστελλε καὶ ἀφώριζεν
they came, he withdrew and separated
ἑαυτόν, φοβούμενος τοὺς   ἐκ
himself,   fearing   those   of the
    περιτομῆς.
circumcision.

For before that certain came from James, he did eat with the Gentiles: but when they were come, he withdrew and separated himself, fearing them which were of the circumcision.

ἐλθεῖν Aor. Act. Infinitive ἔρχομαι
    Meaning = come
συνήσθιεν Imp. Act. Indicative
    3rd. Pers. Sing. συνεσθίω
    Meaning = eat with
ἦλθον Aor. Act. Indicative
    3rd. Pers. Plur. ἔρχομαι
    Meaning = come
ὑπέστελλε Imp. Act. Indicative
    3rd. Pers. Sing. ὑποστέλλω
    Meaning = draw back, shun, withdraw
ἀφώριζεν Imp. Act. Indicative
    3rd. Pers. Sing. ἀφωρίζω Meaning
    = divide, sever, separate, to set off, boundary
φοβούμενος Pres. M/P. Participle Nom.
    Masc. Sing. φοβέω Meaning = fear,
    be afraid, to be alarmed, reverence

Commentary Notes
    Peter had a vision from God and learned that God had bro-

ken down the partition between the Jew and the Gentile. He saw the results with his own two eyes as the first Gentile converts received the Holy Ghost. He understood that the gospel was for all and that all who had received Christ were in Christ, both Jew and Gentile alike. However, when he saw certain Jews coming from Jerusalem whom he was aware of, who were still observing the ceremonial law that eating with Gentiles was unclean, he balked and acted hypocritically. One moment, he was eating with the Gentiles, and the next, he was separating from them. Peter probably did not just abruptly jump up from his table with the Gentiles and run to one by himself. He probably tried to do it nonchalantly so as not to draw any undue attention to it, or to offend any of the Gentile brethren.

Why did Peter suddenly withdraw from eating with the Gentiles? Peter had been assailed by these Jewish brethren before (Acts 11:1-3) and was quite aware of their loyalty to the Jewish ceremonial law. Peter also was aware that these men knew James back in Jerusalem. In context, the wording does not necessarily mean that James had sent them to Antioch, but that they merely were coming from Jerusalem, more specifically, from where James was. Whatever the case, Peter's actions were not directed by the Holy Spirit due to a fear of God, but, rather, by what he thought that man might think of him, and from a fear of man. Since Peter was in a leadership position, he led other brethren astray also.

2. Peter's fraction-2:13

2:13 καὶ   συνυπεκρίθησαν
And [they]acted hypocritically with
αὐτῷ καὶ οἱ   λοιποὶ 'Ιουδαῖοι,
him also the remaining Jews,
ὥστε   καὶ Βαρνάβας
so that also Barnabas
    συναπήχθη   αὐτῶν τῇ
was yielding with [of them]their the
   ὑποκρίσει.
deceitfulness.

And the other Jews dissembled likewise with him; insomuch
that Barnabas also was carried away with their dissimulation.

συνυπεκρίθησαν Aor. Pass. Indicative
  3rd. Pers. Plur. συνυποκρίνομαι
  Meaning = to act hypocritically with, dissemble
  with, to conceal, to answer from under
συναπήχθη Aor. Pass. Indicative
  3rd. Pers. Sing. συναπάγω Meaning = condescend,
  carry away with, lead away with, yield to

Grammatical Notes

In the first part of this verse there are two καὶ's. The first
represents a simple continuative conjunction *(and)* while the
second represents the level of intensity (adjunctive) of the
writer in the statement *(also)*.[10] Another Greek text, however, has the second καὶ in brackets showing that the intensity of dissembling probably was not that important to Paul.
This goes directly against the context. Paul was trying to show
the Galatians just how influencing the dissembling had been
so that it even affected Barnabas.

Commentary Notes

As soon as Peter acted hypocritically by concealing his true
sentiments concerning his relationship with these Gentile
brethren, others followed. In describing Peter's and the other
Jews' actions, Paul employs the word συνυποκρίνομαι, which
from the first part of the word συν we get the word *with*, and
from ὑποκρίνομαι we get our English word hypocrite. The word
actually is describing an actor who is speaking from behind a
mask. The actor is not necessarily speaking what is in his
heart. Likewise, the actions of Peter and the Jews in Antioch
changed when the other Jews from Jerusalem showed up. Peter and the others tried to please Jewish ceremonialists rather
than to reflect the true feelings of their hearts toward the Gentiles. Suddenly Paul noticed that where there had been many
tables with Jew and Gentile brethren seated at them, now there

were only tables with Gentiles and tables with Jews. He understood right away that this was due to the arrival of other Jews who still observed the ceremonial laws of cleanness and uncleanness as concerned the Gentiles. Paul continues to say that they did such a convincing job of acting hypocritically, that even Barnabas changed places. Barnabas was an intimate friend to Paul, and was the very one who sent for him at Tarsus to minister with him in the church at Antioch. This must have offended Paul to see even his partner making such a choice. Other than Paul, Barnabas had been one of the most effective witnesses to the Gentile world. It was all the more clear in Paul's mind, now, that Peter's actions needed to be dealt with publicly, since his actions were affecting the unity of believers publicly. Of course, Paul saw it as his duty being an apostle to bring to Peter's attention his wrong action and its impact on others in the church. So he did just that.

Application
1. We would all be quick to condemn Peter of his hypocrisy here in this verse, but are there any areas of our life in which we act hypocritically?
2. Are you influencing someone to do wrong as Peter did Barnabas? Why not be an example for right in that same persons life?
3. We should make it our goal as Paul did here to influence people to do what is right even when it might cause a tense situation.

Illustration
Although a Christian's false actions may lead others astray, as Peter's did, one's positive example can help to lead others toward good actions. "Example," said Albert Schweitzer, "is not the main thing in influencing others. It is the only thing."

An incident in the life of Ben Franklin is a good illustration of what Schweitzer was talking about. Franklin wanted to install street lighting in Philadelphia, but he knew the city fathers would balk at the expense.

Instead of trying to persuade them, therefore, he simply hung a beautiful lantern on a long bracket in front of his own house.

People picking their way carefully along the streets at night would come out of the dark into the well-lit area in front of Franklin's house and think, "What a great idea." Soon Franklin's neighbors began placing lights in brackets in front of their homes. Before long the entire city awoke to the value of street lighting. Franklin had achieved what he wanted through example without a word being spoken.[11]

3. Peter's Failure-2:14-17
a. Paul's directness with Peter-2:14

2:14 ἀλλ' ὅτε εἶδον ὅτι οὐκ
But when I saw that not

ὀρθοποδοῦσι πρὸς
they were straightforward according to

τὴν ἀλήθειαν τοῦ εὐαγγελίου,
the truth of the gospel,

εἶπον τῷ Πέτρῳ ἔμπροσθεν πάντων,
I said to Peter before them all,

Εἰ σύ, Ἰουδαῖος ὑπάρχων,
If you, a Jew being,

ἐθνικῶς ζῇς καὶ οὐκ
like the Gentiles live and not

Ἰουδαϊκῶς, τί τὰ ἔθνη
the Jews, why the Gentiles

ἀναγκάζεις
do you urge strongly

Ἰουδαΐζειν;
to live as the Jews?

But when I saw that they walked not uprightly according to the truth of the gospel, I said unto Peter before *them* all, If thou, being a Jew, livest after the manner of Gentiles, and not as do the Jews, why compellest thou the Gentiles to live as do the Jews?

> εἶδον 2nd. Aor. Act. Indicative
> > 1st. Pers. Sing. ὁράω Meaning = see, perceive
>
> ὀρθοποδοῦσι Pres. Act. Indicative
> > 3rd. Pers. Plur. ὀρθοποδέω Meaning = walk uprightly, to be straight footed, to go directly forward
>
> εἶπον 2nd. Aor. Act. Indicative
> > 1st. Pers. Sing. λέγω Meaning = say, speak
>
> ὑπάρχων Pres. Act. Participle Nom.
> > Masc. Sing. ὑπάρχω Meaning = after, behave, live
>
> ζῆς Pres. Act. Indicative 2nd. Pers.
> > Sing. ζάω Meaning = live
>
> ἀναγκάζεις Pres. Act. Indicative
> > 2nd. Pers. Sing. ἀναγκάζεις
> > Meaning = compel, constrain, strongly urge
>
> Ἰουδαΐζειν Pres. Act. Infinitive
> > Ἰουδαΐζειν Meaning = live as the Jews, Judaize

Grammatical Notes

One significant difference noted here in our Textus Receptus is the first word of the last section of this verse τί differs from the word πῶς, which is found in its place in some MSS. The first word, τί, is an accusative singular neuter of the interrogative pronoun which is often used adverbially to mean why.[12] Πῶς is an interrogative adverb meaning *how* and is not natural in this sentence structure.[13]

The word used here to describe Peter and the other Jews is ὀρθοποδοῦσι, and it comes from the two Greek words ὀρθός and ποδέω. The Greek word ὀρθός means "straight" and ποδέω means "foot." The word literally means "to walk with straight feet, or to walk a straight course." Wuest says, "It speaks of straightforward, unwavering, sincere conduct in contrast to crooked, wavering, and more or less insincere course which Paul had said Peter and the other Jews were guilty of."[14] The conduct of the Jews here was dishonest.

Commentary Notes

Peter's and the other Jews' conduct was not according to the true spirit of the gospel, which placed both Jew and Gentile on the same level playing field with the ground being level at the foot of the cross. Paul understood this probably better than anyone else at the time because he had been a very zealous Jew who was converted to preach to the Gentiles. He knew there was no barrier, and for these brethren to have one in their mind was not what Christ would have done. These men should have acted as Christ would have by walking a straight path and not a crooked one before these Gentile believers.

Paul addressed Peter publicly on the matter of dishonest conduct. He entered into discourse with him before all who had witnessed Peter's actions. If it had been a private situation, Paul would have addressed Peter privately, but it was not. John R. Rice, in his notes in the *Rice Reference Bible*, says,

Paul rebuked Peter publicly. The incident makes several points:

(1) The wisest, godliest person may fall into sin through some　special love or association. Solomon turned to idolatry through his wives (1 Kgs. 11:1-8). David committed adultery and murder because of his attraction to Bathsheba (2 Sam. 12:4). Paul went to Rome to try to reach the unloved Jews, although forbidden by the Spirit, and offered a Jewish sacrifice (Acts 21:26). Likewise, Peter in associating with the Judaizers at Jerusalem sinned. (2) God surely intended to thus cancel any use of Peter against Paul's gospel... (3) God's man must plainly condemn sin among Christians as well as among the unsaved (1 Tm. 5:20; Tit. 1:9-13; Is. 58:1).[15]

Paul begins his address to Peter with a question to make him consider his actions. His question does not deal with Peter's moral character in this instance, but rather his outward inconsistencies and the effects they might have on the unity between the Jewish and the Gentile Church. Peter has been staying in Antioch with the Gentile church, and eating the food with the Gentiles before those certain men came from Jerusalem. Then Peter's tune changes and he separates himself from the Gentiles and their food and eats separately. Although Peter has not verbally compelled the Gentiles to follow the Jew's customs, he does so externally with his actions. Peter was at the Jerusalem meeting with the other apostles and was part of the solution there. Here he is the cause of the friction, not by way of proclamation, but by action. Paul calls it to his attention because Peter is now sending a completely different message than he has been since he arrived in Antioch, a message that the other Jews understood and followed, heightening the degree of hypocrisy before the Gentile believers.

Illustration

A man sat down to supper with his family, saying grace, thanking God for the food, for the hands which prepared it, and for the source of all life. But during the meal he complained about the freshness of the bread, the bitterness of the coffee and the sharpness of the cheese. His young daughter questioned him, "Dad, do you think God heard the grace today?"

He answered confidently, "Of course."

Then she asked, "And do you think God heard what you said about the coffee, the cheese, and the bread?" Not so confidently, he answered, "Why, yes, I believe so."

The little girl concluded, "Then which do you think God believed, Dad?"

The man was suddenly aware that his mealtime prayer had become a rote, thoughtless habit rather than an attentive and honest conversation with God. By not concentrating on that important conversation, he had left the door open to let hypocrisy sneak in.[16]

Application
1. If we were in Peter's shoes in this verse, how would we handle it?
2. Hypocrisy is bad in and of itself, but when done in front of babes in Christ, it is even worse because it leads new believers astray and sometimes even old.

b. Paul's discourse with Peter-2:15-17
1) Paul's doctrine defined-2:15-16
2:15   ἡμεῖς
We [the ones who are]
    φύσει   'Ιουδαῖοι,
  by natural lineage   Jews,
καὶ   οὐκ ἐξ   ἐθνῶν
and   not   of   the Gentiles
ἁμαρτωλοί,
  sinners,

We *who are* Jews by nature, and not sinners of the Gentiles,

Commentary Notes
    Paul continues his address to Peter and the others attending the fellowship time through verse 21. The Apostle Paul continues his dialogue on justification by faith so that all of those present can understand the true consistency of the gospel and its impact on both Jew and Gentile alike. This understanding would seem most likely since Paul addresses his comments directly to the Galatians in 3:1.
    Paul continues by helping both the Jews and Gentiles to see the distinction that was between them when he states, "We who are Jews by natural lineage, and not sinners as the Gentiles." He is not meaning that the Jews were not sinners like the Gentiles but rather that the Jews had more responsibility since they had been given God's Word from Abraham, on down the line, and had been submitting to the law. The Gentiles were not given God's law to govern their life and, therefore, had been involved in gross and sensual immorality as most of the hea-

then world. The Jews were not ignorant of the law of God and, therefore, should be the ones to set the proper example.

2:16 εἰδότες   ὅτι   οὐ   δικαιοῦται
    Knowing that not is justified
ἄνθρωπος ἐξ   ἔργων   νόμου,
  a man   by the works of the law,
ἐὰν μὴ διὰ πίστεως   Ἰησοῦ Χριστοῦ,
if not   by [the] faith of Jesus Christ,
καὶ   ἡμεῖς εἰς Χριστὸν   Ἰησοῦν
and   we in Christ   Jesus,
ἐπιστεύσαμεν,   ἵνα
we have believed that
    δικαιωθῶμεν   ἐκ   πίστεως
we might be justified   by [the] faith
  Χριστοῦ, καὶ   οὐκ ἐξ   ἔργων
of Christ, and   not by [the] works
  νόμου·   διότι   οὐ
of [the] law; therefore not
δικαιωθήσεται   ἐξ   ἔργων
will be justified according to [the] works
  νόμου πᾶσα σάρξ.
of the law   all   flesh.

Knowing that a man is not justified by the works of the law, but by the faith of Jesus Christ, even we have believed in Jesus Christ, that we might be justified by the faith of Christ, and not by the works of the law: for by the works of the law shall no flesh be justified.

εἰδότες Perf. Act. Participle Nom.
    Masc. Plur. ὁράω Meaning = understanding
δικαιοῦται Pres. Pass. Indicative
    3rd. Pers. Sing. δικαιόω Meaning = free, justify,
    be righteous
ἐπιστεύσαμεν Aor. Act. Indicative

> 1st. Pers. Plur. πιστεύω Meaning
> = believe, put in trust with, commit
>
> δικαιωθῶμεν Aor. Pass. Subjunctive
> 1st. Pers. Plur. δικαιόω Meaning = free,
> justify, be righteous
>
> δικαιωθήσεται Fut. Pass. Indicative
> 3rd. Pers. Sing. δικαιόω Meaning = free,
> justify, be righteous

Grammatical Notes

At the beginning of this verse there is a difference between the Textus Receptus and another Greek rendering of this verse. The Textus Receptus reads εἰδότες ὅτι and another manuscript reads εἰδότες δὲ ὅτι. The difference is the word δὲ. This word is commonly used as an adversative particle.[17] It is not necessary here because of the use of the negative οὐ and ἐὰν μὴ, which already give a sharp antithesis.[18]

Another difference in this verse between the Textus Receptus and other MSS is the first word of the last phrase, διότι. This is the word used in the Textus Receptus while other MSS make use of the word ὅτι. Ὅτι, a "conjunction in form is simply the neuter indefinite relative pronoun ὅ τι. It is very common as a causal particle meaning because or for."[19] However, the use of διότι in the Textus Receptus is a truer reflection of the heart of the apostle in the original language here. Διότι is a combination of διό, which was "formed by uniting a preposition with the neuter relative pronoun δί ὅ, and τι.[20] Διότι and ὅτι both have the meanings because and for, but διότι would be better suited to the context since it has stronger causal force than ὅτι. Since "the turning point or direction of a thought is usually indicated by a conjunction,"[21] it is without a doubt that Paul would use the combination incorporating the "strongest inferential conjunction"[22] (διό), διότι. Why? Paul wanted the final statement of this verse to be in the strongest language possible, for according to the works of the law shall no flesh be justified! He uses a concrete statement saying that absolutely no flesh, none whatsoever, is justified by the works of the law. An extreme statement is deserving of an extreme introduction.

Commentary Notes

Paul does not choose the topic of his theological discourse that he is about to present to these believers. It was chosen for him. He must then continue to help Peter and the other Christians to see that a person's sanctification must link up with his justification. He directs his focus to the Jewish brethren first, because they are more responsible. Paul states, "We who are Jews by nature, knowing that a man is not justified by the works of the law but by the faith of Jesus Christ." Paul believes that this truth concerning salvation is understood by these Jewish brethren, because as far as salvation is concerned, they had seen through the fallacy of the present-day Judaism. Since they saw that its focus was on outward works, he begins here. The Judaism that Paul had grown up learning about was the same legalistic Judaism that Peter and these other Jews were displaying to the Gentiles, one based on works. Paul uses one legalism to confront the other because it is out of a person's understanding of justification that his life will be lived. Paul uses the term ἔργων νόμου, which means the works of the law. This word law is used in the character and legalistic sense. It is used to portray the divine law as a legalistic system in which divine approval is acquired by performing the works.

The very fiber of this legalistic gospel has nothing to do with grace. The way a person is justified is the same way he will continue to live. His very life should be an expression of his salvation (or understanding of it). God nowhere in His Word teaches that works are necessary for salvation or admonishes a man in this direction. However, this belief has been a perverted understanding of justification in man's mind from Cain on. Cain believed that he could bring God the works of his life, the fruit of his labor rather than a burnt animal sacrifice, but he was wrong. He was not wanting to display faith in God but rather appease God and have God's approval on him. The Bible states that out of the abundance of the heart the mouth speaketh, and it also goes without saying that out of the abundance of the heart the life is lived.

The apostle directed everyone's attention to what was causing Peter and these other Jews to act hypocritically and dissemble from the Gentiles and the Christian belief system and action system. These two systems were not lining up with each other on the same foundation. So, Paul reminds the believers of their belief system by stating, "not by works of the law but by the faith of Jesus Christ." Their belief system was based on their faith in Christ, not on their previous misunderstanding of the law (and Paul spoke here from experience as a Pharisee). Paul then focuses on what has unified these Jews with these Gentiles: their faith in Jesus Christ. They had placed their faith in Christ because they had realized that no flesh could be or would be justified by the works of a law. If the Jews turned back to their old system of actions, it would not be in accord with their Christian belief system, and Paul reminded them of that. "True justification of the believing sinner," as Wuest explains, "consists of taking away his guilt and its penalty, since Christ bore both on the cross, and the imputation of a righteousness, even Christ Jesus Himself, in whom the believer stands not only guiltless and uncondemned for time and eternity, but also positively righteous in the sight of the eternal laws of God."23

2) Paul's doctrine defended-2:17

2:17 εἰ δέ,   ζητοῦντες   δικαιωθῆναι
     if But, while we seek to be justified
ἐν Χριστῷ,   εὑρέθημεν   καὶ   αὐτοὶ
by   Christ,   we are found   also   ourselves
ἁμαρτωλοί,   ἆρα   Χριστὸς
  sinners,   therefore   Christ
ἁμαρτίας   διάκονος;   μὴ γένοιτο.
  of sin   the minister?   God forbid!

But if, while we seek to be justified by Christ, we ourselves also are found sinners, *is* therefore Christ the minister of sin? God forbid.

    ζητοῦντες Pres. Act. Participle Nom.
        Masc. Plur. ζητέω Meaning = desire, enquire, seek, seek (by way of worship)
    δικαιωθῆναι Aor. Pass. Infinitive
        δικαιόω Meaning = free, justify, be righteous
    εὑρέθημεν Aor. Pass. Indicative
        1st. Pers. Plur. εὑρίσκω Meaning = find, get, obtain, see, perceive
    γένοιτο 2nd. Aor. Mid. Optative
        3rd. Pers. Sing. γίνομαι Meaning = come into being, be brought to pass, God forbid, happen, be fulfilled

Commentary Notes

Paul described to those listening to him what many people grapple with after trusting Christ as they begin their walk with the Lord by faith. As the new Christian walks more with Him and their relationship grows closer to Him, he realizes more his new freedom in Christ to do what is right out of a heart of love and adoration. However, if this individual who now has a relationship with God gets the idea that he can choose when to walk with God and when not to, then his freedom leads to licentiousness. Thus, some require godly living as an aspect of salvation. They like to add something to the gospel to "insure" that believers live godly lives. Their understanding is that it is right to say that a person is saved by grace, but then he needs to work (obey the law) to keep his salvation or to stay in the good graces of God.

Although Christians are free from the ceremonial law, they still have a moral responsibility to become Christlike. Trusting Christ does not lead to lawlessness, allowing the believer to simply make up his own rules. But, what if a believer does start to follow his own way rather than Christ's? Is Christ the cause of it? No, in fact, Paul uses the phrase μὴ γένοιτο, which means "God forbid" or "let it not be so." God did not design justification by faith to mean that once a person becomes a Christian he can be as morally lax as he wishes, throwing off all restraints. That thinking is antinomianism. Jesus Christ was a man whose life was characterized by being under all God-ordained authority all of the time. He also was a morally pure individual. Trusting Christ for salvation and being baptized into God's forever family will make an individual want to become more Christlike. He will desire to develop character, or, in society, it would be called civic virtue. Paul says if a Christian is found to be a sinner after trusting in Christ, one cannot trace that sin back to his salvation, God forbid.

III. **Interpretation and instruction on law and grace-2:18-4:31**
   A. **The comparison of salvation by the law or by faith-2:18-3:29**
      1. **The Christian's life of faith-2:18-21**
         a. **Paul's personal teaching on justification by faith-2:18-19**

   2:18 εἰ γὰρ ἃ κατέλυσα,
      if For which I demolished
   ταῦτα πάλιν οἰκοδομῶ,
   those things again I build,
      παραβάτην ἐμαυτὸν συνίστημι.
   a transgressor myself I prove.

For if I build again the things which I destroyed, I make myself a transgressor.

   κατέλυσα Aor. Act. Indicative
      1st. Pers. Sing. κατελύω Meaning = destroy,
         dissolve, come to nought, overthrow, demolish
   οἰκοδομω Pres. Act. Indicative

    1st. Pers. Sing. οἰκοδομω Meaning
    = build, edify, embolden
συνίστημι Pres. Act. Indicative
    1st. Pers. Sing. συνίστημι Meaning
    = demonstrate, show, make, bring out, prove

Grammatical Notes

The last word in this verse differs from the last word found in another Greek text. Here συνίστημι is employed while in another text συνιστάνω is found. These two spellings are of the same word; however, one is the real root, the oldest root, while the other is a newer form of it. Συνίστημι is a defective verb having gained various forms later in history.[24] "Συνίστημι and συνιστάνω are later forms of συνίστημι."[25] The Textus Receptus contains the oldest form of the word dating the manuscript that it is based on as older than that of the other Greek text.

Commentary Notes

When Peter and the Jews that Paul had been addressing ate with the Gentiles there in Antioch, they tore down the ceremonial law and the works involved and supported justification by faith. When they failed to follow through, however, by acting hypocritically and separating themselves from the Gentiles, they taught a different gospel. Peter, Paul, and the other Jews knew that the ceremonial law was no longer in effect because Christ had completed it and broken down the barriers between the Jew and Gentile. If they were to rebuild that barrier and return to their old system and wrong understanding of law and works versus their freedom in Christ, they would become transgressors of the higher law of grace.

    2:19 ἐγὼ γὰρ   διὰ   νόμου
       I For through [the] law
    νόμῳ   ἀπέθανον,
 [to the law]   died ,
    ἵνα   Θεῷ   ζήσω.

in order that to God   I should live.

For I through the law am dead to the law, that I might live
unto God.

> ἀπέθανον Aor. Act. Indicative
>   1st. Pers. Sing. ἀποθνῆσκω
>   Meaning = be dead, die, be slain
> ζήσω Aor. Act. Subjunctive
>   1st. Pers. Sing. ζάω Meaning = live

Commentary Notes

Paul reminds the other Jews that the law was the very
agent through which he died to the law. Paul became dead to
the law by trying to keep it. By seeking to be justified by it, he
realized that it would not justify him and he stopped expecting it to. The law did not provide life and righteousness as he
had been expecting to find, but rather condemnation which
drove him to Christ for salvation. Paul became dead to the
law, which meant that it had no influence over him anymore
so far as his justification was concerned. He now had a higher
law governing his life, justification by faith and the grace of
God. He realized that if he continued to look to justification
by the law, his life would be a dead sacrifice with nothing as
the result. But now, having trusted Christ, he looked to God
for direction and consecrated himself to God's service as a living sacrifice so that he might live unto God. Wuest concludes,

> Paul does not say that he is dead to law, that is, a
> law to himself, thus a lawless individual. He still holds
> to the great ethical principles of love and justice, for in-
> stance, which are eternal in their significance, the great
> underlying principles that inhere in God's character and
> in His government. When Paul says that he has died to
> a thing he means that he has ceased to have any rela-
> tion to it, so that it has no further claim upon or control
> over him. It is law as conceived of as a body of legalistic

statutes, that he has died to.[26]

b. Paul's practical teaching on living by faith-2:20

2:20 Χριστῷ   συνεσταύρωμαι·
Christ I have been crucified with:
ζῶ   δέ,   οὐκέτι ἐγώ, ζῇ   δὲ   ἐν
I live but,   yet not I,   lives but in
ἐμοὶ Χριστός·   ὃ   δὲ
me Christ: the one [life] which and
νῦν ζῶ   ἐν σαρκί,   ἐν πίστει
now I live in [the] flesh, by [the] faith
ζῶ τῇ   τοῦ υἱοῦ τοῦ   Θεοῦ,
I live the of the Son of [the] God,
τοῦ ἀγαπήσαντός με καὶ παραδόντος
who   loved   me and   gave
ἑαυτὸν   ὑπὲρ   ἐμοῦ.
himself for [on behalf of]   me.

I am crucified with Christ: nevertheless I live; yet not I, but
Christ liveth in me: and the life which I now live in the flesh I
live by the faith of the Son of God, who loved me, and gave
himself for me.

συνεσταύρωμαι Perf. Pass. Indicative
    1st. Pers. Sing. συνεσταυρόω
    Meaning = crucify with
ζῶ Pres. Act. Indicative 1st. Pers.
    Sing. ζάω Meaning = live
ζῇ Pres. Act. Indicative 3rd. Pers. Sing.
    ζάω Meaning = live
ἀγαπήσαντός Aor. Act. Participle Gen.
    Masc. Sing. ἀγαπάω Meaning = love
παραδόντος Aor. Act. Participle Gen.
    Masc. Sing. παραδίδωμι
    Meaning = give

Grammatical Notes

Paul now directs his audience's attention to Christ's finished work on the cross and its impact in a believer's life. He uses the phrase Χριστῷ συνεσταύρωμαι which means, "I have been crucified with Christ." Paul employed the perfect tense of this phrase to express what had occurred in the past with results extending to the present. He had been crucified with Christ and Christ's crucifixion was affecting his life right then. When Christ died on the cross, he became dead to all of the things around him: the law, the world, and sin. Paul was saying, "I have been crucified with Christ when He was crucified, but I am alive now just as Christ is alive. His resurrection was my resurrection."

Commentary Notes

Paul identified himself with Christ's death on the cross. This truth literally transformed his life. Where he had been trying to find life by the works of the law, he found death. But, when he came to the cross of Christ, which was the most humiliating, excruciating form of death known to man at the time, he found life, resurrected life. A dead man does not try to obey the law. He cannot: he is dead. A dead man does not battle the world or its many lures. He cannot: he is dead. A dead man is not controlled by sin. He cannot be: he is dead. But a man alive to God will be controlled, influenced, and directed by Him. To the law he is inactive, but to God he is alive. Before his conversion Paul had been a very active individual, persecuting Christians and trying to obey the law to find favor with God. After his conversion he did not become a lazy individual, but rather became busy in God's army as a recruiter. He was more active now than he had ever been. We have heard the phrase used before, "Get a life." Well, Paul did just that. What he had before was death, but now he had life and it was a life lived more abundantly! Paul did not get just "any life"— he got the life of Christ. No longer was it Paul's energy or power that he was living by. He could not take any credit for the good that God had done through him. He uses the term ζῇ δὲ ἐν ἐμοὶ Χριστός, which indicates that Christ was the source of everything that was occurring in the life of Paul now, not himself. Every aspect of Paul's life pointed to Christ. Paul was a branch growing and given life by the Vine (John 15). What now was coursing through the Apostle Paul he could take absolutely no credit for since its originator was God Himself.

Paul continued to help others see past the outside and look to the inside by making the transition from flesh to faith. As Paul continued his address to these other believers, he explained the outward (in which they were caught up) with the inward (which was where they were supposed to be). Paul said that everything that he performed in the physical realm (flesh) was traceable only to the spiritual realm (faith). His life, what others saw, was not him but was Christ working through him. The only way that Christ could accomplish all in Paul that He wished to was by faith. Paul's confidence was not in the arm of flesh any longer, but it was in Christ through faith. In fact, it was the faith of Christ that had revolutionized or resurrected Paul's life. Where Paul's persecution brought death to many, now his preaching brought life to all with whom he came in contact. Yes, those to whom he preached were left with the choice of choosing Christ, but Paul fulfilled his responsibility to preach Christ to everyone with whom he came in contact.

The reason that Paul became a living, burning, consumed-up flame for Christ is stated by Paul at the end of this verse. Christ loved Paul and gave Himself for Paul. Paul's Christianity was a genuine, sincere, and personal relationship. He recognized all that it cost Christ to die on that cross. He knew that although Christ was God, He was still a man and had to suffer as a man when He died on the cross. If Jesus Christ loved Paul so much that He gave His life for him, Paul could only hope to give his life for Christ in return. Christ gave His life on a cross for Paul, and Paul hoped to give his life to Christ by carrying His cross. The driving force in the Apostle Paul's life was that Christ loved him so much that He died in his place. Paul understood the depth of this love. He had been beating his head against the wall trying to obey the law for justification. At every corner the law met him saying, "Guilty, guilty." Paul could not find freedom in the law, but when he came to Christ and laid his burden down, he found freedom.

Illustration

I remember the first time I truly understood the truth of being completely justified by faith. I had trusted Christ when I was 13 years old. However, I had been taught that if I did not live a life without any sin and be 100 percent sold out to God all of the time, then there was always the possibility that I could lose my salvation. One day I was sitting in the Commons on the campus of Pensacola Christian College, and a friend and I were discussing this issue. I tried to comprehend the arguments of both sides, but that endeavor is a losing battle. Finally, my friend gave me a list of verses that were used to support each side: either justification by faith plus nothing, or justification by faith plus works to maintain salvation.

As I sat there turning from one Scripture to another, the Word of God shot through my mind and gripped my heart and helped me to see that God loved me so much! When he paid the price for me on the cross and I accepted Him, I became His child forever! I am not one who trusts my emotions much. I do remember, however, that at the very moment I understood that once I had become a child of God's I was His forever, I felt a tingling sensation that went down my spine. I had joy that was that much deeper than when I had trusted Christ at the age of 13. It was a joy that I knew no one could take from me. The truth of justification by grace plus nothing literally revolutionized my life in Christ, and for Christ. At the heart of it all was that Christ loved me so much that He died for me.

Applications
1. As a Christian have you reckoned yourself to be dead with Christ? Do you live a flesh-crucified life daily?
2. Are you still doing what you want to do or have you started allowing the Son of God to live through you?
3. Are you living in the flesh or have you started living by

faith?

c. Paul's primary understanding of righteousness by faith-2:21

2:21 οὐκ   ἀθετῶ   τὴν χάριν
    not I do render null the   grace
τοῦ Θεοῦ· εἰ γὰρ διὰ   νόμου
of [the] God: if for through [the] law
    δικαιοσύνη, ἄρα Χριστὸς
    righteousness, then   Christ
    δωρεὰν ἀπέθανεν.
    in vain   is dead.

I do not frustrate the grace of God: for if righteousness *come* by the law, then Christ is dead in vain.

    ἀθετῶ Pres. Act. Indicative 1st. Pers.
        Sing. ἀθετέω Meaning = cast off, despise, disannul, frustrate,reject, bring to nought, render null
    ἀπέθανεν 2nd Aor. Act. Indicative
        3rd. Pers. Sing. ἀποθνῆσκω Meaning = be dead, die, be slain

Commentary Notes

Paul concludes his address to Peter and the other believers there at Antioch with the solid, fundamental statement, "I do not render null the grace of God." Paul was simply saying that he did not render the grace of God null in any way, shape, or form. He would not render it null with his philosophy because God's grace was exactly what Christ taught to him personally. He would not render it null with his preaching since this was the message that Christ gave to him to preach. He would not render it null with his practice because he understood that people need to see Christ living in us. Paul understood that our thinking, speaking, and living all need to march to the same tune: the grace of God. Paul had previously been duped into believing that by obeying the law he could earn merit with God. He learned it, he taught it, he lived it. But not now, now he understood all of salvation to be by grace. The way that an individual is saved is the same way that he is sanctified. He is birthed into God's family by grace and must learn to mature in grace. Paul understood this and concluded his argument to Peter by stating that Christians must be consistent in what they believe, say, and do.

Paul helped Peter and the other Jewish brethren to see that although they believed they were saved by grace and were teaching that they were saved by grace, their practice did not match their philosophy or their preaching. Paul would not nullify the grace of God in any of these areas whether it was by sin or by observance of the ceremonial law, and he did not want the other brethren to do this either. Paul understood that if righteousness could be obtained through the observance of the law, then the death of Christ on the cross would be in vain: it would be useless. If man could point to himself for any merit, whether of works or of morality, then Christ's death on the cross would be rendered void and thus the grace of God also would be rendered void. Thus, Paul reminds Peter that to step backward to religion rather than forward in his relationship with God would send the wrong message to all, Jew and Gentile alike.

1 Barnes, 926.
2 Dana and Mantey, 168.
3 Ibid., 170.
4 Ibid.
5 Barnes, 927.
6 Dana and Mantey, 139.
7 Ibid., 29.
8 Hindson and Kroll, 2379.
9 Wuest, 68-69.
10 Dana and Mantey, 250.
11 Arthur Lenehan, "To Illustrate," *Leadership Journal* 18, no. 1, 14 January
   1997 [journal on-line]; available from http://www.christianity.net/leadership/
   features/illustrate.html; Internet; accessed February 1997.
12 Machen, 172.
13 Dana and Mantey, 238.
14 Wuest, 74.
15 John R. Rice, *The RICE Reference Bible* (Nashville, TN: Thomas Nelson
   Publishers, 1981), 1262.
16 Parsons, *Bible Illustrator.*
17 Dana and Mantey, 244.
18 Robertson, 1187.
19 Dana and Mantey, 245.
20 Ibid.
21 Ibid., 240.
22 Ibid., 245.
23 Wuest, 78.
24 A. T. Robertson and W. Hersey Davis, *A New Short Grammar of the Greek
   Testament* (Grand Rapids, MI: Baker Book House, 1977), 287.
25 Zodhiates, *The Complete Word Study Dictionary: New Testament,* 1344.
26 Wuest, 80.

2. The Galatians' forgotten faith-3:1-5
a. Paul's question concerning their betrayer-3:1

3:1 Ὦ ἀνόητοι Γαλάται, τίς ὑμᾶς
    O foolish Galatians, who you
ἐβάσκανε   τῇ   ἀληθείᾳ
has bewitched that the   truth
μὴ πείθεσθαι,   οἷς κατ'
not you should obey, whose before
ὀφθαλμοὺς 'Ιησοῦς Χριστὸς
   eyes   Jesus   Christ
    προεγράφη   ἐν
has been clearly proclaimed among
ὑμῖν ἐσταυρωμένος;
you   crucified?

O foolish Galatians, who hath bewitched you, that ye should
not obey the truth, before whose eyes Jesus Christ hath been
evidently set forth, crucified among you?

    ἐβάσκανε Aor. Act. Indicative 3rd.
        Pers. Sing. βασκαίνω
        Meaning = bewitch, malign, mislead by pretense

πείθεσθαι Pres. Mid. Infinitive
πείθω Meaning = obey, trust, yield, rely
προεγράφη Aor. Pass. Indicative
    3rd. Pers. Sing. προγράφω
    Meaning = before ordain,
    clearly proclaim, evidently set forth
ἐσταυρωμένος Perf.Pass.Participle
    Nom. Masc. Sing. σταυρόω
    Meaning = crucify

Grammatical Notes

The first place that the *Textus Receptus* clearly differs from another Greek text in this verse is the omission of the following phrase: τῇ ἀληθείᾳ μὴ πείθεσθαι, translated "that you should not obey the truth." While the *Textus Receptus* records it, in the other text it is missing. Here the Apostle Paul is revealing the result in the life of the Galatians who had practiced what the false teachers had taught them. They had stopped obeying the truth that since they had been saved by faith they should live by faith. However, the other Greek text does not include this phrase, thus invalidating the end result of being taught a lie, disobedience to the truth. Paul has just stated that he lives by the truth, the faith of the Son of God. He points out that they have rejected this truth in practice because they have rejected it in faith. Without this phrase the clause is incomplete. It shows the passivity of the Galatian believers, but it does not reveal the outcome of their passivity. Passivity in the Christian life does produce results, the wrong kind of results. Lack of full obedience is clearly disobedience. The next portion of this verse that is left out in some MSS is the phrase ἐν ὑμῖν, translated "among you." This prepositional phrase is important since it is ἐν with the locative case signifying the direction of the action of the verb προεγράφη meaning "clearly proclaim."[1] Christ's crucifixion had been clearly proclaimed expressly by Paul to the Galatian churches.

Commentary Notes

Paul had just shown in Galatians 1 and 2 that his apostleship, his aim (grace), and his actions came from Christ. He also showed how the other leading apostles supported and agreed with him wholeheartedly. Now, he will question the Galatians about their own salvation and sanctification by way of the Holy Spirit of God. He will then go on to support his message to the Galatians by showing that justification by grace was true before the Old Testament was written, during the writing of it, and after it was written. Then, he will show them that the Old Testament law and New Testament grace are not at odds with each other, but rather that the Old Testament law was given to direct men to their need of a Savior, Jesus Christ.

Paul now directs his address solely to the Galatians. He does not give them a word of commendation once in this letter, but instead points to their problem. In fact, he highlights their problem throughout the whole letter. He calls them foolish. "It is an expression of surprise mingled with indignation."[2] The original word that is used here is ἀνόητοι and does not mean that they were naturally stupid or lacked a normal level of intellect, but rather it means that they were acting without reason, showing a real lack of understanding. What caused them to act without reason? What caused them to leave the doctrine of justification by grace that the Apostle Paul had taught them, as well as what the other apostles had been teaching? Why did they not use their reason or their sober judgment? They had been charmed. The word that describes what happened to them is ἐβάσκανε and has the idea of being under the spell of an evil eye or being fascinated to the point of confusion. Paul knew that the Galatians' decision did not include asking the Holy Spirit what truth was, nor did it include the simple thought process of asking why Christ died on the cross.

Anytime truth is set aside there are side effects in an individual's life. The Galatians set aside the truth that Paul had taught them; and when this happened, they stopped living according to the truth and began disobeying it. They had

defected from believing the truth, which resulted in their disobedience to the truth.

Paul presented Christ crucified to the Galatians as clearly
as he possibly could. In fact, Paul says that he presented it so
clearly that it was as if it had occurred in their very presence,
before their eyes. When Paul preached, he preached Christ.
He set forth no one or no thing other than Christ. Paul set
forth Christ before them in such a vivid way that they could
not just simply dismiss it from their minds.

Application
1. Is there something that has you out of God's will, Christian?
2. Has the Devil got you lured into this world with some confusion or fascination?

b. Paul's question concerning the Spirit-3:2

3:2 τοῦτο μόνον θέλω   μαθεῖν   ἀφ'
      This only I wish to learn from
ὑμῶν, ἐξ   ἔργων   νόμου   τὸ
you, by the works of the law the
Πνεῦμα ἐλάβετε,   ἢ ἐξ
Spirit Did you obtain, or by
   ἀκοῆς   πίστεως;
the hearing of faith?

This only would I learn of you, Received ye the Spirit by the
works of the law, or by the hearing of faith?

> θέλω   Pres. Act. Indicative 1st.
>   Pers. Sing. θέλω Meaning = desire, wish, will,
>   intend
> μαθεῖν Aor. Act. Infinitive μανθάνω
>   Meaning = learn, understand
> ἐλάβετε   Aor. Act. Indicative 2nd.
>   Pers. Plur. λαμβάνω Meaning =
>   accept, attain, obtain, receive

Commentary Notes

Paul continues his severe reproof of the Galatians here by presenting a question to them. In fact, Paul understands that they had only one way they could possibly answer this question, which would be a truth that they could not so easily dismiss. He asked them how they obtained the Holy Spirit of God in their heart. Did they receive the Holy Spirit by obeying and doing the work of a law, maybe even the law of Moses, or did they receive the gift of the Holy Spirit and all of the wonderful benefits that He bestows in the life of a believer by faith in God? Paul introduces this one argument with the word μόνον, which means "only." He understood that this question of how the Galatians received the Holy Spirit was enough to clinch the truth in their mind. Paul appealed to their remembrance of His renewal of their hearts and His sanctifying of their souls. The Holy Spirit was the One who comforted them in affliction. He was the One whom they received at their conversion by faith.

c. Paul's question concerning their maturity-3:3

3:3 οὕτως ἀνόητοί   ἐστε;
      so   foolish Are you?

ἐναρξάμενοι Πνεύματι,   νῦν
Having begun in the Spirit, now
   σαρκὶ
by the flesh
      ἐπιτελεῖσθε;
are you being made complete?

Are ye so foolish? having begun in the Spirit, are ye now made perfect by the flesh?

ἐστε   Pres. Act. Indicative 2nd. Pers.
    Plur. εἰμι Meaning = is, are
ἐναρξάμενοι Aor. Mid. Participle
    Nom. Masc. Plur. ἐνάρξομαι
    Meaning = to commence on, rule

ἐπιτελεῖσθε Pres. Mid. Indicative 2nd.
Pers. Plur. ἐπιτελέω Meaning = accomplish, do, finish, perform, make perfect

Commentary Notes

Once again, when describing the Galatians, Paul employs ἀνόητοί, which means "foolish, void of understanding, or unwise." He asks them if they are so foolish as to be void of understanding the clarity of the gospel and the impact that the Holy Spirit is to have on an individual's life. The Holy Spirit baptizes an individual into the family of God. He is the beginning for a new Christian. These Galatians had experienced this baptism when Paul first preached Christ to them. They understood Paul's question. There is no doubt that they had been sanctified and had grown to a degree as the Spirit is the One who guides believers into all truth. Paul questions the actions of the Galatians, "Can you who trusted Christ by faith and were baptized into the body of Christ by the Spirit now perfect your spirituality or make it complete by obeying the ordinances of the Jewish system in the flesh?" Paul knew the answer to the question before he asked it, but he was not too sure that the Galatians did. The Greek word ἐπιτελεῖσθε is in the middle voice, which means making yourselves perfect or complete by way of self-effort. When Christianity moves from the spiritual realm to the physical realm, it becomes just like any other religion, made up of outward works that need to be done by the individual. If the summation of true spirituality in Christendom can be completely comprehended in the physical realm, then where does the Holy Spirit come in? The Galatians had moved in their Christianity from a holy and spiritually consecrated worship of God to an outward conformity of the Jewish rites and ordinances. Paul knew that would not be the true means for a Christian to grow then and it still is not today. The Bride of Christ is not only an organization but more importantly it is an organism, and the Holy Spirit is the very life of its being. We cannot ignore Him and His work and expect to be complete and mature believers in Christ.

d. Paul's question concerning their suffering-3:4

3:4 τοσαῦτα   ἐπάθετε
so many things Have you endured
εἰκῆ; εἴ γε   καὶ   εἰκῆ.
in vain? if it was really in vain?

Have ye suffered so many things in vain? if *it be* yet in vain.

ἐπάθετε   Aor. Act. Indicative 2nd.
      Pers. Plur. πάσχω Meaning =
      feel, passion, suffer, (be) vex

Commentary Notes
   Acts 13:45, 50; 14:2, 5, 19, and 22 all record some of the
many hardships that the Galatians went through because of
their identification in Christ. Paul questioned them about these
hardships, because he refused to believe that they had suffered
for Christ for no reason. In fact, Paul questioned whether or
not it was even vain to question the Galatians at all. He refused to give up hope on the Galatian believers or to think that
they were going to completely abandon Christ for Judaism.

e. Paul's question concerning the miracles-3:5

3:5   ὁ   οὖν
[the one] who therefore
    ἐπιχορηγῶν ὑμῖν   τὸ Πνεῦμα
He fully supplies to you the   Spirit
καὶ ἐνεργῶν δυνάμεις ἐν   ὑμῖν,
and   works miracles among you,
ἐξ ἔργων   νόμου,   ἢ ἐξ
by the works of the law, or by
  ἀκοῆς   πίστεως;
the hearing   of faith?

He therefore that ministereth to you the Spirit, and worketh
miracles among you, *doeth he it* by the works of the law, or by
the hearing of faith?

ἐπιχορηγῶν Pres. Act. Participle Nom.
 Masc. Sing. ἐπιχορηγέω
 Meaning = add, minister, fully supply
ἐνεργῶν   Pres. Act. Participle Nom.
 Masc. Sing. ἐνεργέω Meaning = do, work, show
 forthself, be mighty in, (be) effectual (fervent)

Commentary Notes

When Paul preached Christ in Galatia, many believed on Christ. Not only did many believe on Christ, but there were miracles performed that could point only to God (Acts 14:3, 9-10). These were the two signs: that God had saved many people in Galatia and that He was working in them. In fact, Paul used the present tense in both ἐπιχορηγῶν and ἐνεργῶν to show that God was still abundantly supplying the Holy Spirit and still working miracles among them. The Galatians were saved by faith and sealed by the Holy Spirit, not when they performed the works of the law, but when they trusted Jesus Christ by faith. The Holy Spirit is the One who had been supplied abundantly to them and had worked the miracles among them. Paul had to help them understand this contrast of works of the law versus grace by faith in Christ. Paul knew that they could answer the question in only one way honestly, by faith.

3. The example of Abraham's faith-3:6-9
a. Abraham's belief in God-3:6

3:6 καθὼς Ἀβραὰμ   ἐπίστευσε
Inasmuch as Abraham put his trust
τῷ Θεῷ, καὶ   ἐλογίσθη   αὐτῷ
in God, and it was reckoned to him
εἰς δικαιοσύνην.
for justification.

Even as Abraham believed God, and it was accounted to him for righteousness.

ἐπίστευσε   Aor. Act. Indicative 3rd.
    Pers. Sing.   πιστεῦω   Meaning = believe, commit (to
    trust), put in trust with
ἐλογίσθη   Aor. Pass. Indicative 3rd.
    Pers. Sing.   λογίζομαι   Meaning
    = conclude, count, impute, reckon

Grammatical Notes

The only difference here between the *Textus Receptus* and other MSS is that the *Textus Receptus* follows the standard rule found in all Byzantine manuscripts in that it does not have a movable final consonant on ἐπίστευσε before another consonant and the Alexandrian type text does, reading ἐπίστευσεν τῷ Θεῷ.[3]

Commentary Notes

Paul employed the example of Abraham so the Galatians could understand how God brought salvation to them: the same way that He did to Abraham, by faith. Abraham was saved the only way that God ever intended any one to be saved, by faith. By trusting God that He would send a Messiah long before Christ came or even the giving of the Law, Abraham was saved. Paul used the best example from the Old Testament that he possibly could to explain the difference between faith and works. He went directly to the Patriarchal head of the nation of Israel who lived about 430 years before the giving of the law. He quoted directly from Gen. 15:6, exactly what God had recorded about Abraham at Moses' hand. Abraham had believed, placed his faith in God, and God counted it as righteousness. He was saved, not by the works of the law (it had not been given yet), but by faith in God's Word. The Judaizers were teaching that the deeds of the law were also necessary to salvation; if this fallacy were so, then even the patriarch they pointed to as the physical and spiritual father of their nation and religion, Abraham, could not have been saved. Paul did not simply end the use of this example in this verse, but goes on to explain more implications from this tes-

timony of Abraham in the very lives of these Galatian believers, both Jew and Gentile alike.

b. Abraham's children of faith-3:7

3:7 γινώσκετε ἄρα ὅτι   οἱ
    Know ye   then that they which
ἐκ πίστεως, οὗτοί εἰσιν
[are] of faith, the same are
υἱοὶ   Ἀβραάμ.
[the] sons of Abraham.

Know ye therefore that they which are of faith, the same are
the children of Abraham.

    γινώσκετε Pres. Act. Imperative
      2nd. Pers. Plur. γινώσκω
      Meaning = know, be aware, understand
    εἰσιν   Pres. Act. Indicative 3rd. Pers.
      Plur. εἴμι Meaning = are

Commentary Notes
    Paul states imperatively that those who have trusted Christ
as their Savior are the sons, literally children or descendants
of Abraham. These same people and no others. Becoming a
son of Abraham means receiving all of the rights, privileges,
and responsibilities that come with sonship. In this case, Paul
was writing to people who had been deceived into focusing only
on the outward physical world (at natural descendants) and
those who had been circumcised as Abraham's sons. Yes, these
were the descendants of Abraham, physically, but that relationship did not make them descendants spiritually. God did
not want them to focus only on the physical, so Paul directs
their attention to the spiritual. All who have trusted Christ
by faith, whether Jew or Gentile, whether circumcised or not,
all of these have become the spiritual sons of Abraham. These
and these only receive the spiritual benefits, responsibilities,
and blessings as the sons of Abraham.

c. Abraham's blessing to all-3:8

3:8 προϊδοῦσα   δὲ ἡ γραφὴ
seeing before   And the Scripture
ὅτι ἐκ πίστεως   δικαιοῖ
that by   faith   He would justify
τὰ ἔθνη ὁ Θεός,
the Gentiles [the] God,
πρευηγγελίσατο
proclaimed the good news in advance
τῷ Ἀβραὰμ ὅτι* Εὐλογηθήσονται
to Abraham,   "theywill be blessed
ἐν σοὶ πάντα   τὰ ἔθνη.
In you   all   the nations."

*When introducing direct discourse (God speaking to Abraham), it is not to be translated but represented by quotation marks.

And the scripture, foreseeing that God would justify the heathen through faith, preached before the gospel unto Abraham, *saying,* In thee shall all nations be blessed.

> προϊδοῦσα 2nd. Aor. Act. Participle
>> Nom. Fem. Sing. προΐδω
>> Meaning = saw before, foresee
> δικαιοῖ Pres. Act. Indicative 3rd.
>> Pers. Sing. δικαιόω Meaning = free, justify
> πρευηγγελίσατο Aor. Mid. Indic. 3rd.
>> Pers. Sing. προευαγγελίζομαι
>> Meaning = preach before the gospel, proclaim
>> before the good news
> Εὐλογηθήσονται Fut. Pass. Indicative
>> 3rd. Pers. Plur. ἐνευλογέω
>> Meaning = bless, to confer a benefit on

Commentary Notes
Paul wrote this verse with a specific reference to the Old

Testament. He said that the Scripture was written with the understanding that the Gentile world would have the same blessings and benefits as that of Abraham's physical descendants who trusted in the Messiah. Abraham was to be the Gentile's spiritual progenitor too. Abraham received this good news from God. We do not know whether Abraham had the gospel itself preached to him by God, but we do have record of God's telling Abraham that he would be the channel through which all of the nations of the earth would be blessed (Gen. 12:3). Abraham did understand that the Messiah would come through his seed and that the Messiah and everything included with Him would be the blessing to all nations.

d. Abraham's companions by faith-3:9

3:9 ὥστε   οἱ   ἐκ
       Therefore they which [are]   of
πίστεως εὐλογοῦνται σὺν τῷ
   faith   are blessed with the
πιστῷ   Ἀβραάμ.
believing   Abraham.

So then they which be of faith are blessed with faithful Abraham.

εὐλογοῦνται Pres. Pass. Indicative
      3rd. Pers. Plur. εὐλογέω
      Meaning = bless, praise, thank or invoke a
      benediction upon, prosper

Commentary Notes
    That which characterized Abraham's life was to characterize other believers' lives: faith. Abraham was blessed because he was a man of faith. He was saved by faith and walked by faith in God. Those whose lives are also characterized by faith will enjoy the same benefits now that Abraham did once he

had trust in the Messiah by faith in God's Word. The wording here in the original language implies that those whose lives are characterized by faith will be blessed by association with faith in God just like Abraham and that they will also enjoy the same type of fellowship.

Application
1. Why was Abraham blessed? He was a man who exercised his faith in God so much he was called "faithful Abraham."
2. Christian, do you see the hand of God's blessing in your life? Are you living by faith, faithfully?

4. The curse of the Law without faith-3:10-13
a. A curse for those under the law-3:10

3:10 ὅσοι   γὰρ ἐξ ἔργων   νόμου
whosoever For of the works of the law

εἰσίν, ὑπὸ   κατάραν   εἰσί·
are, beneath the curse they are:

γέγραπται γάρ,   'Επικατάρατος
it is written for ,   Cursed [is]

   πᾶς   ὃς οὐκ ἐμμένει   ἐν
everyone who not does continue in

   πᾶσι τοῖς   γεγραμμένοις ἐν τῷ
all things that   are written   in the

βιβλίῳ τοῦ νόμου, τοῦ ποιῆσαι αὐτά.
book   of the law, to   do   them.

For as many as are of the works of the law are under the curse: for it is written, Cursed *is* every one that continueth not in all things which are written in the book of the law to do them.

   εἰσίν Pres. Act. Indicative 3rd. Pers.
      Plur. εἰμι Meaning = are
   εἰσί Pres. Act. Indicative 3rd. Pers.
      Plur. εἰμι Meaning = are

γέγραπται Perf. Pass. Indicative
    3rd. Pers. Sing. γράφω
    Meaning = describe, write
ἐμμένει Pres. Act. Indicative 3rd.
    Pers. Sing. ἐμμένω
    Meaning = continue, to stay
    in the same place, persevere
γεγραμμένοις Perf. Pass. Participle
    Dat. Masc. Plur. γράφω
    Meaning = describe, write
ποιῆσαι Aor. Act. Infinitive ποιέω
    Meaning = do

Grammatical Notes

No less than four places in this verse the *Textus Receptus* and the Alexandrian type Greek text differ from each other. The first is a movable final consonant, ν, located at the end of εἰσί before γέγραπται in the other text. Notice here in this verse, in the *Textus Receptus*, are located two examples of the rule for the movable final consonant: εἰσίν, ὑπὸ in which the movable final consonant is located before a word beginning with a vowel and εἰσί· γέγραπται in which it is absent before a word beginning with a consonant.[4]

Commentary Notes

Anyone who is attempting to be justified by yielding himself to the law will find himself still under the curse. Whether a person is attempting to be justified by the moral law or the ceremonial law makes no difference. All who attempt to be justified by their works have been condemned by their works already (John 3:18). Man's works are like quicksand: with enough gathered around him he is sure to be lost. This is in stark contrast to what Paul has already shared about Abraham. Abraham was a man whose faith was not in himself or his works, but in God. His faith was his character. Today, when Abraham's name is mentioned, it is generally in the context of faith just as it is in the Book of Hebrews. Anyone who seeks to be justified by performing the works of the law will find himself under the curse, resting on sin. Each time a man tries to fulfill the whole law, he comes up short, thus being reminded of the law which denounces a cursing on the guilty. The curse that man finds himself under is the punishment of the law that he has broken. If he attempts to be saved by works, then he must face the cursing or penalty for not meeting God's criteria. Any partial obedience by man, no matter how great or little the degree, will not save him from the penalty that he faces. Partial obedience is at best just that, partial. Any violator of the law whether great or small is guilty of all and is condemned to be punished for all. This man is cursed to eternal destruction or death.

b. The just live by faith-3:11

3:11 ὅτι   δὲ   ἐν νόμῳ   οὐδεὶς
that Now by the law   no man
δικαιοῦται παρὰ   τῷ Θεῷ, δῆλον·
is justified before [the] God,[is] certain:
ὅτι ʽΟ δίκαιος ἐκ πίστεως ζήσεται·
for, The just   by   faith   shall live.

But that no man is justified by the law in the sight of God, *it is* evident: for, The just shall live by faith.

δικαιοῦται Pres. Pass. Indicative 3rd.
    Pers. Sing. δικαιόω Meaning = free, justify, be
    righteous, to render just or innocent
ζήσεται Fut. Mid. Indicative 3rd.
    Pers. Sing. ζάω Meaning = live

Commentary Notes
    Paul directs his reader's attention back to the one way that man obtains life: through faith. Paul quotes Hab. 2:4 as he continues to drive home to these believers that there is only one way to be justified before God. The works of the law will get a man nowhere with God: only faith will bring life to a

man. God is the Great Judge of all mankind, who will observe
a man as being just only because He observes his faith. Without this faith a man is not justified and is condemned to eternal punishment.

Illustration

When John Paton was translating the Bible for a South
Seas island tribe, he discovered that they had no word for trust
or faith. One day a native who had been running hard came
into   the missionary's house, flopped himself in a large chair
and said, "It's good to rest my whole weight on this chair."

"That's it," said Paton. "I'll translate faith as 'resting one's
whole weight on God.'"5

Application

1. Christian, you who have been justified, do you live by faith?
   Are you resting your whole weight on God?
2. If you've entrusted your eternity to God, will you also do it
   with your day-to-day affairs?
3. If your faith will work when you die, are you exercising it
   now while you are alive?

c. Christ's redemption from the Curse-3:12-13

3:12 ὁ   δὲ   νόμος οὐκ ἔστιν ἐκ
      the And   law   not [it] is of
πίστεως, ἀλλ'   Ὁ   ποιήσας
   faith,   but The one   doing
αὐτὰ ἄνθρωπος ζήσεται
them   man   shall live
      ἐν   αὐτοῖς.
according to   them.

And the law is not of faith: but, The man that doeth them shall
live in them.

ἔστιν   Pres. Act. Indicative 3rd. Pers.
    Sing. εἰμι Meaning = is
ποιήσας Aor. Act. Participle Nom.
    Masc. Sing. ποιέω Meaning = do
ζήσεται Fut. Mid. Indicative 3rd. Pers.
    Sing. ζάω Meaning = live

Grammatical Notes

The difference between the *Textus Receptus* and another Greek text in this verse is the word ἄνθρωπος. The *Textus Receptus* has this word and the other Greek text does not. The significance of this word being here is so that it can qualify precisely what is the subject of the verb. It is not simply "a man" or "he" only, but rather ἄνθρωπος signifies any person of the human race, whether male or female, a human being. This is very similar to God's choice of words in Gen. 1:27, "So God created man in his *own* image, in the image of God created he him; male and female created he them." In this verse God uses אתו as a qualifying statement pointing to self meaning "he himself" in reference to all of mankind. He then distinguishes man's separate parts as distinctively זכר "male" and נקבה "female." Hence, the need for the word ἄνθρωπος, since it is the Greek word for all of mankind, both male and female.

Commentary Notes

A man will find himself attempting to get into heaven by only one of two ways: either by some kind of work that he has done, which is legalism, or by faith in God, which is grace. A man did not have to believe the Old Testament law in order to live by it. There was no faith involved in living by the law. However, to be justified in that system a man would have to live in total obedience. He would have to know and act out every jot and tittle to be legally just; however, it is not possible for any man to fulfill the law in this manner. The law and faith are diametrically opposed. One does not exist as part of another, nor can they coexist as equals. Before God's eyes man can only be justified by faith. The law has nothing to do with faith; therefore, God does not observe man's obedience to it.

3:13 Χριστὸς ἡμᾶς   ἐξηγόρασεν
  Christ   us   He has redeemed
ἐκ   τῆς κατάρας   τοῦ   νόμου,
from   the   curse   of the   law,
 γενόμενος   ὑπὲρ   ἡμῶν
having become   in behalf of   us
κατάρα·   γέγραπται   γάρ,
a curse: it is written   for,
Ἐπικατάρατος πᾶς   ὁ
Cursed [is]   everyone who
κρεμάμενος   ἐπὶ ξύλου·
 hangs   on   a tree:

Christ hath redeemed us from the curse of the law, being made a curse for us: for it is written, Cursed *is* every one that hangeth on a tree:

ἐξηγόρασεν Aor. Act. Indicative 3rd.
 Pers.Sing. ἐξαγοράζω Meaning
 = redeem, buy up, set free
γενόμενος Aor. Mid. Participle Nom.
 Masc. Sing. γίνομαι Meaning = be made
γέγραπται Perf. M/P. Indicative 3rd.
 Pers. Sing. γράφω Meaning = describe, write
κρεμάμενος Pres. Mid. Participle
 Nom. Masc. Sing. κρεμάννυμι
 Meaning = hang

Grammatical Notes
 The one difference between the *Textus Receptus* and some MSS in this verse is the phrase γέγραπται γάρ. In other MSS it reads ὅτι γέγραπται. The positions of the two different words in reference to the verb are not significant because they follow their syntactical rules, but their translations are. Both

conjunctions can be classified in a Causal way; however, when ὅτι is classified this way, it is translated as "because,"[6] which is not a logical interpretation; or it could simply stand as quotation marks around the conclusion of the verse in English, but the syntax requires a stronger connection. If it were to be classified as a Continuative, it would be translated as "that."[7] The Continuative classification of this word does not do the statement justice in the Greek.

Γάρ, on the other hand, "is most frequently used in the *illative* sense introducing a reason."[8] When used in this manner and context it would express a *confirmation* and would be translated "for."[9] In this sense does Paul confirm the previous statement of the verse that Christ had paid our price by becoming a curse for us.

Also, Paul uses a different Greek word here to describe Christ's redemption of mankind from the law rather than the normal word, which is λυτρόω. The word that Paul uses here is ἐξαγοράζω. Both words carry the connotative meaning of "to buy up or to redeem"; however, they each have more expressive, precise meanings that differentiate their appropriateness for use in different areas of Scripture.

When God wanted to emphasize who or what the individual or individuals were being redeemed from, he used λυτρόω, as he did in Luke 24:21 where the disciples on the road to Emmaus had been expecting Christ to redeem Israel from the Roman Empire. This word was also used in Titus 2:14 to show that Christ redeemed a Christian from iniquity. This word also focused on the captive being released because of the receipt of a ransom as in 1 Pet. 1:18, where Christ's redemption of mankind was not with corruptible things but rather with His precious blood. This word clearly was used to depict the understanding of redemption by focusing on the Redeemer, the means of redemption, and the captivator, Satan.

On the other hand, ἐξαγοράζω does not deal with these aspects of redemption primarily. The Greek word ἐξαγοράζω emphasizes the extent of the redemption. This characteristic is seen in the four places in Scripture that it is found, which are here in Gal. 3:13, 4:5, Eph. 5:16, and Col. 4:5.

Here in Gal. 3:13 this word deals with Christ's redeeming those who had been held captive by the curse of the law and in 4:5 with those who were under the law. The extent of redemption is shown in these verses to be to those who have accepted Christ's finished work on the cross. Although Christ's redemption was extended to all in bondage to the curse of the law, only those who received Him received it.

In Eph. 5:16 and Col. 4:5, the apostle employs this word to help the readers understand how important time is and that they should be redeeming it. In essence, Paul told these believers that they needed to buy up every moment that they could because they would have only one time to purchase or redeem that exact moment. Paul was emphasizing that each moment will count for either good, or it will not. Each moment must be bought back gaining as much time and opportunity as is possible to witness, to do right, and to act based on wisdom, according to these two verses.

When I was about eight or nine years old, I remember my dad coming home with cases of oil for the car. Zayre (a Wal-Mart-like store) was having a sale, and he bought all of the oil that they had out on the shelf. Since he changed the oil in our cars himself, this was a great opportunity to save money; so he seized the opportunity when it occurred this one time. It just so happened that the store went out of business, but dad still had the oil that he had purchased at a reduced price. If he had waited until another sale to buy the oil, he would have been too late. Opportunities do not wait.

Besides teaching the importance of seizing the moment, these verses also show the importance of the duration of redemption: it occurs only once in the life of a believer, just as a Christian is redeemed from the curse of the law just once. Just as we have only one life to live for Christ, so He paid the price once for all. Christ's one act on the cross, in that one moment of time, paid for all who have and will place their faith in Him. Christ paid for all who possibly could have been bought, but it covers only those who trust Him. Christ has redeemed all, all who accept Him.

Commentary Notes

Paul is trying to paint the most important picture that these believers will ever view in helping them understand the results that accepting Christ as their personal Savior has already had on them. He tells them that Christ has redeemed them, those who are saved, from the curse of the law. The law condemns all who are under it as guilty of sin (Rom. 3:19, 20), who will one day have to accept the penalty of sin, which is death (Rom. 6:23). Paul displays this fact before the eyes of the Galatian believers in his choice of words describing their redemption. Salvation is a one-time event that cannot be reversed, and it will never need to be done again. Christ became our Substitute (Rom. 5:8) and took on the curse of death for us. He took on the curse as if he had been one of the most depraved sinners on this earth. Christ was treated as if He had committed a sin worthy of death (Deut. 21:23). The Book of Deuteronomy describes the sins which are worthy of death by being hanged on a tree (cross). The verse also stipulates that anyone worthy of this type of death was not to remain suspended overnight. A person who was executed in this manner was determined to be a recipient of God's divine judgment in his life for his heinous crime. He was considered to be accursed of God.

Christ was crucified in this same manner. When Deuteronomy was recorded by Moses, crucifixion was not even a form of execution that was being practiced in Hebrew culture, yet God knew exactly what death Christ must die and how it must take place, thus fulfilling this passage in Deuteronomy. Paul quotes this verse to help the Galatians see just what Christ went through for all of mankind. Not only was it the most cruel and humiliating form of execution that the Roman Empire used, but it was also known to the Jews as the most degrading death a man could die. Jesus knew this, and He understood it all too well. Paul wanted to help the Galatians understand it also.

5. The reception of the promise by faith-3:14-18
a. The Gentiles receive it-3:14

3:14 ἵνα   εἰς τὰ   ἔθνη   ἡ
In order that on the   Gentiles the
εὐλογία τοῦ Ἀβραὰμ   γένηται
blessing of Abraham   might come
ἐν   Χριστῷ   Ἰησοῦ, ἵνα τὴν
through Christ   Jesus, that the
ἐπαγγελίαν τοῦ Πνεύματος
promise   of the   Spirit
λάβωμεν   διὰ   τῆς πίστεως.
we might receive through [the] faith.

That the blessing of Abraham might come on the Gentiles through Jesus Christ; that we might receive the promise of the Spirit through faith.

γένηται Aor. Mid. Subjunctive 3rd.
     Pers. Sing. γίνομαι Meaning = be brought (to pass), come (to pass)
λάβωμεν Aor. Act. Subjunctive 1st.
     Pers. Plur. λαμβάνω Meaning = receive, obtain

Commentary Notes
The whole reason that Christ died on the cross was not only to save the Jewish people but the Gentiles also. People who receive the blessing of Abraham, salvation, are considered his spiritual children and also receive by faith the Holy Spirit. The Comforter was promised by Christ to His Church, and all those who become a part of His Church by faith receive the Holy Spirit. It is interesting that Paul mentions specifically receiving the wonderful gift of the Holy Spirit by faith, right alongside of salvation. It is a beautiful picture of how God intended Christians to live. Since they are saved by faith, they must live by faith. The most wonderful gift that God ever gave to us is Himself. First, He promised the Spirit, then He

gave us the Spirit, desiring us to see just how significant we
are to Him.

b. The example is of a man's covenant-3:15

3:15 Ἀδελφοί,   κατὰ
    Brethren,   after the manner
ἄνθρωπον λέγω·   ὅμως
of men I speak: though
ἀνθρώπου   κεκυρωμένην
a man's   having been confirmed
διαθήκην   οὐδεὶς   ἀθετεῖ   ἢ
covenant, no one   disannuls   or
ἐπιδιατάσσεται.
    adds to it.

Brethren, I speak after the manner of men; Though *it be* but a
man's covenant, yet *if it be* confirmed, no man disannulleth,
or addeth thereto.

    λέγω Pres. Act. Indicative 1st. Pers.
       Sing. λέγω Meaning = speak
    κεκυρωμένην Perf. Pass. Participle
       Acc. Fem. Sing. κυρόω Meaning = confirm, ratify
    ἀθετεῖ Pres. Act. Indicative 3rd. Pers.
       Sing. ἀθετέω Meaning = cast off,
       despise, disannul, reject, bring to nought,
       disesteem, violate, neutralize, set aside
    ἐπιδιατάσσεται Pres. Mid. Indic. 3rd.
       Pers. Sing. ἐπιδιατάσσομαι
       Meaning = add to, to appoint besides, supplement
       (as a codicil)

Commentary Notes
    The apostle continues his analogy on Abraham in this verse
as he turns the corner from a distant proclaimer of truth to a
kindly affectionate brother who tries to settle a disagreement
in a kind manner. It is almost as if we can sense his emotions

in this verse as Paul tries to make it personal. He, himself, must write as if he were present and speaking to them. He writes, "Brethren."

To help differentiate the promise made to Abraham from the giving of the law to Moses, he speaks to them with a simple human example. When a man writes out his last will and testament, it becomes a legal binding document. At the man's death the will is followed to the tee. Also, when one man commits to another by word of mouth, the words spoken are binding words. Paul helps the Galatians see that if it is this way with men, how much more so is it with God. Once the covenant is confirmed or ratified, it cannot be broken. God's Word is as good as He is. Just as God spoke the world into existence, He made, or literally cut, the covenant with Abraham planning to bless him and his descendants both physically and spiritually. No man can disannul or make void the agreement that has been made by God. God has chosen to bind Himself to faithfully fulfilling all of the conditions that He has promised.

c. The Promise is made to Christ-3:16

3:16 τῷ δὲ ᾿Αβραὰμ ἐρρήθησαν
     to Now Abraham were spoken
αἱ ἐπαγγελίαι, καὶ τῷ σπέρματι
the promises, and to [the] seed
αὐτοῦ. οὐ λέγει, Καὶ τοῖς
his[of him]. not He does say, And to
σπέρμασιν, ὡς ἐπὶ πολλῶν, ἀλλ᾽ ὡς
   seeds, as to many, but as
ἐφ᾽ ἑνός, Καὶ τῷ σπέρματί
to one, And to the seed
σου, ὅς ἐστι Χριστός.
your [of you], which is Christ.

Now to Abraham and his seed were the promises made. He saith not, And to seeds, as of many; but as of one, And to thy seed, which is Christ.

ἐρρήθησαν Aor. Pass. Indicative 3rd.
        Pers. Plur. ῥέω Meaning =
        command, make, say, speak (of)
λέγει Pres. Act. Indicative 3rd. Pers.
        Sing. λέγω Meaning = say, speak, show
ἐστι Pres. Act. Indicative 3rd. Pers.
        Sing. εἰμι Meaning = is

Commentary Notes

God promised Abraham that in him would all the nations of the earth be blessed. This promise meant that all would be beneficiary of a special blessing through Abraham, that is, Abraham's seed. Paul understood the Abrahamic covenant. He also understood the blessing because he had experienced Christ's saving grace in his own life. Paul knew that the Jews, themselves, would not be the fulfillment of the Abrahamic covenant, but that only Christ could be. Hence, the distinction Paul makes here between the plural seeds and the singular seed.

d. The law does not disannul the promise-3:17

3:17 τοῦτο δὲ   λέγω,   διαθήκην
        this And I say,   the covenant
προκεκυρωμένην   ὑπὸ τοῦ Θεοῦ
which was confirmed before   God
εἰς Χριστόν   ὁ   μετὰ ἔτη
in   Christ, which after years
τετρακόσια καὶ τριάκοντα γεγονώς
four hundred and   thirty   was
νόμος οὐκ   ἀκυροῖ, εἰς τὸ
the law, cannot invalidate, that it
καταργῆσαι   τὴν ἐπαγγελίαν.
should make void the   promise.

And this I say, *that* the covenant, that was confirmed before of God in Christ, the law, which was four hundred and thirty years after, cannot disannul, that it should make the promise of none effect.

λέγω Pres. Act. Indicative 1st. Pers.
    Sing. λέγω Meaning = say,
    shew, speak, put forth, tell
προκεκυρωμένην Perf. Pass. Participle
    Acc. Fem. Sing. προκυρόω
    Meaning = confirm before, to ratify previously
ἀκυροῖ Pres. Act. Indicative 3rd. Pers.
    Sing. ἀκυρόω Meaning =
    disannul, make of none effect, to invalidate
καταργῆσαι Aor. Act. Infinitive
καταργέω Meaning = make invalid,
    make ineffective or powerless

Commentary Notes

When God made the covenant with Abraham, He Himself ratified it. He was not simply ratifying it with a man, Abraham, but with the specific seed of Abraham that would fulfill the covenant, Christ. This verse tells us that the covenant was validated by God in Christ 430 years before the law was given. If God made a promise to Himself, it is as if He ratified it. Abraham understood that when God stated something would happen, Abraham could count on it to happen. God substantiated His promise before Abraham's eyes and in his presence, but the covenant, the promise, was given to Christ.

e. The inheritance is received by the promise- 3:18-29

3:18 εἰ γὰρ ἐκ νόμου ἡ
    if For out of the law the
κληρονομία, οὐκέτι ἐξ ἐπαγγελίας·
inheritance, no longer of promise:
τῷ δὲ Ἀβραὰμ δι'
to but Abraham according to
ἐπαγγελίας κεχάρισται ὁ Θεός.
    promise He gave it God.

For if the inheritance *be* of the law, *it is* no more of promise:
but God gave *it* to Abraham by promise.

κεχάρισται Perf. M/Pass. Indicative
    3rd. Pers. Sing. χαρίζομαι
    Meaning = give, grant

Commentary Notes
   Paul displays once again before the Galatians' eyes the difference between salvation by keeping a law and accepting God's
grace. The inheritance that Abraham was promised, the Jews
expected, and that the whole world would be blessed by was
not simply a physical inheritance but rather the messianic
blessing. A Messiah would be born that would save the people,
whosoever believed on Him, from their sins. Paul helped the
Galatians see that this blessing could not be received by the
keeping of the law because the blessing was already granted
by a promise given 430 years previous. The one major difference is revealed as works versus faith, once again. Either salvation is by works of the law, or salvation comes by grace
through the promise.
   Paul sends a resounding message to the Galatians when
he focuses their attention on God again. He uses the perfect
tense to state that God gave the inheritance to Abraham by
promise, which means that it has already transpired, it has
already happened and nothing could change it. For them not
to believe this would be distrust in God!

   3:19 τί   οὖν ὁ νόμος; τῶν
       Why then the law?   the
   παραβάσεων χάριν   προσετέθη,
   violations because of It was added,
   ἄχρις οὗ   ἔλθη   τὸ σπέρμα ᾧ
     until   would come the seed to whom
       ἐπήγγελται,
   the promise was made;

διαταγεὶς   δι'   ἀγγέλων
it was appointed through   angels
ἐν   χειρὶ   μεσίτου.
in   the hand   of a mediator.

Wherefore then *serveth* the law? It was added because of transgressions, till the seed should come to whom the promise was made; *and it was* ordained by angels in the hand of a mediator.

προσετέθη Aor. Pass. Indicative 3rd.
    Pers. Sing. προστίθημι
    Meaning = add, increase
ἔλθη Aor. Act. Subjunctive 3rd. Pers.
    Sing. ἔρχομαι Meaning = come
ἐπήγγελται Perf. Pass. Indicative 3rd.
    Pers. Sing. ἐπαγέλλω Meaning = profess, (make)
    promise
διαταγεὶς Aor. Pass. Participle Nom.
    Masc. Sing. διαγγέλλω
    Meaning = declare, preach,
    signify, to herald thoroughly, ordain

Commentary Notes

As the apostle continues his treatise on justification by grace, he so defeats the legalists' idea that justification might be by the works of the law that the overwhelming question is, "So what was the law for?" Now there is sufficient understanding for Paul to remove the wrong picture of the law that the legalists had painted in the minds of the Galatian believers and to begin painting a clear, precise, and true picture of the law. This picture does not simply represent what Paul understood it to be, but what God's intended purpose was for it and how it directed the unsaved to God's wonderful gift of salvation by His grace.

The law was given to help man see his sinful nature (Rom. 4:15, 7:7-11). The law was never intended to be a means of justification but rather to allow man to realize that his sin was indeed very awful and that he needed a Messiah. The advent of the Old Testament law given to Moses was to carry out a purpose in God's plan till the Messiah would come (not that it would not be important after His coming, but that it would achieve its purpose before it).

Now it is important to understand what portion of the law Paul is describing here: it is not the ceremonial law, but the moral law.[10] The ceremonial law or larger portion of the law of Moses was "given to accomplish important purposes among the Jews until the Messiah should come."[11] It was an important part, not because it brought salvation but because it pointed mén toward the Savior while fulfilling the promise to Abraham about the Messiah. After Jesus came, this portion of the law was no longer needed because the Savior had come, hence the unveiling of exactly who He would be and what He has done for us on the cross. This portion of the law, the sacrificial or ceremonial, will be brought back and added alongside the moral law for all mankind living on the earth during the Millenium when Jesus Christ reigns with a rod of iron; however, during the Church Age it has been set aside.

The part of the law that cannot be set aside is God's moral law, not that the moral law stands on its own structurally because it does not. It is an important part of a whole. God's moral law is given because of men's transgressions, or to display before man what the nature of sin is and to deter him from following it. If a man in the Old Testament came to a clear understanding of this law and did not have Someone to turn to for forgiveness of sins, he would not be able to be released of the guilt of his sins, hence the need of the ceremonial law in the Old Testament. The Jews or Gentiles that were saved by faith were not saved by bringing animals to be sacrificed for sin offerings. That was only the evidence of their faith in God's Word in which he promised a Messiah would come and shed His blood for their sins. It is the evidence that they understood the sacrifice as a type of the Messiah.

Today, God's moral law is still at work in men's lives showing them the nature of sin as well as its results and pointing them to a Savior, Jesus Christ, and not to the sacrifices of the ceremonial law. The moral law fulfilled its purpose in the Old Testament in the lives of many Jews and Gentiles alike, such as Joshua, Caleb, King David, Rahab, and Ruth. God's moral law was understood by those in Old Testament times just as it is today, and this Old Testament understanding can be seen in the reading of Psalm 119. Nearly all the verses in this chapter mention the Word of God, and the different terms used to describe the law show its different purposes. The author, although not named in the text, is probably David. But, whoever it might be, this Psalm shows clearly that the Hebrews understood the different aspects or purposes of the Law of God in their lives. If they understood it, should not we as Christians all the more?

God used angels, who were present at the giving of the law, to order and arrange (διαταγεὶς is a military term meaning to arrange or to order) His Law at its communication to Moses (Deut. 33:2; Acts 7:53; Heb. 2:2), who was the mediator between God and man (Deut. 5:5; Ex. 32:15-16). It is possible that the angels were used of God to help communicate God's law to man, but there is more Scriptural support that they were present as God communicated it Himself.[12]

3:20 ὁ   δὲ   μεσίτης   ἑνὸς
    the Now mediator for one
οὐκ ἔστιν, ὁ   δὲ Θεὸς εἱς ἐστίν.
not is,   but God is   one.

Now a mediator is not *a mediator* of one, but God is one.

ἔστιν Pres. Act. Indicative 3rd. Pers.
    Sing. εἰμι Meaning = is

Commentary Notes

A mediator is a middleman. Moses, at the giving of the law, was the middleman or mediator between God and Israel.

Paul is signifying in this verse that there was an agreement
by the two parties: God and Israel. Moses took the Law to
Israel and told them that God had promised to bless them so
long as they obeyed it. Israel promised to obey the Law, and,
when they did, God blessed them. During the times they chose
not to obey the Law, God did not bless them.

This covenant stands in stark contrast with the Abrahamic
covenant in that God cut the Abrahamic covenant with Himself, not Abraham. When God did this, there was no need of a
mediator because God is One and covenanted with Himself
and no other. Abraham just happened to be present and got
to be the recipient of many blessings. The Abrahamic covenant
was made with the Seed, singular, of Abraham, Jesus Christ.
God made the covenant with Himself; therefore, God is One
and there was no need of a mediator.

> **3:21** ὁ   οὖν   νόμος κατὰ τῶν
>   the   therefore law against the
>   ἐπαγγελιῶν τοῦ Θεοῦ; μὴ γένοιτο.
>   promises   of God? God forbid.
>   εἰ γάρ   ἐδόθη   νόμος   ὁ
>   if For had been given a law which
>   δυνάμενος ζωοποιῆσαι,   ὄντως
>   could have given life,   indeed
>   ἂν ἐκ νόμου   ἦν
>   according to the law would have been
>   ἡ δικαιοσύνη.
>   righteousness.

Is the law then against the promises of God? God forbid: for if
there had been a law given which could have given life, verily
righteousness should have been by the law.

> γένοιτο 2nd. Aor. Mid. Optative 3rd.
>   Pers. Sing. γίνομαι
>   Meaning = God forbid

ἐδόθη   Aor. Pass. Indicative 3rd. Pers.
> Sing. δίδωμι
> Meaning = give, grant

δυνάμενος   Pres. M/P. Participle Nom.
> Masc. Sing. δύναμαι   Meaning = be able, can, could, may, might, be of power, be possible

ζωοποιῆσαι   Aor. Act. Infinitive
ζωοποιέω   Meaning = make alive, give life, quicken

Grammatical Notes

The phrase τοῦ Θεοῦ at the end of the first part of this verse distinguishes who made the promises. This is an important phrase because it points directly to God. In another Greek text this phrase is in brackets, again decreasing the significance of God.

Commentary Notes

After all that has just been written, the question, then, in the forefront of the reader's mind would have been about the relationship of the promise to Abraham and the law given to Moses. They were not contradictory but complementary. They were not against each other because they both had different purposes. The law was given to help bring about the fulfillment of the promise. In fact, Paul uses the strongest declarative sentence to keep this clear in his readers' minds, "μὴ γένοιτο" which literally means "It cannot be." However, this phrase includes the strength of "It is impossible" or even "God forbid."

If there had been a law on earth that could have given life, surely the law of Moses could. It was perfect in nature, pure in character, equal in fairness, and just in its penalty. Every law on earth was inferior to this law. However, no law ever gave life; only the new birth brought life (John 3). The law was not designed to give life. Not one human who has ever lived has complied completely with it, so not one human could be justified by it. The promise produced life but the law demanded death. If it were possible, then justification or righteousness could have come by the law. These two worked together toward the same goal, but the law could not reach the goal standing alone. If man could not be justified by this law then there was never a law, that he could be justified by.

3:22 ἀλλὰ συνέκλεισεν   ἡ   γραφὴ
       But has enclosed   the Scripture
τὰ πάντα ὑπὸ ἁμαρτίαν, ἵνα   ἡ
   all   under sin, in order that the
ἐπαγγελία   ἐκ   πίστεως 'Ιησοῦ
promise according to faith in Jesus
Χριστοῦ   δοθῇ   τοῖς
Christ   might be given to those who
πιστεύουσι.
believe.

But the scripture hath concluded all under sin, that the promise by faith of Jesus Christ might be given to them that believe.

συνέκλεισεν Aor. Act. Indicative 3rd.
       Pers. Sing. συγκλείω
       Meaning = conclude, enclose, shut up
δοθῇ Aor. Pass. Subjunctive 3rd. Pers.
       Sing. δίδωμι Meaning = give, grant, commit,
       deliver
πιστεύουσι Pres. Act. Participle Dat.
       Masc. Plur. πιστεύω Meaning
       = believe, commit (to trust)

Commentary Notes
    This verse stands in stark contrast to the hypothesis stated in the previous verse that man might be able to be justified by the law. It says, "But the Scripture has enclosed all under sin." The word used here, συνέκλεισεν, means "shut up, enclosed, concluded," as in, "there are no other options or choices." It is a term that describes best a prisoner locked up in a prison

cell. He has been concluded or enclosed in that cell. So it is
with all humanity, regardless of what they might accomplish
while here on the earth, or what position they might attain—
all are enclosed under sin (Deut. 27:26; Rom. 3:9, 19, 22-23).
There are no exceptions to this law, none.

This verse shows us the purpose of the law. It must help
man see that he is a sinner and cannot fulfill the law on his
own. He must then turn to the Savior, the One who has fulfilled the law completely! Why? So that by faith, man can
receive the promise that God has offered. This Biblical truth
of salvation was the direct opposite of what the legalists were
saying. They wanted the Galatians to turn their back on their
faith and rely solely upon their works.

> **3:23** Πρὸ τοῦ δὲ ἐλθεῖν τὴν πίστιν,
>   before [the] But came [the] faith,
> ὑπὸ νόμον   ἐφρουρούμεθα,
> by the law we were kept under guard,
> συγκεκλεισμένοι εἰς τὴν μέλλουσαν
>   confined   unto the is destined
> πίστιν ἀποκαλυφθῆναι.
> faith   to be revealed.

But before faith came, we were kept under the law, shut up
unto the faith which should afterwards be revealed.

> ἐλθεῖν Aor. Act. Infinitive ἔρχομαι
>   Meaning = come, appear
> ἐφρουρούμεθα Imp. M/P. Indicative
>   1st. Pers. Plur. φρουρέω
>   Meaning = keep (with a garrison), guard
> συγκεκλεισμένοι Perf. Pass. Participle
>   Nom. Masc. Plur. συγκλείω
>   Meaning = conclude, enclose, shut up
> μέλλουσαν Pres. Act. Participle Acc.
>   Fem. Sing. μέλλω Meaning =
>   shall, should, be yet, will, would

ἀποκαλυφθῆναι   Aor. Pass. Infinitive
ἀποκαλύπτω   Meaning = reveal

Commentary Notes

Before an individual realizes he needs to place his faith in Jesus Christ as his only means to heaven, he is kept by the law. This truth can be seen in men's lives all around the world. Moral laws restrain man from total depravity and help him to see the wickedness of his ways. This truth also was implied by Paul here on a testamental basis: that before faith or the Christian religion came, men were kept under the law. Only the law could help man fully understand his condition. Man was guilty, condemned to death, with only one way of escape: faith in Jesus Christ and His finished work on Calvary.

This explanation becomes all the more obvious as Paul's choice of words here is studied. The word ἐφρουρούμεθα, which is translated "kept," has the fuller meaning of "kept by a garrison or in jail or prison, confined without any way of escape." According to Paul, the law is the sheriff, judge, and jury. The law points out to man his condition: he is a sinner. In this sinful condition the law guards him and keeps him shut up in his jailhouse: the law. The person being held in this prison is there for one of two reasons. Either he is simply being held captive for his protection until he realizes that the law is pointing him to Christ as his only means of escape from the penalty of his sin; or if he rejects Christ, then he is being held until his appointed time with death. The law has condemned him to death because man cannot keep the law, yet it also diverts the man's attention away from himself and toward the Savior, his only means of escape. The law did this with such rigid scrutiny that there was no possible means of escape, except through faith in Christ, Who is the only hope of pardon from the death penalty.

Then the prisoner has the opportunity to receive that pardon when Christ is revealed to him. This is just like the pardon that a condemned prisoner with the death penalty would receive from the governor of the state that he is in. If the governor calls to pardon the individual on his deathbed, that person must accept the pardon in order not to face his sentence. If he rejects the pardon, he dies. The revealing of faith in Christ is just like receiving that telephone call from the governor. It reveals the prisoner's only way of escape from the coming judgment.

3:24 ὥστε   ὁ νόμος παιδαγωγὸς
    Therefore the law a schoolmaster
    ἡμῶν   γέγονεν εἰς   Χριστόν,
    of us [our]   was   up to   Christ,
    ἵνα ἐκ πίστεως   δικαιωθῶμεν.
    that by   faith   we might be justified.

Wherefore the law was our schoolmaster *to bring us* unto Christ, that we might be justified by faith.

γέγονεν Perf. Act. Indicative 3rd. Pers.
    Sing. γίνομαι Meaning = is, be
δικαιωθῶμεν Aor. Pass. Subjunctive
    1st. Pers. Plur. δικαιόω Meaning = free, justify, be righteous

Word Study
    The word παιδαγωγὸς is the Greek word from which we get the word *pedagogue*. This word does not reflect the meaning of one who is the instructor, but, rather, that of the one to whom the care of the boys were given regarding school. A pedagogue, usually a trustworthy slave, was one who had been given the responsibility to take the boy to school. He was to make sure that the boy was protected, and, yet, he was also to make sure that the boy did not get into any mischief. The pedagogue also helped prepare the lessons for the child whom he cared for. His central focus was not to teach but to watch over. Although this word is translated "schoolmaster" here, in the sense of our understanding of the word Christ is our schoolmaster and the law is our pedagogue. It is God's law which directs us to

our need of a Savior. God's law restrains us from sin, it convicts us of sin, and it condemns us of sin, but nowhere do we find in Scripture that it saves us from sin. Salvation through the law would be legalism. The law is our pedagogue. It leads us to Christ. This is its God-given responsibility and purpose, to bring men to Christ so that we might be justified by faith.

I remember as a young boy of twelve years old trying to be a good person and to find favor in God's eyes simply because I did not want to humble myself in front of the people at church and walk down an aisle. The more and more that I tried to "be a good boy," the more that I realized I was not. Did I get in trouble? Yes, in fact, it seemed that I found myself getting into more trouble since I started trying to justify myself by my works. The law kept showing me that I was in need of a Savior. It kept pointing me away from myself and toward Christ. When I was thirteen, one Sunday evening my uncle preached a piercing message on hell. I knew that I was not saved and that I needed to be. I went home that night under great conviction and realized that since I was still under conviction, I could still accept Christ as my Savior. So right there in my room I bowed my knees and prayed and asked Christ to save me. I knew when I got up that I had needed to do that all along. The next Sunday guess what I was doing? I was walking down front to share my testimony in church as to what had happened the week before. The one thing that I was sure of, though, was that it was a decision that I made on my own and no one forced me into it. It was but three years later that I found myself down front in the same church sharing my testimony of how God had called me to preach. God's law directed my attention from my "good works" to my sinful nature and my need of a Savior. It was my pedagogue.

3:25 ἐλθούσης   δὲ τῆς πίστεως,
   [it] having come But [the]   faith,
οὐκέτι   ὑπὸ   παιδαγωγόν ἐσμεν.
no longer under   a tutor   we are.

But after that faith is come, we are no longer under a school-master.

ἐλθούσης Aor. Act. Participle Gen.
    Masc. Sing. ἔρχομαι
    Meaning = come, appear
ἐσμεν Pres. Act. Indicative 1st. Pers.
    Plur. εἰμι Meaning = am, is, are

Commentary Notes

Once the pedagogue has led us to Christ, our schoolmaster or instructor, in whom we have placed our faith, the job of the pedagogue is finished and his work over. Once we have placed our faith in Christ, we are free from the guilt and condemnation of the law. When a Jew in the first century trusted Jesus Christ as his Savior, he no longer had to continue performing the ceremonies and rites of the Jewish law because he had been set free from them. So it is with us today. "Free from the law, O happy condition! Jesus has died and there is remission. Cursed by the fall yet purged by the cross, Christ has redeemed us once for all. Once for all, O sinner, receive it. Once for all, O Christian, believe it." Rom. 8:1 says it best, "There is therefore now no condemnation to them which are in Christ Jesus, who walk not after the flesh, but after the Spirit."

3:26 πάντες γὰρ   υἱοὶ   Θεοῦ
    all   For the children of God
    ἐστὲ   διὰ   τῆς πίστεως
  [you pl.] are through [the] faith
    ἐν Χριστῷ Ἰησοῦ.
    in   Christ   Jesus.

For ye are all the children of God by faith in Christ Jesus.

ἐστε Pres. Act. Indicative 2nd. Pers.
    Plur. εἰμι Meaning = am, is, are

Commentary Notes

Now that we have placed our faith in Christ Jesus we are no longer under a pedagogue. Paul's understanding here in context is not simply that now we have been born into the family of God as Jesus described to Nicodemus in John 3. He wants these Galatian believers to understand that they are now of age and are no longer under a pedagogue. He helps them to see that now they are considered a son, an heir of God since they have placed their faith in Christ.

3:27 ὅσοι   γὰρ εἰς Χριστὸν
as many of you For into   Christ
ἐβαπτίσθητε,   Χριστὸν
have been baptized, Christ
ἐνεδύσασθε.
have put on.

For as many of you as have been baptized into Christ have put on Christ.

ἐβαπτίσθητε Aor. Pass. Indicative 2nd.
    Pers. Plur. βαπτίζω Meaning = baptize, wash
ἐνεδύσασθε Aor. Mid. Indicative 2nd.
    Pers. Plur. ἐνδύω Meaning =
    array, clothe (with), endue, have (put) on

Commentary Notes

The baptism that is being referred to here is the baptism of the Holy Spirit and not water baptism. The aorist passive here indicates that this baptism had been done to the Galatian believers, at least as many Jews and Gentiles alike who had trusted Christ as their Savior. The Holy Spirit had baptized them into the family of God, and they had put on Christ.

The phrase "put on" someone was used many times by those in the ancient Roman world to show that they were following that person, or that they had taken on that person's beliefs and practices as their own. When Paul writes this to these converts, he realizes precisely what he is saying and he knew which Galatians he was talking about and which Galatians he was not talking about. Those who had put on Christ were the ones who had followed Christ both in teaching and in action. When a boy became of age in the Jewish culture, he was then able to wear a garment that would display to others that he was of age and was to be treated with the full status of a grown-up son and a citizen. The Greek verb here is an aorist middle which shows the reflexive action or continuation of their putting on Christ themselves. They had been baptized by the Holy Spirit, but they themselves chose to follow Christ from that point on and to continue to put on Christ. Paul knew exactly who had decided to put on Christ. The true Galatian converts had; and the legalists, those desiring to stay under the law, had not.

3:28 οὐκ   ἔνι   Ἰουδαῖος οὐδὲ
      neither   There is   Jew   nor
Ἕλλην,   οὐκ   ἔνι   δοῦλος οὐδὲ
Greek,   neither there is   slave   nor
ἐλεύθερος, οὐκ   ἔνι   ἄρσεν καὶ
citizen,   neither there is   male   nor
θῆλυ·   πάντες γὰρ   ὑμεῖς   εἷς
female;   all   for   ye   one
ἐστὲ   ἐν   Χριστῷ   Ἰησοῦ.
ye are   in   Christ   Jesus.

There is neither Jew nor Greek, there is neither bond nor free, there is neither male nor female: for ye are all one in Christ Jesus.

ἔνι   Pres. Act. Indicative 3rd. Pers.
     Sing. ἔνεστι   Meaning = there is
ἐστὲ   Pres. Act. Indicative 2nd. Pers.
     Plur. εἴμι   Meaning = are

Commentary Notes

All in Christ are on the same level. The ground at the foot of the cross is level. Whether Jew or Gentile (anyone who is not a Jew), a slave or a free citizen, man or woman, all can come to Christ for salvation. Although there might be some nationality differences or maybe societal status differences or even gender differences, all are one in Christ. These outward physical barriers and distinctions all break down once a person is in Christ. In Christ, no one receives preferential treatment over another, all receive the "preferred" treatment as children of God.

3:29 εἰ δὲ ὑμεῖς Χριστοῦ, ἄρα
      if And ye [are] Christ's, then
τοῦ   Ἀβραὰμ σπέρμα ἐστέ, καὶ
[the] of Abraham seed ye are, and
   κατ'   ἐπαγγελίαν κληρονόμοι.
according to [the] promise   heirs.

And if ye *be* Christ's, then are ye Abraham's seed, and heirs according to the promise.

ἐστε Pres. Act. Indicative 2nd. Pers.
   Plur. εἰμι Meaning = are

Commentary Notes

Writing to churches in a Gentile region, Paul knew that both Jews and Gentiles alike would read his letter. He also knew that those who were claiming that he was not an apostle would read the letter. So he concludes this section by beginning this sentence with the word *if.* He knew that some were claiming he was an apostle and some were not, so he makes that distinction clear. They would all like to know who is in line to receive the inheritance according to the promise and who is not. It is conviction to the legalists and encouragement to the true believers. Paul wanted all in these churches to know that being Abraham's seed far surpassed the extent

of the law since Abraham received the promise 400 years before the giving of the law. Now the true believers were the
heirs. They had nothing to worry about because they were
Abraham's true spiritual seed, not those who attempted to keep
the law for salvation's sake.

[1] Dana and Mantey, 97.
[2] Wuest, 83.
[3] Robertson, 220.
[4] Robertson, 220.
[5] Parsons, *Bible Illustrator.*
[6] Dana and Mantey, 257.
[7] Ibid.
[8] Ibid., 243.
[9] Ibid., 242.
[10] Barnes, 940.
[11] Ibid.
[12] Barnes, 427.

B. The change in position from being a servant to a son-4:1-20

1. Christ has redeemed the servant and made him a son-4:1-7

4:1 Λέγω δέ, ἐφ᾽ ὅσον χρόνον ὁ
    I say Now,   as long as   the
κληρονόμος νήπιός ἐστιν, οὐδὲν
    heir   a child he is, nothing
  διαφέρει δούλου, κύριος
he differs from a slave, master
πάντων ὤν·
  of all   he is,

Now I say, *That* the heir, as long as he is a child, differeth nothing from a servant, though he be lord of all;

    Λέγω Pres. Act. Indicative 1st. Pers.
       Sing. λέγω Meaning = say, speak, tell
    ἐστιν Pres. Act. Indicative 3rd. Pers.
       Sing. εἴμι Meaning = is
    διαφέρει Pres. Act. Indicative
       3rd. Pers. Sing. διαφέρω
       Meaning = be better, carry, differ from, be (more) excellent

Commentary Notes

In the last verse of the previous chapter Paul differentiates who are heirs and who are not. He now goes on in this and the following six verses (through verse 7) to describe in greater detail what the privileges of a son or an heir are, and draws a greater distinction between those who are mature heirs and those who are not. He writes that the heir, as long as he is a child (νήπιός), or how we would understand and describe as a minor today, does not have any input as to the disposing of the property he should one day inherit. He has not come of age; therefore, just as the servants in the house make no decisions on the property or inheritance, so the child who is still a minor makes no decisions on it. He is simply taken care of and given directions what to do.

> **4:2** ἀλλὰ ὑπὸ   ἐπιτρόπους
> But under tutors [domestic
>   ἐστὶ καὶ οἰκονόμους,
> managers]   he is and governors
> ἄχρι τῆς   προθεσμίας   τοῦ
> up to the   time appointed   of the
> πατρός.
> father.

But is under tutors and governors until the time appointed of the father.

> ἐστὶ Pres. Act. Indicative 3rd. Pers.
>   Sing. εἰμι Meaning = is

Commentary Notes

Domestic managers were common in the Middle East during Bible times. A man who had many servants and much property needed help in overseeing it all. He also usually set up his most trusted servants to oversee his sons as they grew up, assigning different servants to different boys to help challenge his children to be mature. The man would also have stewards set up to govern his personal affairs and property. They would manage their master's estate. This was the case with Joseph. Potiphar set him up as a steward, not over the children, but over all of his personal affairs and possessions. The domestic managers or tutors who oversaw the children were the ones who were father-appointed guardians, given the supervision of that child. The child growing up in this atmosphere is overseen by the domestic managers and has no say over the property that will one day be his inheritance, because that responsibility has been delegated to the stewards. As long as the child is a minor, this is the authority structure that he must work within until the time appointed by the father that he should obtain his inheritance. The child, so long as he was a minor, was under government and restraint.

4:3 οὕτω καὶ ἡμεῖς, ὅτε   ἦμεν
so Even we, when we were
        νήπιοι,
children [simple-minded or immature],
ὑπὸ τὰ   στοιχεῖα   τοῦ   κόσμου
under the   principles   of the   world
ἦμεν   δεδουλωμένοι·
we were   enslaved.

Even so we, when we were children, were in bondage under the elements of the world:

ἦμεν   Imp. Act. Indicative 1st. Pers.
    Plur. εἰμι Meaning = is, am, was, were
δεδουλωμένοι Perf. Pass. Participle
    Nom. Masc. Plur. δουλόω
    Meaning = to enslave, bring into
    bondage, become (make) servant

Grammatical Notes
    The one difference in this verse between the *Textus Receptus* and another Greek text is the choice between an older or newer

form of a word. Here in this text ἦμεν is used; this is the older Imperfect Active Indicative First Person Plural of the word εἰμί. The newer form, which can be found in the Papyri and is used in this same verse in the Alexandrian type Greek text is ἤμεθα.[1] This form is also declined the same way as that found in this text. This form is not found at all in the *Textus Receptus* yet can be found in this other Greek text here and three other places (Matt. 23:30, Acts 27:37, and Eph. 2:3).[2] The form found here in the *Textus Receptus* is the same form found in the eleven places this declension of this word is used; however, the other text is split between the two using the older declension seven times and the newer one four times. This displays the greater consistency of the *Textus Receptus*.

Commentary Notes

Next Paul makes this simple lesson practical to the Galatians by helping them see that he is talking about all saved individuals before they became Christians. All unsaved individuals are under the basics or ABC's of the first principles of this world.[3] The verbiage that Paul uses depicts a sorrowful picture of slavery of the worst kind in the spiritual realm, a focus on our works and not on the grace of God. Paul, here, uses a common Jewish analogy to remind the reader that the rites of the law were like the things of this world in that they were passing, momentary, and of little value. "They were unsatisfactory in their nature, and were soon to pass away, and to give place to a better system—as the things of this world are soon to give place to heaven."[4]

4:4 ὅτε   δὲ   ἦλθε   τὸ   πλήρωμα
    when But had come the   fullness
τοῦ χρόνου, ἐξαπέστειλεν   ὁ   Θεὸς
  of   time, [He] sent forth [the] God
τὸν υἱὸν   αὐτοῦ,   γενόμενον
the Son   of Him [His Son],   born
ἐκ γυναικός, γενόμενον ὑπὸ   νόμον,
of a woman,   born   under the law,

But when the fulness of the time was come, God sent forth his Son, made of a woman, made under the law,

ἦλθε Aor. Act. Indicative 3rd. Pers.
        Sing. ἔρχομαι Meaning = come
ἐξαπέστειλεν Aor. Act. Indicative 3rd.
        Pers. Sing. ἐχαποστέλλω
        Meaning = to send away forth
        (on a mission), to dispatch, or
        to dismiss, to send (away, forth, out)
γενόμενον Aor. Mid. Participle Acc.
        Masc. Sing. γίνομαι Meaning =
        be made, born, produced, brought about

Grammatical Notes

A movable final consonant added on to the end of ἦλθε in the Alexandrian type text is the only difference in this verse between the *Textus Receptus* and the other text. It is not necessary to be here since ἦλθε occurs before a word that begins with a consonant.

Commentary Notes

Within its context, this verse has much meaning and significance. Paul has been discussing the heir who has not yet reached the age of accountability; therefore, he is not yet fully mature. He now turns the perspective of the reader just a little to show that Christ was sent by God, not because He was now mature, but because the time was now mature or full. It was the proper time on earth for God to send His Son to this earth. It was the predicted time. "The exact period had arrived when all things were ready for His coming."[5]

It is interesting to see in this verse how Paul describes Christ. First, Christ was "sent forth" implying that Christ existed before His incarnation. This also signifies that Christ was sent by God. Second, Christ was made of (became out of), ἐκ, or birthed from a woman. Christ, the God-man, was born into this world by a natural, human birth. In this birth from a woman, Christ fulfilled the promise of Gen. 3:15: He was the Seed that would bruise Satan's head. He became incarnate (John 1:14) and took upon him the form of a servant (Phil. 2:7). Christ was also made under the law of God. He had to become subject to it to secure the redemption of those under it.

> **4:5** ἵνα   τοὺς   ὑπὸ   νόμον
> In order that those under the law
>   ἐξαγοράσῃ,   ἵνα τὴν
> they might be redeemed, that the
>   υἱοθεσίαν   ἀπολάβωμεν.
> adoption as sons we might receive.

To redeem them that were under the law, that we might receive the adoption of sons.

> ἐξαγοράσῃ Aor. Act. Subjunctive
>   3rd. Pers. Sing. ἐξαγοράζω
>   Meaning = redeem
> ἀπολάβωμεν Aor. Act. Subjunctive
>   1st. Pers. Plur. ἀπολαμβάνω
>   Meaning = receive, take

Commentary Notes

Christ had a purpose for coming to earth and being made out of a woman under the law of God: to redeem mankind who was under the law. He came to purchase mankind out of sin and death's slave market (Gal. 3:13). His atoning sacrifice was meant to buy back all who were sinners and were facing the dreaded penalty of death under God's law. The end result in the lives of those slaves to sin and death, facing its penalty, was that they would then become God's sons, not servants, but sons by way of adoption. This adoption occurs when we receive it. We have been adopted by God not as a minor, or as a servant, but as a full adult son with heirship privileges, position, and power. We know we have a spiritual inheritance in heaven because Christ went to prepare a place for us. We are seated in the heavens with Christ because we are in Christ. Only Christians can pray to their Heavenly Father and have the assurance that He will hear and answer their prayers always.

4:6 ὅτι   δέ ἐστε υἱοί,
because And ye are sons,
ἐξαπέστειλεν ὁ   Θεὸς τὸ Πνεῦμα
has sent forth [the] God   the Spirit
τοῦ υἱοῦ αὐτοῦ εἰς τὰς καρδίας
of [the] Son of Him into the hearts
ὑμῶν, κρᾶζον, 'Αββᾶ, ὁ πατήρ.
of you, intreating, Abba, [the] Father.

And because ye are sons, God hath sent forth the Spirit of his Son into your hearts, crying, Abba, Father.

ἐστε Pres. Act. Indicative 2nd. Pers.
    Plur. εἰμι Meaning = are
ἐξαπέστειλεν Aor. Act. Indicative
    3rd. Pers. Sing. ἐξαποστέλλω
    Meaning = send (away, forth, out)
κρᾶζον Pres. Act. Participle Nom.
    Neut. Sing. κράζω
    Meaning = cry (out), intreat

Grammatical Notes
    One letter differentiates other Greek MSS. from the *Textus Receptus* here in this verse; however, it also changes the form of the word from ὑμῶν "your" to ἡμῶν "our." As it stands in the *Textus Receptus* it is in agreement with the verb used in the first part of this verse, ἐστε "ye are." Although this change which includes the heart of the apostle might be theologically appropriate, grammatically it does not follow the consistency of the rest of the text.

Commentary Notes
    Since we are now the full adult sons of God by adoption

into His forever family, God has commissioned the Holy Spirit, which is the Spirit of Christ, His Son, into our hearts. Is it possible for someone to ask Jesus into his heart, as is so often the way that it is explained to little children? Yes, according to this verse. Just as the Holy Spirit is the Spirit of Christ, so He is commissioned by God to enter the hearts of His sons when they trust Christ to save them, or simply ask Jesus into their hearts.

The Holy Spirit upon entering now cries out to God the Father, "Abba, Father." Not only is God the Creator of the individual but now He is also his Heavenly Father. The term *Abba* was never to be used by a slave in the house in which he worked when referring to the master of the house. However, this phrase was reserved for the children to use, those who were free from the bondage of the law of God and its penalty. This term was not simply used to describe Dad when the child felt a warm fuzzy feeling in his stomach. Although it is a very emotional term, it was used more often by children who had become mature and had a greater respect for their father. This was the phrase that was used when a mature child wanted to have a deep intimate moment with his father. God wanted this idea of intimate sonship to be conveyed to Jew and Gentile alike; thus, everywhere this Aramaic (Jewish) word occurs in Scripture, its Greek counterpart or interpretation (for the Gentile) occurs also.

4:7 ὥστε   οὐκέτι   εἶ   δοῦλος,
   So that no longer you are a slave,
ἀλλ᾽ υἱός· εἰ δὲ υἱός, καὶ
but a son; if and a son, then
κληρονόμος Θεοῦ   διὰ   Χριστοῦ.
   an heir   of God through Christ.

Wherefore thou art no more a servant, but a son; and if a son, then an heir of God through Christ.
   εἶ Pres. Act. Indicative 2nd. Pers.
      Sing. εἰμι Meaning = art, be

Grammatical Notes

As this verse appears here in the *Textus Receptus,* it teaches that each of us individually is an heir of God by means of or through Christ. This is consistent with the picture that Paul portrays in Rom. 8:16-17a when he writes, "The Spirit itself beareth witness with our spirit, that we are the children of God: And if children, then heirs; heirs of God, and joint-heirs with Christ." The two thoughts in Rom. 8:16-17a that the apostle pieces together as two pieces of the puzzle are (1) we are heirs of God and (2) joint-heirs with Christ. So here in Gal. 4:7 he states that these believers are heirs of God, but he shows Jesus Christ not simply as our accompaniment but specifically as the agent through which or by the means of how we have become heirs. He articulates this clearly so that these believers could see lucidly what Christ has done for them and they cannot do for themselves. It is a beautiful word picture painted for these believers concerning the result of their salvation.

This important picture of Christ's work never comes into view in the other Greek text. Where the *Textus Receptus* reads καὶ κληρονόμος Θεοῦ διὰ Χριστοῦ another text reads καὶ κληρονόμος διὰ Θεοῦ, leaving out the word Χριστοῦ hence, not making a believer individually the "heir of God through Christ" but simply an "heir through God." The detailed picture of how the Galatian believers have become the heirs in this verse has been murkied by the exclusion of the work of Christ represented here by His presence. Paul, throughout this whole book, is explicitly pointing the attention of his audience to Christ; why then, would he not have done the same in this verse? He did. The correct Greek text reveals this just as clearly as the incorrect text conceals it.

Commentary Notes

This verse is a continuation in thought from the previous one. In that God sent His Son to die for mankind, so man can receive God's Son and become God's son. Because God sends His Spirit to dwell in man when he receives His Son, man can now experience the blessings, the inheritance, of being God's child.

All three persons of the Trinity are involved in making a person to be a child of God. The Father commissioned the Son to die on the cross and pay the price. He then commissioned the Spirit to indwell the believer to guide him into all truth and to bless him with his portion of the inheritance. All that the believer has to do is simply humble himself and accept God's Son and then stay humbly in tune with His Spirit and accept His guidance. The believer is no longer a servant. This is truly a personal message, and at this point the Apostle Paul turns from an all-inclusive second person plurality in the previous verse to a second person singular and says, "Thou art no more a servant, but a son." How much more personal can a Triune God get to an individual? I guess He could take him to Heaven to dwell with Him eternally! The full inheritance experienced at last! We have become the heirs of God through Christ. We will enjoy the full line of God's blessings for all eternity simply because we asked Jesus into our hearts!

2. The son must not turn back to the world as its servant-4:8-11

4:8 Ἀλλὰ   τότε μέν, οὐκ
Nevertheless then   indeed, not
   εἰδότες   Θεόν,   ἐδουλεύσατε
having known   God,   you served
   τοῖς   μὴ   φύσει
those which not by nature
   οὖσι   θεοῖς·
[they] are   gods.

Howbeit then, when ye knew not God, ye did service unto them which by nature are no gods.

εἰδότες Perf. Act. Participle Nom.
Masc. Plur. εἴδω Meaning = know

ἐδουλεύσατε Aor. Act. Indicative
  2nd. Pers. Plur. δουλεύω Meaning
  = be in bondage, (do) serve (-ice)
οὖσι Pres. Act. Participle Dat. Masc.
  Plur. εἰμι Meaning = are

Commentary Notes

On the one hand, before the Galatians got saved, they did not know God. Since they did not know God, they were serving someone or something and Paul declares to them here that those things they served were not deity or God. Paul is simply stating the facts of their previous condition before they received the truth of the gospel. Each person today is serving either the God of this Universe or a god or gods. It is important to note that Paul refers to these gods in other portions of Scripture as so- called gods (1 Cor. 8:4-6) and as demons (1 Cor. 10:19, 20). Many people around the world are still in this state today.

My grandparents, missionaries to Haiti, lived back up in the mountains. Almost every night they could hear the voodoo drums beating because the people were holding voodoo services with their witch doctors. Invariably, it was demon worship. My grandma told me a story of a time a service was held in the same village in which they were living. At the end of the ceremony, a zombie came to her door. She said the only thing that kept it from coming in was prayer. I went to Haiti the summer following my junior year of college to preach through an interpreter. As soon as I stepped off the plane, I could sense the spiritual bondage of the country; yet shortly after, the eagerness with which many Haitians wanted to escape their spiritual bondage also became evident. The Haitian pastor with whom I stayed for the week had grown up as an adopted son in my grandparents' home, where God had saved him and called him to preach. The church and school that I preached in was the third active church that he had started. People would walk up to five to seven miles to come to church on Sunday. He took me out even farther into a little forty-foot-wide by seventy-foot-long building where he was starting another church. We had one hundred people in that building on a Wednesday night and not one of them had a vehicle. Again, they all had walked to church from up to five miles away.

As wonderful as these victories were, however, the spiritual bondage in that country was still great. At night we could hear the voodoo drums in the mountains. The pastor even took me by a spot, in the daytime, where Haitians held their voodoo services, not too far from his church. Although Catholicism, which is one form of idolatry, and demon worship have a hold in the country, voodoo is predominant. It is the national religion of Haiti, and most of its people are in bondage to it.

> **4:9** νῦν δέ,   γνόντες   Θεόν,
>   now But, after you have known God,
> μᾶλλον δὲ   γνωσθέντες ὑπὸ Θεοῦ,
>   or   rather are known by   God,
> πῶς ἐπιστρέφετε πάλιν ἐπὶ τὰ
> how do you turn again   to the
> ἀσθενῆ καὶ   πτωχὰ   στοιχεῖα,
> weak   and   beggarly   elements,
>   οἷς   πάλιν   ἄνωθεν
> to which once more   again
>   δουλεύειν   θέλετε;
> to be in bondage   you choose?

But now, after that ye have known God, or rather are known of God, how turn ye again to the weak and beggarly elements, whereunto ye desire again to be in bondage?

> γνόντες Aor. Act. Participle Nom.
>   Masc. Plur. γινώσκω
>   Meaning = know, perceive
> γνωσθέντες Aor. Pass. Participle Nom.
>   Masc. Plur. γινώσκω
>   Meaning = know, perceive

ἐπιστρέφετε Pres. Act. Indicative
   2nd. Pers. Plur. ἐπιστρέφω
   Meaning = to revert (literally, figuratively,
   or morally)
δουλεύειν Pres. Act. Infinitive
   δουλόω Meaning = be in bondage, (do) serve (-ice)
θέλετε Pres. Act. Indicative 2nd. Pers.
   Plur. θέλω Meaning = desire, wish,
   choose, prefer, intend

Commentary Notes

Paul has just taken the Galatians back in thought to what it was like before they were saved: they served things that were not God. Now he goes on to show them in the form of a question what it is like after having trusted Christ as their personal Savior to turn back to those same things for salvation. After they had known God, or even better yet, been known by God, who is the one who initiated grace in their life, how could they return to living the way they had before God made them His children? The word γνωσθέντες is employed here and reflects on the person initiating the action rather than the recipient. God is the "Knower" and man, or the Galatians in this case, are the "known" just as God is the grace-giver and mankind is the recipient. Paul asks the Galatians how after being born into God's forever family could they turn again to the weak (destitute of strength) and beggarly (destitute of resources) elements of this world. The elements neither have power to save nor the substance to keep and house for all eternity. Why get into the process of turning from God the Creator to the law, the created? The verbiage that is used here to describe the Galatians shows that they were in the process of turning but that they had not completely turned from God to the works of the law for saving grace. As far as salvation was concerned, the law was both unable to save and insufficient to keep the Christian. The Galatians were turning from freedom and liberty in Christ to the bondage and servitude of the law.

4:10 ἡμέρας παρατηρεῖσθε, καὶ
     days   You observe,   and
μῆνας, καὶ καιρούς, καὶ ἐνιαυτούς.
months, and   seasons, and   years.

Ye observe days, and months, and times, and years.

παρατηρεῖσθε   Pres. Mid. Indicative
     2nd. Pers. Plur. παρατηρέω
     Meaning = observe, watch

Commentary Notes

Paul states here that the Galatians were observing days, months, seasons, and years. Notice that the verb is in the middle tense. This usage shows that they were observing these times for themselves, not for God. That is an important point because serving self is what trying to be saved by the works of the law rather than the grace of God is all about. A person does not have to focus on God but rather focuses on himself to see if he is good enough to get to heaven. If he is not, then he continues to focus on what he can do to get there. But, God simply does not work that way. The legalists had been successful to a degree in turning these Galatian believers aside from the grace of God.

4:11 φοβοῦμαι ὑμᾶς, μή πως εἰκῆ
     I fear for you, lest to no avail
       κεκοπίακα
I have labored to the point of
          εἰς ὑμᾶς.
exhaustion   in   you.

I am afraid of you, lest I have bestowed upon you labour in vain.

φοβοῦμαι   Pres. Mid. Indicative
> 1st. Pers. Sing. . φοβέω   Meaning = be (+sore)
> afraid, fear, to frighten, to be alarmed

κεκοπίακα   Perf. Act. Indicative
> 1st. Pers. Sing. κοπιάω   Meaning = (bestow) labor,
> toil, to feel fatigue, to work hard, labor to the point of
> exhaustion

Commentary Notes

Paul gets down to the bottom line with the Galatians. He tells them here that he has a fear concerning them and indicates with the word *lest* that he will tell them what that fear is. Paul has a hard time believing that all the time that he had spent with the Galatian churches, in which he thought he saw miracle after miracle among the people as they were converted, was wasted time. It was hard for this preacher of the gospel to believe that these converts were not turning from their pagan religion to the Christian principles he had taught them. He had heard that they were leaving the servitude of their old pagan idolatry and turning to the servitude of the ceremonies and rites of annulled legalism of the Jews. By turning to legalism as a means of justification, they were rejecting the gospel and renouncing Jesus Christ as their Savior. There is not a pastor, evangelist, or missionary alive who has not felt the same way as the apostle here, wondering if the time invested in the life of one of his converts was to no purpose.

3. Paul chastises the Galatians for their following the false brethren-4:12-20

4:12 Γίνεσθε   ὡς   ἐγώ,   ὅτι   κἀγὼ
become [ye]   as   I am,   for   I also
    ὡς   ὑμεῖς, ἀδελφοί,   δέομαι   ὑμῶν.
[am] as ye   Brethren, I beseech   you.
    οὐδέν   με   ἠδικήσατε·
not at all   to me   Ye have done hurt.

Brethren, I beseech you, be as I *am;* for I *am* as ye *are:* ye have not injured me at all.

> Γίνεσθε   Pres. M/P. Imperative
> > 2nd. Pers. Plur. γίνομαι
> > Meaning = be, become
>
> δέομαι   Pres. M/P. Indicative
> > 1st. Pers. Sing. δέομαι
> > Meaning = beg, petition, beseech,
> > make request, pray to
>
> ἠδικήσατε   Aor. Act. Indicative
> > 2nd. Pers. Plur. ἀδικέω
> > Meaning = hurt, injure, to be unjust,
> > do wrong (morally, socially or physically)

Commentary Notes

Paul refuses to believe that the Galatians have completely rejected Christ for the principles of Judaism and begs them to continue becoming as he is. The word *become* is in the present middle imperative, which indicates that Paul believes that they have turned to Christ from their paganism, yet he wants them to continue in Christ and become as committed to Christ as he is. He cast away the filthy garb of his righteousness (serving the Jews' law, his legalism) for the liberty that he received in Christ. He wants the Galatians to continue doing the same thing. Paul reminds them that he is in the same situation that they are in. They have trusted Christ and he has trusted Christ. Paul was a Jew; they are Gentiles. Paul had not taken their lack of faith as a personal harm or hurt to him, so he tells them that they have not hurt him. Their actions were not considered by Paul to be a personal offense against him, which was a very mature response after all the personal time that he had spent with them.

4:13 οἴδατε   δὲ   ὅτι   δι᾽
     You know even   that   through

ἀσθένειαν τῆς σαρκὸς
feebleness of the   flesh
    εὐγγελισάμην   ὑμῖν
I preached the gospel   to you
τὸ   πρότερον.
the   at first.

Ye know how through infirmity of the flesh I preached the gospel unto you at the first.

οἴδατε Perf. Act. Indicative 2nd. Pers.
    Plur. εἴδω Meaning = know, perceive
εὐγγελισάμην Aor. Mid. Indicative
    1st. Pers. Sing. εὐγγελίζω
    Meaning = to announce good news,
    declare, bring glad tidings, preach (the gospel)

Commentary Notes
    Paul brings back to memory in the minds of these Galatian believers in the churches that he spent time with them and preached the gospel to them when he states, "You know." He was attempting to set aside their views of a legalistic salvation for a moment by pulling back the curtain of what stood between him and them in their mind to help them see how much he cared for them. "People do not care how much you know until they know how much you care." This was evidently what Paul understood and was going back to the first time that he spent with them. Some believe that his infirmity of the flesh was either malaria, epilepsy, or even ophthalmia, an eye disease commonplace in their locale. Since Paul doubled back and retraced his steps after preaching in Derbe, he probably saw the churches of Galatia twice before moving on during his first missionary trip.

    4:14 καὶ τὸν πειρασμόν μου
        And the   trial   of me

τὸν   ἐν τῇ σαρκί
[the one] which [was] in the flesh
μου   οὐκ   ἐξουθενήσατε
of me   not   you did despise
οὐδὲ   ἐξεπτύσατε,
or   reject with contempt [lit. spit out],
ἀλλ'   ὡς   ἄγγελον   Θεοῦ
but   as   an angel   of God
ἐδέξασθέ   με,   ὡς
you accepted   me,   as
Χριστὸν   Ἰησοῦν.
Christ   Jesus.

And my temptation which was in my flesh ye despised not, nor rejected; but received me as an angel of God, *even* as Christ Jesus.

ἐξουθενήσατε   Aor. Act. Indicative
     2nd. Pers. Plur. ἐξουθενέω
     Meaning = contemptible, despise,
     least esteemed, set at nought
ἐξεπτύσατε   Aor. Act. Indicative
     2nd. Pers. Plur. ἐκπτύω   Meaning
     = to spit out, spurn, reject
ἐδέξασθέ   Aor. Mid. Indicative
     2nd. Pers. Plur. δέχομαι
     Meaning = accept, receive, take

Grammatical Notes

In this verse we find a variant reading that can be found in other Greek manuscripts. In place of πειρασμόν μου (which means "my trial"), some manuscripts have the phrase πειρασμόν ὑμῶν which means "your trial." There is no doubt here both in the Greek and in the English, with this verse being connected in thought and paragraph to the previous one, that with the first reading, that of the *Textus Receptus*, there is a unified contour in the language that is used. Paul reminds the Galatian churches of his infirmity and then continues in the next verse to refer to it as his trial. However, if we accept the second reading or "your trial," then the continuity of the paragraph is broken as well as the balance of what Paul is saying.

The trial of Paul, which was in his flesh, was neither despised nor rejected with an attitude of contempt by the Galatians. However, if we say that their trial was in Paul's flesh, which is implied by the other MSS, then it must readily be admitted that Paul's flesh as well as his preaching of the gospel was at best a nuisance to the Galatians. And though he was a nuisance, they still did not despise him nor reject him. This negative reaction toward Paul's flesh does not seem to be the case at all since Paul goes on to say that they received him as an angel or messenger of God, even as Jesus Christ himself. In the context it becomes very obvious that the Galatians had no reserves about Paul whatsoever. Yes, he did have an infirmity, which was his trial in his flesh, yet to the Galatians it meant nothing. They received him as if he had been Christ himself! There were absolutely no reservations or hesitations in their reception of him. Acts 14:11-18 tells us that they accepted him with veneration as Christ, which is the highest honor possible. Which reading in the Greek best reveals the mind of the Spirit and of Paul in this sense? No doubt the first reading, the one found in the *Textus Receptus*.

4:15 τίς οὖν ἦν ὁ μακαρισμὸς
    where Now is the   blessing
ὑμῶν; μαρτυρῶ γὰρ ὑμῖν
of you? I bear witness For to you
ὅτι, εἰ δυνατόν, τοὺς ὀφθαλμοὺς
that, if possible, the   eyes
ὑμῶν   ἐξορύξαντες
of you [ye] would have plucked out
ἂν ἐδώκατέ μοι.
[and] given them to me.

Where is then the blessedness ye spake of? for I bear you record, that, if *it had been* possible, ye would have plucked out your own eyes, and have given them to me.

ἦν Imp. Act. Indicative 3rd. Pers.
    Sing. εἰμι Meaning = is
μαρτυρῶ Pres. Act. Indicative
    1st. Pers. Sing. μαρτυρέω Meaning = to be witness,
    testify, bear record, (be, bear, give, obtain) witness
ἐξορύξαντες Aor. Act. Participle Nom.
    Masc. Plur. ἐξορύσσω Meaning = to dig out, to
    extract, remove, break up, pluck out
ἐδώκατέ Aor. Act. Indicative
    2nd. Pers. Plur. δίδωμι Meaning = give, grant,
    commit, offer

Grammatical Notes

The first word of this verse is the only difference that presents itself here between the *Textus Receptus* and the other Greek text. Here in this text the word τίς is used, which is the "regular pronoun for introducing questions."[6] However, the other text employs the word ποῦ, which is an interrogative adverb. In this structure, either word could be translated *where*.

Commentary Notes

What happened to all the joy that the Galatians had expressed because they had Paul the Apostle? Paul then reminds them of their desire to honor him when he was there. He reminds them that, if it had been possible, some of them would have given him their very eyes. This was probably in reference to his infirmity in the flesh. They did not view Paul's trial as a nuisance but, rather, wished that there was a way in which they could help him with it. If it would have helped him, they would have dug out or gouged out their own eyes and given them to Paul because they esteemed him so highly.

4:16 ὥστε   ἐχθρὸς ὑμῶν
So then an enemy to you
γέγονα   ἀληθεύων
have I become I an telling the truth
ὑμῖν;
to you?

Am I therefore become your enemy, because I tell you the truth?

γέγονα Perf. Act. Indicative
1st. Pers. Sing. γίνομαι
Meaning = become

Commentary Notes

After reminding the Galatians of how close he was to them and how they felt toward him, he then points out to them the attitude that they were now displaying toward him. They were treating him as if he were their enemy. The Greek perfect here signifies that they had felt that he had become their permanent, hostile, personal enemy. He was not their enemy when he came preaching the gospel to them, and he was not their enemy when he wrote the truth to them. He asked them this question almost chiding them for their wrong attitude toward him simply because he tells them the truth. He had been accused by the legalistic Jews of not telling the truth, yet he has just spent the last two thirds of this letter telling the truth to them again and substantiating it with Scriptural examples.

Illustration

The elderly countess was very happy with her own chauffeur. He was courteous, prompt and efficient. The only complaint she had concerned his personal appearance. One day she said to him diplomatically, "Randall, how frequently do you think oneshould shave in order to look neat and proper?"

"Well, madam," said Randall, also trying to be diplomatic, "with a light beard like yours, I'd say every three or four days would be enough."[7]

Application

1. Sometimes the truth hurts. When it does, Christian, do you take offense at it, do you get defensive, do you attack the truth giver?

4:17 ζηλοῦσιν   ὑμᾶς οὐ
They zealously desire you,   not
καλῶς,   ἀλλὰ   ἐκκλεῖσαι   ὑμᾶς
for good, indeed to shut out you
θέλουσιν,   ἵνα αὐτοὺς
they wish,   that them
        ζηλοῦτε.
you may be jealous over.

They zealously affect you, *but* not well; yea, they would exclude you, that ye might affect them.

ζηλοῦσιν Pres. Act. Indicative
    3rd. Pers. Plur. ζηλόω Meaning =
    to have warmth of feeling for or
    against, affect, be jealous over, be zealous, desire
ἐκκλεῖσαι Aor. Act. Infinitive ἐκκλείω
    Meaning = exclude, to shut out
θέλουσιν Pres. Act. Indicative
    3rd. Pers. Plur. θέλω Meaning =
    choose, prefer, to wish, will, desire
ζηλοῦτε Pres. Act. Subjunctive
    2nd. Pers. Plur. ζηλόω Meaning =
    to have warmth of feeling for or
    against, affect, be jealous over, be zealous, desire

Commentary Notes

The Apostle Paul, as being guided by the Spirit, chose his wording ever so carefully, but wrote with mighty word pictures. Here, in this verse, the Apostle paints a picture of the Judaizers that could not have been presented any clearer. At the first, he simply states, "They zealously desire you." The word here ζηλοῦσιν that Paul uses means to be zealous toward something or someone usually in a good sense or for a good reason. So Paul tells the Galatians that they (the others, the Judaizers, the ones wedging themselves in between the Galatian believers and Paul) are eager for the Galatians; they zealously desire them. The apostle points out that in this instance, however, the Judaizers' desire for the Galatians is not for the right reason: the Judaizers have mixed motives. Their desire is not of God, for God authors good and allows bad that will eventually work for good, but the result here is against God. Although the Judaizers zealously desired the Galatian believers to follow them, yet they would shut them out from other teachers and especially from the true gospel of Christ and keep them only to themselves and false doctrine. The Galatian believers would then turn nowhere else, except to the Judaizers, who would then be able to manipulate them in whatever way they wanted to. The key here is why they wanted to befriend the Galatian believers: to teach them that Paul was wrong and they were right. They really did not care about the Galatians, except for getting them to become another notch in their "spiritual" book.

> **4:18** καλὸν   δὲ τὸ ζηλοῦσθαι ἐν
> [it is] good But to be zealous in
> καλῷ   πάντοτε, καὶ μὴ μόνον
> a good [thing] always, and not only
> ἐν   τῷ   παρεῖναί   με
> in [when] the   to be present me
> πρὸς ὑμᾶς.
> with you.

But *it is* good to be zealously affected always in *a* good *thing,* and not only when I am present with you.

> ζηλοῦσθαι **Pres. M/P. Infinitive** ζηλόω
> Meaning = to have warmth of feeling for or
> against, affect, be jealous over, be zealous, desire

Commentary Notes

Paul, then, reminds the Galatians of his relationship that he has established with them. He reminds them that he had zealously worked with them and he wants them to continue in that relationship as long as it is in a good thing and always. He wants them to know that although he cannot be with them, he still zealously desires to spend quality time with them. He would not treat them one way while he was with them and a completely different way when he was absent.

4:19 τεκνία   μου,   οὓς   πάλιν
     little children   of me, for whom again
     ὠδίνω,   ἄχρις οὗ   μορφωθῇ
     I labor in birth,   until   is formed
Χριστὸς ἐν ὑμῖν,
Christ   in   you,

My little children, of whom I travail in birth again until Christ be formed in you,

     ὠδίνω   Pres. Act. Indicative 1st. Pers.
        Sing. ὠδίνω Meaning = to experience the pains of
        parturition, travail in (birth)
     μορφωθῇ   Aor. Pass. Subjunctive
        3rd. Pers. Sing. μορφόω
        Meaning = form, to fashion

Grammatical Notes

The first word is the first difference in this verse between the *Textus Receptus* and an Alexandrian type text. Here in our text τεκνία is employed, which comes from the root τεκνίον, meaning "little child." The other uses the word τέκνα, which comes from the root τέκνον meaning "child." It is the same basic root; however, a greater degree of immaturity among the Galatians, spiritually speaking, or figuratively (not literal age), is displayed by the Holy Spirit in the choice of the *Textus Receptus* term. "Τεκνία [meaning "little child"] is the usual word for maternal endearment. It expresses the tenderness of Paul and the immaturity of the Galatians."[8]

The second difference that appears here between the two texts is the word ἄχρις, which is used as a conjunction meaning "until" (the time when). In place of this word the other text uses μέχρις, which is also used as a conjunction meaning "until." Both words point toward Christ being formed in the Galatians and both are used as conjunctions. However, ἄχρις is an adverb showing the time when the verb will be accomplished or when Paul will be done with the birthing and after-birth process, while μέχρις is simply a preposition which moves in that direction without fully qualifying the verb. "It differs, therefore, from ἄχρις in that ἄχρις fixes the attention upon the whole duration up to the limit, leaving the further continuance suspect, while μέχρις refers solely to the limit implying that the action terminates there."[9]

Commentary Notes

Paul shows the Galatians his concern for them by his simple personal address to them, calling them his little children. Paul had shared the gospel with the Galatians. They had trusted Christ under his ministry. He feels very close to them. He also addresses their spiritual state when he calls them little children (τεκνία). The Galatians obviously were not mature believers just yet, because they were wavering in the face of false doctrine. Paul knew this and continues to display his maternal care for them when he tells them that he is experiencing the same labor pains that he felt when he preached the gospel to them. He goes through this same pain as he cares for these believers, and he wishes to see them move on to have Christ formed in them, an outward picture of an inward experience. Paul wants the Galatians to allow God to mold their inner beings to be Christlike just as a potter molds or fashions clay.

4:20 ἤθελον   δὲ   παρεῖναι   πρὸς
I wish   Even to be present with

ὑμᾶς ἄρτι, καὶ   ἀλλάξαι   τὴν
you   now, and   to change the
φωνήν μου,   ὅτι
tone of me, because
    ἀποροῦμαι   ἐν ὑμῖν.
I stand in doubt of   you.

I desire to be present with you now, and to change my voice;
for I stand in doubt of you.

ἤθελον Imp. Act. Indicative
    1st. Pers. Sing. θέλω Meaning =
    desire, intend, will, choose, prefer
παρεῖναι Pres. Act. Infinitive πάρειμι
    Meaning = to be near, present
ἀλλάξαι Aor. Act. Infinitive ἀλλάσσω
    Meaning = to make different, change
ἀποροῦμαι Pres. Mid. Indicative
    1st. Pers. Sing. ἀπορέω Meaning =
    (stand in) doubt, be perplexed

Commentary Notes

Paul is not very happy with the situation that the Galatians
have allowed themselves to get into. He continues his maternal instinct in this verse yet he changes his tender, compassionate concern into a rigid reprimand just as a mother would
to her son who just tracked mud in on the carpet after coming
home from his first day of school. She would be happy to see
him home, but her mood would change when she saw the mud
on the carpet, since she has repeatedly asked him before to
wipe his feet off. Here we see Paul tell the Galatian believers
that he desires to be present with them, yet not to give them a
kind, loving embrace. He changes his attitude here with them
in this verse and tells them that he would change his voice
with them, if he were in their presence. Paul was not joying in
the situation that the Galatians had placed themselves in. He
was perplexed that they had so quickly turned from Christ to

works. How was Paul to know the best way to help keep the Galatians from drifting away from Christ? They had placed him in a tough situation so far as how he could help them back to the truth.

C. The challenge given in the allegory of Ishmael and Isaac-4:21-31
1. Bondage due to the flesh-4:21-25

4:21 Λέγετέ μοι,   οἱ
    You tell   me, the ones who
ὑπὸ νόμον   θέλοντες   εἶναι,
under the law   ye desire   to be,
τόν νόμον οὐκ   ἀκούετε;
the   law   not   do you hear?

Tell me, ye that desire to be under the law, do ye not hear the law?

> Λέγετέ Pres. Act. Imperative
>   2nd. Pers. Plur. λέγω
>   Meaning = tell, say, utter, speak
> θέλοντες Pres. Act. Participle Nom.
>   Masc. Plur. θέλω Meaning = wish, desire, prefer, choose
> εἶναι Pres. Act. Infinitive εἴμι
>   Meaning = be, is, are
> ἀκούετε Pres. Act. Indicative
>   2nd. Pers. Plur. ἀκούω
>   Meaning = to hear, give audience

Commentary Notes

Paul now turns his focus on the people in the church who desire to be under the law, and who are about to put off Christ to do so. He wants them to realize the importance of the lesson that he is about to teach them. The true difference between law and grace will be seen here as he reminds them of

Abraham and his two prominent children, Ishmael and Isaac, and their mothers, Hagar and Sarah.

4:22 γέγραπται   γάρ, ὅτι ᾿Αβραὰμ
    it is written For, that Abraham
δύο υἱοὺς ἔσχεν· ἕνα ἐκ τῆς
two sons [he] had: one by a
  παιδίσκης,   καὶ   ἕνα   ἐκ
slave woman, and the other by
τῆς ἐλευθέρας.
a free woman.

For it is written, that Abraham had two sons, the one by a bondmaid, the other by a freewoman.

γέγραπται Perf. Pass. Indicative
    3rd. Pers. Sing. γράφω
    Meaning = describe, write
ἔσχεν Aor. Act. Indicative 3rd. Pers.
    Sing. ἔχω Meaning = to hold, have

Commentary Notes

Paul gives a brief overview of the facts recorded in Gen. 16:15 and Gen. 21:1, 2 so that he can get to the lesson that he wants to teach. It was not that Abraham did not have any other sons. One, however, was by faith in the promise, Isaac, and the other was a product of Abraham's disbelief, a work of the flesh, Ishmael. Ishmael was born to Abraham by Hagar, an Egyptian bondwoman or slave, Sarah's handmaid. Isaac was born to Abraham by Sarah, Abraham's wife, a free woman.

4:23 ἀλλ'   ὁ   μὲν ἐκ τῆς
    But he who indeed of the
  παιδίσκης   κατὰ   σάρκα
slave woman according to the flesh
γεγέννηται, ὁ δὲ ἐκ τῆς ἐλευθέρας
  was born, he but of the free woman

διὰ   τῆς ἐπαγγελίας.
according to the   promise.

But he *who was* of the bondwoman was born after the flesh;
but he of the freewoman *was* by promise.

γεγέννηται Perf. Pass. Indicative
3rd. Pers. Sing. γεννάω Meaning = to procreate,
bear, beget, be born, bring forth, make, spring,
gender, conceive, be delivered of

Commentary Notes
Even though both sons had the same father, because they
had different mothers they were completely different. Sarah
made the choice that could be made by a married woman who
had no children: to give her handmaid to her husband to bare
children in her name. The husband could not make this choice;
only the wife could. Sarah, losing faith in the promise of God
due to her age and the number of years past since the promise, gave Hagar to Abraham to "raise up a seed," the wrong
seed. This was not from God and was simply a natural event.
God could have chosen to work in the natural, but His spe-
cialty is always in the supernatural. God would rather make
a promise to a seventy-five-year-old man and see it fulfilled
when he is one hundred and his wife is ninety. God dwells in
the supernatural. This is where He receives the glory and
honor. When man cannot explain events, he must simply direct his focus heavenward.

Illustration
Ben Patterson, in "Waiting," writes:
In 1988, three friends and I climbed Mount Lyell,
the highest peak in Yosemite National Park. Two of us
were experienced mountaineers. I was not one of the experienced two. Our base camp was less than 2,000 feet
from the peak, but the climb to the top and back was to
take the better part of a day, due in large part to the

difficulty of the glacier one must cross to get to the top. The morning of the climb we started out chattering and cracking jokes.

As the hours passed, the two mountaineers opened up a wide gap between me and my less-experienced companion. Being competitive by nature, I began to look for shortcuts to beat them to the top. I thought I saw one to the right of an outcropping of rock — so I went, deaf to the protests of my companion.

Perhaps it was the effect of the high altitude, but the significance of the two experienced climbers not choosing this path did not register in my consciousness. It should have, for thirty minutes later I was trapped in a cul-de-sac of rock atop the Lyell Glacier, looking down several hundred feet of a sheer slope of ice, pitched at about a forty-five degree angle. . . . I was only about ten feet from the safety of a rock, but one little slip and I would not stop sliding until I landed in the valley floor some fifty miles away! It was nearly noon, and the warm sun had the glacier glistening with slippery ice. I was stuck and I was scared.

It took an hour for my experienced climbing friends to find me. Standing on the rock I wanted to reach, one of them leaned out and used an ice ax to chip two little footsteps in the glacier.

Then he gave me the following instructions: "Ben, you must step out from where you are and put your foot where the first foothold is. When your foot touches it, without a moment's hesitation swing your other foot across and land it on the next step. When you do that, reach out and I will take your hand and pull you to safety."

That sounded real good to me. It was the next thing he said that made me more frightened than ever. "But listen carefully:

As you step across, do not lean into the mountain! If anything, lean out a bit. Otherwise, your feet may fly out from under you, and you will start sliding down."

I do not like precipices. When I am on the edge of a cliff, my   instincts are to lie down and hug the mountain, to become one with it, not to lean away from it! But that was what my good friend was telling me to do. I looked at him real hard. . .

Was there any reason, any reason at all, that I should not trust him? I certainly hoped not! So for a moment, based   solely on what I believed to be the good will and good sense of my friend, I decided to say no to what I felt, to stifle my impulse to cling to the security of the mountain, to lean out, step out, and traverse the ice to safety. It took less than two seconds to find out if my faith was well founded. It was.[10]

Just as Ben had to trust his friend's counsel on the side of that mountain for even his very life, so we must trust God's Word in our everyday situations. Abraham saw God work the supernatural in his life because he learned to wait on God and trust Him. So can you and I.

4:24 ἅτινά   ἐστιν ἀλληγορούμενα·
   Which things is [are]   an allegory:
αὗται γάρ εἰσιν αἱ δύο διαθῆκαι·
these for   are   the two covenants;
μία μὲν ἀπὸ ὄρους Σινᾶ,
one indeed from mount Sinai,
εἰς δουλείαν   γεννῶσα,
to   slavery   such as begets,
ἥτις ἐστὶν Ἄγαρ.
which is   Hagar.

Which things are an allegory: for these are the two covenants; the one from the mount Sinai, which gendereth to bondage, which is Agar.

ἐστιν Pres. Act. Indicative 3rd. Pers.
　　Sing. εἴμι Meaning = is
γεννῶσα Pres. Act. Participle Nom.
　　Masc. Sing. γεννάω Meaning = to procreate, bear,
　　beget, be born, bring forth, make, spring,
　　gender, conceive, be delivered of

Commentary Notes

The two historical stories that Paul has just referenced his readers' minds to were not allegories; they were facts. Paul uses them allegorically, to illustrate a point he is trying to get across to his readership, the servitude of the bond to the free. This was an illustration that all Jews would understand since their home country was near the descendants of Ishmael, Hagar's son. Paul uses these two women to represent the bondage of the law of Moses to the freedom of the gospel. The two women represent the two covenants, as Paul is using them here as illustrations. He uses the word "are" signifying that the two women are "representations of" the two different covenants or testaments (complete).

Paul directs the attention of his readers first, to the covenant that God made with the Jews at Mt. Sinai. This covenant tends to produce bondage, servitude, or slavery. Hagar represented the Mosaic covenant because she was a servant, a slave girl, and this same condition of servitude was very much like that produced by the law.

4:25 τὸ γὰρ Ἄγαρ Σινᾶ ὄρος ἐστὶν
　　this For Hagar Sinai mount is
ἐν τῇ Ἀραβίᾳ, συστοιχεῖ δὲ τῇ
in Arabia, corresponds and to which
νῦν Ἱερουσαλήμ, δουλεύει δὲ
now Jerusalem, in slavery and
μετὰ τῶν τέκνων αὐτῆς.
with the children of her.

For this Agar is mount Sinai in Arabia, and answereth to Jerusalem which now is, and is in bondage with her children.

ἐστὶν Pres. Act. Indicative 3rd. Pers.
    Sing. εἰμι Meaning = is
συστοιχεῖ Pres. Act. Indicative
    3rd. Pers. Sing. συστοιχέω
    Meaning = to file together
    (as soldiers in ranks), answer to, to correspond to

Commentary Notes

Hagar represents Mt. Sinai, located in Arabia, and in Paul's day Mt. Sinai was in direct correspondence to Arabia. Paul wrote here that just as Hagar was a slave, so too were the Jews living in Jerusalem, because they had rejected their Messiah. Since they had rejected their Messiah, they and their children were now in bondage to the Old Testament rites and ceremonies. They could have had freedom and liberty which Christ, their Messiah, brought, but they foolishly chose the works of the flesh, obedience to the law, over faith in Jesus Christ. Paul was painting a word picture of the Jews during his day for the Galatian churches here, and it is one that we can all learn from.

Anytime someone rejects Jesus Christ as his personal Savior, the only thing left to depend upon for salvation is his crummy works of the flesh. Just as Hagar was nothing more than a slave in Abraham's house, so also the Jews, who rejected Christ, plunged their future generations into slavery to the law in the flesh. The Jerusalem that Paul speaks of in this verse is the earthly Jerusalem, the one located in Israel. If you have had a chance to go to visit this Jerusalem, you will see that it is still in the same bondage today, to the works of the flesh, as it was in Paul's day. Since Israel rejected Jesus Christ, the Jews are still looking for their Messiah.

Illustration

One afternoon, down by the "Wailing Wall," I had an opportunity to speak with a Jewish rabbi. I asked him many questions about what he believed, and specifically, what it was that he was looking for in the Messiah, what the Jews were still looking for. I can not forget his response. Not one aspect of his answer had to do with spiritual items, but rather only with the physical. His description of what the Jews were looking for in their "Messiah" was almost a word-for-word description of the Antichrist in Revelation. As best I could, without causing a scene, I tried to witness to this fifty-one-year-old man who had devoted the last twenty years of his life to Judaism. His spiritual eyes were closed to such a degree, that the only way that I could think of him, was how Jesus had said in John 12:35, "Yet a little while is the light with you. Walk while ye have the light, lest darkness come upon you: for he that walketh in darkness knoweth not whither he goeth." If this Jewish rabbi only knew where his darkness was taking him. Even though I have no way of communicating with him, I am still reminded to pray for him often, because of what Jesus said to Paul in Acts 26:18, "To open their eyes, and to turn them from darkness to light, and from the power of Satan unto God, that they may receive forgiveness of sins, and inheritance among them which are sanctified by faith that is in me." There is no greater bondage than that of spiritual darkness.

2. Freedom results from faith-4:26-28

4:26 ἡ   δὲ   ἄνω Ἰερουσαλὴμ ἐλευθέρα
       the But above Jerusalem   free
ἐστίν, ἥτις ἐστὶ μήτηρ   πάντων ἡμῶν.
[it] is, which is the mother of all   of us.

But Jerusalem which is above is free, which is the mother of us all.

ἐστίν Pres. Act. Indicative 3rd. Pers.
    Sing. εἰμι Meaning = is
ἐστι Pres. Act. Indicative 3rd. Pers.
    Sing. εἰμι Meaning = is

Commentary Notes

Paul now turns his reader's eyes from the physical Jerusalem to the spiritual Jerusalem in direct contrast to the previous verse. All true believers are children of the true, spiritual Jerusalem. Since the heavenly Jerusalem is free, and not in bondage, so also are her children independent from the Mosaic law.

4:27 γέγραπται γάρ, Εὐφράνθητι στεῖρα
it is written For, Rejoice you barren
ἡ οὐ τίκτουσα· ῥῆξον καὶ βόησον
that not do bear; break forth and shout
ἡ οὐκ ὠδίνουσα· ὅτι
[the one] who not travail in labor: for
πολλὰ τὰ τέκνα τῆς ἐρήμου
many [are] the children of the deserted
μᾶλλον ἢ τῆς ἐχούσης τὸν ἄνδρα.
more than she who has a husband.

For it is written, Rejoice, *thou* barren that bearest not; break forth and cry, thou that travailest not: for the desolate hath many more children than she which hath an husband.

γέγραπται Perf. Pass. Indicative
    3rd. Pers. Sing. γράφω
    Meaning = describe, write
Εὐφράνθητι Aor. Pass. Imperative
    2nd. Pers. Sing. εὐφραίνω Meaning = fare, make
    glad, be merry, rejoice, to (be) put in a good frame
    of mind
τίκτουσα Pres. Act. Participle Nom.
    Fem. Sing. τίκτω Meaning = to produce, bear, bring
    forth
ῥῆξον Aor. Act. Imperative 2nd. Pers.
    Sing ῥήγνυμι Meaning = break forth
βόησον Aor. Act. Imperative 2nd. Pers.
    Sing. βοάω Meaning = shout, cry

ὠδίνουσα Pres. Act. Participle Nom.
    Fem. Sing. ὠδίνω Meaning = to
    experience the pains of parturition, travail in birth
ἐχούσης Pres. Act. Participle Gen.
    Fem. Sing. ἔχω Meaning = have, hold

Commentary Notes

Again we find the phrase "It is written." In verse 22 it was
not a direct quotation, but, rather, a summation of historical
facts. Here, however, it is a direct quotation from the Old Testament in Greek, the Septuagint, of Isa. 54:1. Isa. 53 is one of
the greatest detailed descriptions of the Messiah found in the
Old Testament. The last part of verse 12 of Isaiah 53 describes
Christ as "numbered with the transgressors; and he bare the
sin of many, and made intercession for the transgressors." It
was directly after this last description of Christ that Isaiah
wrote the next verse, the one Paul quotes, Isa. 54:1. Directly
after this description of Christ, Isaiah wrote, "Sing" in the Hebrew or "Rejoice" in the Greek. Paul was directed by the Holy
Spirit to quote this verse for two reasons. The first being that
the Judaizers, who were misleading the Galatians, were Jews
who were too proud to admit that their nation had rejected
their true Messiah, as was described in Isaiah 53, with the
result then being that, the Gentiles would then come to Christ
by the droves. Isaiah had painted this same picture of the
spiritual Jerusalem as being a mother desolate for many years
of her own until the Gentiles believed, she would break forth
with rejoicing, just as a mother who had been barren rejoiced
to have children. The desolate here being a description of her
(spiritual Jerusalem) without many Jewish believers. However, this all changes as the Gentiles trust Christ as their personal Savior. Second, this verse would serve as a reminder to
the Judaizers of the proof of Christ as their Messiah from their
Scriptures too. The prophecy given by Isaiah in 54:1 was that
there would be more believers from the Gentile world than
there had ever been from the Jews. This prophecy has already
been fulfilled.

The grace of God puts a song in the heart and results in men rejoicing as is described both in Isa. 54:1 and here in Gal. 4:27. It gives men something to sing about!

4:28 ἡμεῖς δέ,   ἀδελφοί,   κατὰ   ᾿Ισαάκ,
       we   Now,   brethren,   just as   Isaac,
ἐπαγγελίας   τέκνα   ἐσμέν.
of promise   children   we are.

Now we, brethren, as Isaac was, are the children of promise.

ἐσμέν   Pres. Act. Indicative 1st. Pers.
       Plur. εἰμι   Meaning = are

Grammatical Notes
   In this verse the differences that make themselves known between the *Textus Receptus* here and other Greek MSS are the first and last words, their person. The first and last words in this text, ἡμεῖς and ἐσμέν, are first person plural verbs with the understood subject of "we", as is translated here. However, some MSS read ὑμεῖς and ἐστέ, which are second person plural verbs with the understood subject of "ye" (you plural). One commentary, that was supposedly based on the King James Version, that I read to see which of these readings it accepted, accepted the latter and included the following statement, "The best texts have 'ye' instead of 'we.' "[11] Such a comment undermines the English text on which it was based. This commentary then goes on to describe how Paul was directing his comments to the Galatians as the intended "ye."[12] This might have been a possibility if this verse had been isolated from the paragraph that it finds itself in. But it cannot be a possibility simply because of its context. Paul begins this paragraph of text in verse 21 directing his comments toward those who "desire to be under the law" as "Tell me, ye that. . .". This whole paragraph is about displaying before them and the true believers at Galatia the contrast, the totally opposite viewpoints of those desiring to be in bondage under the law and

those who are not and are free. In this verse, Paul makes a
sharp contrast from those to whom he has directed this paragraph by saying, "Now, we, brethren. . .are. . ." Again in verse
31, same paragraph still, Paul writes, "ἄρα, ἀδελφοί, οὐκ ἐσμὲν
παιδίσκης τέκνα, ἀλλὰ τῆς ἐλευθέρας," meaning "So then, brethren, we are not children of the bondwoman, but of the free."
Paul concludes in verse 31 the same concept that he does in
this verse. He shows that true believers are children of the
promise and children of the free and he includes himself in
this group of true believers there also.

Commentary Notes
     Paul states clearly here that those of us who are born again
are of the promise. We resemble Isaac who was promised to
Abraham to be born of Sarah. We are not Ishmael's, to whom
no promise was made.

3. The flesh and faith and their children contrasted
   -4:29-31
   4:29 ἀλλ᾽ ὥσπερ τότε ὁ   κατὰ
          But just as when he according to
   σάρκα   γεννηθείς   ἐδίωκε
   the flesh was conceived persecuted
               τὸν   κατὰ
   [the one] who [was born] according to
   Πνεῦμα, οὕτω καὶ   νῦν.
   the Spirit, so   even [it is] now.

But as then he that was born after the flesh persecuted him
that was born after the Spirit, even so *it is* now.
     γεννηθείς Aor. Pass. Participle Nom.
          Masc. Sing. γεννάω Meaning = to
          procreate, be born, bear, conceive
     ἐδίωκε Imperf. Act. Indicative
          3rd. Pers. Sing. διώκω
          Meaning = ensue, follow, persecute

Commentary Notes

Paul now relates the story of what happened between Ishmael and Isaac to what he sees happening there in the Galatian churches. Those whose salvation had been after the flesh, according to the law, who really were not truly saved, were persecuting those who were born after the Spirit, according to the promise. They were after the Spirit because they had received Christ according to the Word of God, just as Abraham had believed God's promise and saw it come to pass in his life. Those after the flesh most obviously were Jews, just as Paul as a devout Jew had persecuted the church before his conversion. The persecution Paul now faced himself when he went out preaching the gospel was nearly always mainly from the Jews or Jewishly induced Gentiles. This conflict came because the Jews had not appropriated in their own lives the promises that God gave concerning their Messiah. Therefore, they felt that since they had to "obey the law" for salvation that there was no other way.

4:30 ἀλλὰ   τί λέγει ἡ
Notwithstanding what says   the
   γραφή; Ἔκβαλε τὴν παιδίσκην
Scripture? Cast out the slave woman
καὶ τὸν υἱὸν αὐτῆς, οὐ γὰρ μὴ
and the son of her: for by no means
κληρονομήσῃ ὁ υἱὸς τῆς   παιδίσκης
shall be heir the son of the slave woman
μετὰ τοῦ υἱοῦ τῆς   ἐλευθέρας.
with the son of the   free woman.

Nevertheless what saith the scripture? Cast out the bondwoman and her son: for the son of the bondwoman shall not be heir with the son of the freewoman.

λέγει Pres. Act. Indicative 3rd. Pers.
      Sing. λέγω Meaning = say, shew, speak, utter, tell

Ἔκβαλε Aor. Act. Imperative
2nd. Pers. Sing. ἐκβάλλω Meaning = to eject, cast
out, send away

Commentary Notes

Paul now brings this most familiar story of his Jewish coun-
terparts to a conclusion for his Galatian readership. He asked
first what happened in the story of Abraham, Isaac, and
Ishmael, so that the decision made in that instance will help
them make the right decision in their instance. A lesson needed
to be appropriated from Scripture in their lives and the choice
must be completely theirs. Sarah saw Ishmael mocking Isaac
at the time that Isaac was being weaned and went to Abraham
with the same request the Paul now turns to the Galatians
with. "Cast out the bondwoman and her son." Anything that
had been brought in that led to servitude and slavery needed
to be cast out. Whoever was not compelling the Galatians to
be free in Christ was not living according to the promise nor
were they directed by the Spirit of God. They needed to be
left at the entrance of the churches and never be allowed in.

4:31 ἄρα,   ἀδελφοί, οὐκ ἐσμὲν
So then, brethren, not we are
παιδίσκης   τέκνα,
of the slave woman   children
ἀλλὰ   τῆς ἐλευθέρας.
but   of the   free.

So then, brethren, we are not children of the bondwoman, but
of the free.
ἐσμὲν Pres. Act. Indicative 1st. Pers.
Plur. εἰμι Meaning = are

Commentary Notes

Deduced, not only from the preceding verse and allegory,
but from all that Paul has taught here, is the fact that we who
are Christians are not children of the slave woman, but of the

free. We cannot be children of both women. Christians have been liberated by Christ from the law of sin, not to be in bondage to the law but to be free.

1 Robertson, 312.
2 Seedmaster for Windows Ver. 3.1 Beta 6, White Harvest Software, Raleigh, NC.
3 Hindson and Kroll, 2389.
4 Barnes, 945.
5 Ibid.
6 Dana and Mantey, 132.
7 Parsons, *Bible Illustrator.*
8 Hindson and Kroll, 2393.
9 Zodhiates, *The Complete Word Study Dictionary: New Testament*, 976.
10 Kevin Miller, "To Illustrate," *Leadership Journal* 15, no. 1, 16 July 1996 [journal on-line]; available from http://www.christianity.net/leadership/7L1/7L1022.html; Internet; accessed July 1997.
11 Hindson and Kroll, 2394.
12 Ibid.

IV. Liberation in Loving Action-5:1-6:10
A. Circumcision or Christ-5:1-6

5:1 τῇ ἐλευθερίᾳ   οὖν   ᾗ
in the liberty Therefore by which
Χριστὸς ἡμᾶς ἠλευθέρωσε,
Christ   us   has made free,
στήκετε, καὶ μὴ πάλιν   ζυγῷ
stand firm,and not again with the yoke
δουλείας   ἐνέχεσθε.
of slavery be ensnared.

Stand fast therefore in the liberty wherewith Christ hath made us free, and be not entangled again with the yoke of bondage.

> ἠλευθέρωσε Aor. Act. Indicative
> 3rd. Pers. Sing. ἐλευθερόω Meaning
> = deliver, make free, liberate, except
> στήκετε Pres. Act. Ind/Imper.
> 2nd. Pers. Plur. στήκω Meaning =
> stand, to be stationary, to persevere
> ἐνέχεσθε Pres. M/P. Imperative
> 2nd. Pers. Plur. ἐνέχω Meaning = to hold in or
> upon, ensnare, to keep a grudge, entangle with,
> have a quarrel against

Commentary Notes

Based on all of the doctrine that the apostle has just taught the Galatians, he now tells them that this is the place in which they are to remain: in the liberated freedom that Christ has given them. In Christ an individual truly is free. If a person does not know he is free, however, or has been taught differently, then he may be ensnared by the yoke of slavery without even realizing it. He can be trapped just as a fur trader would set traps for the animals whose fur and flesh he is seeking. Likewise, the enemy would like those of us who have been freed not to know that we are.

If a person does not know that he is free, then he is in slavery, not simply bondage but slavery. Slavery gives us not only the position but the motivated force behind our actions. A person who is free is able to make his own choices just as a Christian is willing, of his own free volition, to dedicate his life to what Christ would have him do. A slave, however, is in bondage and does not make his own choices, but rather must succumb to the will of the one who has him held captive. He is not only a captive but a slave. Since Paul understood this principle, he commands the Galatians to stand firm in their liberty, their position in Christ. It is time for them to back away from the snare of the law and the flesh and stand firmly grounded in their freedom in Christ.

Illustration

While taking a prisoner from a Guelph, Ontario, correctional center to be arraigned on charges of attempted armed robbery, police constable John Bolton noticed a cross around the neck of the convict. Knowing the man was not religious, he took a closer look. The prisoner attempted to conceal something protruding from the top of the cross. When questioned, he said it was a good luck charm designed to look like a spoon for sniffing cocaine. But Constable Bolton was sure it looked like a handcuff key. By experimentation he found that the protuberance would open most handcuffs. The discovery led to the exposure of an attempt by prisoners in the correctional center to make a number of these cross-keys.

There is a cross that sets men free, free from the bondage of the law, and that cross is the cross of Calvary. Unfortunately many are more concerned about freedom for the body than they are about freedom for the soul. Whether inside or outside prison, all men need the cross that sets us free.[1]

> **5:2** Ἴδε,   ἐγὼ Παῦλος λέγω ὑμῖν,
>   Behold, I   Paul   say to you,
> ὅτι ἐὰν   περιτέμνησθε,
> that if   you become circumcised,
> Χριστὸς ὑμᾶς οὐδὲν   ὠφελήσει.
> Christ you nothing   will profit.

Behold, I Paul say unto you, that if ye be circumcised, Christ shall profit you nothing.

> Ἴδε Pres. Act. Imperative 2nd. Pers.
>   Sing. εἴδω Meaning = behold, lo, see
> λέγω Pres.Act. Indicative 1st. Pers.
>   Sing. λέγω Meaning = say, shew, speak, tell, utter
> περιτέμνησθε Pres. Pass. Subjunctive
>   2nd. Pers. Plur. περιτέμνω
>   Meaning = circumcise
> ὠφελήσει Fut. Act. Indicative 3rd. Pers.
>   Sing. ὀφελέω Meaning = to be useful,
>   to benefit, better, advantage, profit, prevail

Commentary Notes

The whole crux of the Book of Galatians can be summed up right here in this verse as it is taken in context. Paul says to the Galatians, "Look and see, based on all that I have written to you, if you add circumcision to Christ for salvation, the only thing you get is slavery." Nothing is to be added to Christ for the means of salvation. Paul was not saying that circumcision in and of itself would nullify what Christ had done for these believers. He was saying that if they were trusting anything other than Christ and Christ alone for salvation, then He would not benefit them anything. As Paul said in Rom. 3:20, "By the deeds of the law shall no flesh be justified." Paul was dealing with people in Galatia who were being taught that in order to really truly be justified, Christ was not all they needed: they should be physically circumcised and obey the rites of the Old Testament law as well. But that is not true. Paul was not tossing out the act of circumcision completely; he himself circumcised Timothy, but not for justification. Justification comes in Christ, and Christ only. Paul spent his whole energies trying to fully persuade these believers of this truth with this letter.

5:3 μαρτύρομαι δὲ πάλιν παντὶ
    I testify For again to every
ἀνθρώπῳ περτεμνομένῳ, ὅτι ὀφειλέτης
   man being circumcised, that a debtor
ἐστὶν ὅλον τὸν νόμον ποιῆσαι.
   he is whole the law to keep.

For I testify again to every man that is circumcised, that he is a debtor to do the whole law.

μαρτύρομαι Pres. M/P Indicative
    1st. Pers. Sing. μαρτύρομαι
    Meaning = take to record, testify, witness
περτεμνομένῳ Pres. M/P. Participle
    Dat. Masc. Sing. περτέμνω
    Meaning = circumcise
ἐστὶν Pres. Act. Indicative 3rd. Pers.
    Sing. εἰμι Meaning = is
ποιῆσαι Aor. Act. Infinitive ποιέω
    Meaning = do, commit, fulfill, exercise

Commentary Notes
    When a person ensnares himself in the law for the purpose of justification, he becomes a slave to the law. He is not

only indebted to keep part of the law but all of it! Every jot and every tittle must be kept for justification. To do such is humanly impossible because all have sinned! Paul had already preached this message to the Galatians, and now he is preaching it again (πάλιν) to them on paper or parchment. This message of freedom from the law must be kept within context, however. Paul was not saying he no longer practiced helping his neighbor find his lost ox if he saw it go astray, as is directed in Deut. 22:1, 2. Paul was stating that the law was no means of justification and had never been meant to be. If a person wanted to put himself back in this position as a debtor to the law, he would assume upon himself all obligation to the law and in turn he would be abandoning the liberty that he had been given in Christ.

5:4 κατηργήθητε   ἀπὸ τοῦ
You have withdrawn from [the]
Χριστοῦ, οἵτινες ἐν   νόμῳ
Christ,   which by   the law
δικαιοῦσθε·   τῆς χάριτος
are declared righteous; from grace
ἐξεπέσατε.
you are fallen.

Christ is become of no effect unto you, whosoever of you are justified by the law; ye are fallen from grace.

κατηργήθητε Aor. Pass. Indicative
    2nd. Pers. Plur. καταργέω Meaning
    = abolish, do away, become (make)
    of no (none, without) effect, make
    void, (render) entirely idle (useless)
δικαιοῦσθε Pres. M/P. Indicative
    2nd. Pers. Plur. δικαιόω Meaning =
    free, justify, declare righteous

ἐξεπέσατε Aor. Act. Indicative

    2nd. Pers. Plur. ἐκπίπτω Meaning = to drop away,
    be driven out of someone's course, to lose, be cast,
    fail, fall (away, off), take none effect

Grammatical Notes

This verse differs in the two Greek texts by the article τοῦ in front of Χριστοῦ. The other Greek text excludes it. The article is helpful because it helps to keep the reader's attention focused on the one true Christ, the Anointed One, the Messiah.[2]

Commentary Notes

If it were possible to be justified by Christ plus anything else, then Christ would not be necessary for salvation. He would be made void and His death on the cross rendered useless. A person who tries to justify himself both by Christ and something else cannot find justification in that fashion according to Rom. 11:6. A person in this position has withdrawn his faith in Christ to save him and has placed it in obedience to the law. Paul clarifies that those in this position have brought into nothing their relationship with Christ and its blessings, but they have turned to themselves and their works and really are not justified. They seek to be justified by their works, but they really are not.

A person in this situation also leads himself logically into a system of law and out of a system of grace. The Apostle Paul was not affirming that this person had lost the grace of God personally as a means of salvation but that he had lost the system of grace and picked up the system of law as a means to live by on a daily basis. Not all of the Galatians had fallen into this trap, however, some had. The whole Book of Galatians is all about being justified by Christ plus nothing, not the law, not anything! A person seeks justification either as a free gift from God, or by the works of the law. Paul points out here that salvation does not come by the works of the law, but by grace, a pure belief system.

Illustration

Dr. Johnny Pope was preaching at a Bible conference at Pensacola Christian College and explained the phrase "ye are fallen from grace" as thus:

Let's suppose I am a 19-year-old young man and I have this girlfriend named Grace. She just turned 18 and we are really in love. One day we decide that we are going to elope that night. It's 9:00 p.m. and I creep up to her house and place a ladder up to her second-story bedroom window. I climb up the ladder to take her things and to give her a kiss. Just as I get to the top of the ladder, she changes her mind about even being in love with me and pushes the ladder backwards. As I am falling backwards, I reach out and try to grab onto the window ledge once more. I miss. I have fallen from Grace. I never really had her to begin with!

Application
1. Christian, are you doubting your salvation today? Is it because you have sin in your life?
2. Or is it because you've never really accepted the grace of God for salvation?

> **5:5** ἡμεῖς γὰρ Πνεύματι ἐκ
> we For through the Spirit by
> πίστεως ἐλπίδα δικαιοσύνης
> faith [the] hope of righteousness
> ἀπεκδεχόμεθα.
> eagerly await.

For we through the Spirit wait for the hope of righteousness by faith.

> ἀπεκδεχόμεθα Pres. Mid. Indicative
> 1st. Pers. Plur. ἀπεκδέχομαι
> Meaning = to expect fully

Commentary Notes

We, who are true believers, are fully expectant of the hope of justification by faith in our Redeemer. John R. W. Stott writes,

> What we are waiting for is termed "the hope of righteousness," the expectation for the future which our justification brings, namely   spending eternity with Christ in heaven. For this future salvation we wait. We do not *work* for it; we *wait* for it by faith. We do not strive anxiously to secure it, or imagine that we have to earn it by good works. Final glorification in heaven is as free a gift as our initial justification. So by faith, trusting only in Christ crucified, we wait for it.[3]

We have hope that no one else does. Those looking to works to save them have no hope except that they might be able to keep the whole law. However, this is impossible since all have sinned and come short of the glory of God. We do not wait passively, but rather we have the down payment, the Holy Spirit as our earnest, and with that we know that our hope shall be fulfilled. "Faith is the substance of things hoped for," according to Heb. 11:1. We could replace faith with Holy Spirit in reference to salvation, because He is our earnest; therefore we, through the Spirit, expect fully to be justified by faith.

> **5:6** ἐν γὰρ Χριστῷ Ἰησοῦ οὔτε
>   in For Christ   Jesus neither
>   περιτομῇ   τι   ἰσχύει, οὔτε
>   circumcision anything avails, nor
>   ἀκροβυστία,   ἀλλὰ   πίστις
>   uncircumcision, but   faith
>   δι' ἀγάπης ἐνεργουμένη.
>   by love   working.

For in Jesus Christ neither circumcision availeth any thing, nor uncircumcision; but faith which worketh by love.

ἰσχύει Pres. Act. Indicative 3rd. Pers.
>   Sing. ἰσχύω Meaning = to have (or exercise) force,
>   be able, can do, could, might, be of strength
ἐνεργουμένη Pres. M/P. Participle Nom.
>   Fem. Sing. ἐνεργέω Meaning = to be active,
>   efficient, do, be mighty in, work (effectually in)

Commentary Notes

When a person is saved and placed in Christ, he is not justified because of circumcision nor is he condemned because of circumcision. When a person is in Christ, circumcision has no force or strength to accomplish anything in his spiritual life. A person in Christ, however, is affected very much by exercising his faith. His faith is to work by love. Faith is to be effectually active in that person's life in displaying love toward God and compassion toward man, because faith without works is dead. This faith accomplishes through this person all that it has accomplished in this person. He realizes that God has extended His grace to him in that he is saved. He in turn reciprocates this active love back to God and mankind.

B. Circumcision or the cross-5:7-12

5:7 ἐτρέχετε καλῶς· τίς ὑμᾶς ἀνέκοψε
>   You ran   well. Who you hindered
τῇ ἀληθείᾳ μὴ   πείθεσθαι;
>   the truth not ye should be persuaded?

Ye did run well; who did hinder you that ye should not obey the truth?

>   ἐτρέχετε Imp. Act. Indicative 2nd. Pers.
>   >   Plur. τρέχω Meaning = run or walk hastily
>   ἀνέκοψε Aor. Act. Indicative 3rd. Pers.
>   >   Sing. ἀνακόπτω Meaning = to beat back, hinder
>   πείθεσθαι Pres. M/P. Infinitive πείθω
>   >   Meaning = believe, obey, trust, yield,
>   >   have confidence, persuade

Word Study

The term ἀνέκοψε that Paul uses here to describe what has been done to the Galatians by an outsider, a Judaizer, is a military term. It means "to beat back, hinder, check, retard, or to drive back." In warfare it best describes an army on its offensive attack driving back an army that is steadily advancing against it. Paul takes this military term, however, and transposes it into the Olympic arena. Many are running in the race and there is only one leader at a time. Paul says here to the Galatians, "You were running well," possibly even leading the race in the area for God, advancing into the enemy's territory with the gospel. "Who set you back or who is the enemy who has impeded your progress and is preventing you from reaching your goal by cutting in on your path and knocking you off course?" Paul asked this question with such a vivid word picture to help them better see the situation. Since the Galatians did not have the enemy marked, they were being greatly affected by him.

Commentary Notes

Paul knew that the Galatians were on the right track and making much progress, so here he likens their Christian experience to a footrace. He says that they were running in their lane at their own pace and someone tripped them up. He asked them who this person was that tripped them up probably for two reasons. The first reason was so that they would be able of their own accord to identify which person (the leader of the Judaizers there at Galatia) had infiltrated their churches and been taking them off course in their race for God. The second reason was that Paul wanted to help them see that the person responsible for tripping them up could not have done it without their approval and allowance of it.

Paul gets to the heart of the matter of what is truly happening in the last part of his question. The enemy that had infiltrated their camp and thrown them off track in their race had also turned them aside from the right course of obedience to the truth. The Galatians had turned from truth to error, from fact to fiction, from reality to illusion. No one could ever possibly, since the time of creation to present, or in the future, be justified by the law. This was a lie from the enemy to get the Galatian believers off the path of the truth and onto that of error. Paul asked this question in such a way as to make them think of what has been happening. He caused their minds to focus on the key individual who has been hindering them. After stopping to consider this person, the Galatians must have wondered more about this individual, and maybe even the question why he would try to hinder them. So Paul goes on to tell them why, but in a much later verse because he has other things that he wants to tell them first. He wants to challenge them to grow in Christ.

5:8 ἡ   πεισμονὴ   οὐκ ἐκ   τοῦ
    This persuasion not from [the one]
           καλοῦντος   ὑμᾶς.
Him who   calling   you.

This persuasion *cometh* not of him that calleth you.

    καλοῦντος Pres. Act. Participle Gen.
       Masc. Sing. καλέω
       Meaning = bid, call

Commentary Notes
    God calls men to liberty not legalism. The Galatians were being flattered in the wrong way in the wrong direction, away from the truth. They had been pursuing the truth, but now were being persuaded by a lie. The Galatians should not have been listening to the legalists who were servants of their own flesh, and not of God.

    5:9 μικρὰ   ζύμη ὅλον τὸ   φύραμα
        A little   leaven whole the   lump

ζυμοῖ.
leavens.

A little leaven leaveneth the whole lump.

ζυμοῖ   Pres. Act. Indicative 3rd. Pers. Sing. ζυμόω
        Meaning = to cause to ferment, leaven

Commentary Notes

Just as when a small portion of leaven or yeast is mixed into the container of ingredients for bread, at first it is not noticeable because it blends so well and there is so little. So it is that later on its effects can be seen on the whole mixture of ingredients. Just a small portion of leaven has affected a whole loaf. False doctrine works the same way in a church or group of churches as is the case at hand. Just as leaven, if left in the other ingredients long enough, will corrupt and ferment all of the other ingredients, so one false doctrine will corrupt many other truths in Scripture in the mind of the person who believes the one false doctrine. Soon that one false doctrine becomes the pair of glasses that the individual focuses on every other truth through. All other truth must then in some way or another line up with that one falsity. Paul is trying to help the Galatians see that the one false belief, that man can get to heaven by obedience to the law, will become the wrong pair of glasses for the Galatians to use, and it will throw their focus off God and onto themselves. However, if they believe that Christ, and Christ alone, can save them, then they will have clearer vision when it comes to the other truths in Scripture.

5:10 ἐγὼ   πέποιθα   εἰς ὑμᾶς
      I   have confidence in   you
     ἐν   Κυρίῳ,   ὅτι οὐδὲν ἄλλο
  through the Lord that no   other
     φρονήσετε·   ὁ   δὲ
  you will have mindset; the one who but

ταράσσων ὑμᾶς βαστάσει
disturbs   you   shall bear
τὸ   κρίμα,   ὅστις ἂν ἦ.
the judgment, whoever he is.

I have confidence in you through the Lord, that ye will be none
otherwise minded: but he that troubleth you shall bear his
judgment, whosoever he be.

πέποιθα Perf. Act. Indicative 1st. Pers.
   Sing. πείθω Meaning = believe,
   have confidence, rely, persuade
φρονήσετε Fut. Act. Indicative
   2nd. Pers. Plur. φρονέω Meaning =
   set the affection on, care, to exercise
   the mind, have an opinion
ταράσσων Pres. Act. Participle Nom.
   Masc. Sing. ταράσσω Meaning =
   trouble, to stir, disturb, or agitate (roll water)
βαστάσει Fut. Act. Indicative
   3rd. Pers. Sing. βαστάζω
   Meaning = bear, carry, take up, to lift
ἦ Pres. Act. Subjunctive 3rd. Pers. Sing.
   εἰμι Meaning = be

Commentary Notes
   Paul has heard what choices the Galatians had been led to
make by the legalists, but he is not satisfied with the choices.
The Galatians, Paul is confident and trusting, will make the
right decision: to turn from the falsities back to the truth and
not be swayed again. However, Paul's confidence is not in the
Galatians, but is in the Lord. The Lord can keep the Galatians
following the truth. I am sure that Paul had been praying for
them already and was planning to continue praying for them.
When he put them in God's hands, he knew everything would
be all right. Paul's confidence was in the Lord, not in the
Galatians. When we place our confidence in people, instead of

the Lord, they will let us down every time, but God will not.

Illustration

I was counseling a parent once about her child who was trying to overcome a sin in her life. The parent was carrying verse cards and quotations on faith with her and even setting them up where she worked, so that she would have more faith. I told the parent that until she were willing to trust her child to the Lord when she was not around, then she would continue to worry about this child. A major problem with her continuing worry was that the parent was communicating to the child that she had no confidence in her overcoming the sin, even when the child truly wanted to be free.

So what did this parent do? She prayed and committed her daughter and this situation to the Lord. She confessed her pride in believing that her worry was stronger than faith in God to do the job. After that she could put away the verse cards, not because she did not believe them, but because she had appropriated the truth on them from her head to her heart in God. Since then that mother has told me that her joy is wrapped up in the Lord since that is where her faith is. She said the one statement that helped her release her daughter to the Lord when she could not be there was that "the Lord was truly better able to mother her child than she was." Later, she thanked me again for the counsel.

Paul might have known these particular Judaizers who were baffling the Galatians, or maybe not. In either case, he gives them no recognition in his letter, as if to say that their time is up and they do not belong there anymore teaching lies. He does, however, help the Galatians and these Judaizers to see that the false teachers will be punished for their leading the Galatians astray. He especially points out the ringleader, because as James says, "He will face the greater damnation."

5:11 ἐγὼ δέ, ἀδελφοί, εἰ περιτομὴν
   I But, brethren, if circumcision

ἔτι κηρύσσω, τί ἔτι
still I preach, why still
     διώκομαι;   ἄρα
do I suffer persecution? Then
κατήργηται τὸ σκάνδαλον
has ceased the offense
τοῦ σταυροῦ.
of the cross.

And I, brethren, if I yet preach circumcision, why do I yet suffer persecution? then is the offence of the cross ceased.

κηρύσσω Pres. Act. Indicative
    1st. Pers. Sing. κηρύσσω Meaning = to herald,
    especially divine truth, preacher, proclaim, publish
διώκομαι Pres. M/P. Indicative
    1st. Pers. Sing. διώκω Meaning = ensue, follow,
    persecute, press forward,
κατήργηται Perf. Pass. Indicative
    3rd. Pers. Sing. καταργέω
    Meaning = cease, abolish, to be (render) entirely
    idle(useless), do away, become of no effect

Commentary Notes

The Judaizers were accusing Paul of preaching the necessity of circumcision to salvation, but Paul separates himself
from them here. They were probably directing the Galatians'
attention to Timothy, who Paul himself circumcised, but Paul
has just spent the last four and one half chapters dispelling
the idea that he could ever believe works were necessary for
salvation. Now he attacks the issue of circumcision directly
as he distinguishes himself from the Judaizers. Christianity
has never been intended to focus on the flesh, the outward
appearance, without first changing the inward. Paul knew this,
and, in fact, it was what he preached. However, the Judaizers
did not want to clean up the inside; they simply wanted to
make some outward changes and leave their focus there. Yet,

Paul would not allow that to be the case. To change the inside of an individual it took the spiritual impact, not of physical circumcision, but of spiritual circumcision which came only by way of the cross.

So Paul continues to reason with the Galatians when he asks, "If I still preach circumcision, why do I still suffer persecution?" Since Paul wants to help the Galatians deal with the root of the problem, he enters into the direct challenge of the Judaizers, who continually focus on the physical part of man. Paul takes the Galatians to the root of the matter by focusing on the spiritual part of man. When asking this question, he automatically distinguishes fact from fiction. Why would the Judaizers be persecuting him in his absence, if he were propagating the same religious belief as they? They would not. He not only points out to the Galatians here that he is the one being persecuted or being charged with inconsistency, but he goes on to reveal to the Galatians what part of Christianity the Judaizers were having problems with, the centrifugal part, the cross of Christ.

He knew what was offending the Judaizers: it was not circumcision; it was the cross. The cross and circumcision could never be preached in the same breath out of the mouth of Paul, because the two are contradictory. The cross offends pride. Circumcision bolsters pride. Paul knew that if he were preaching circumcision, then it would not bristle the hairs on the back of the Judaizers. But if he preached the cross, as the only way to heaven, then the Judaizers would have to confess their sins, and the sins of the previous generation, for putting Christ to death on the cross. In other words, not only did they have to recognize themselves as sinners in the sight of God, but they also had to remit the statement that the Jews said before Pilate, "His blood be on us and our children." That is a double hurdle to have to jump to get to the point of being ready to accept Christ as their personal Savior. If I had been a Jew, that would have been a pretty big offense to my pride, and so it was to the Judaizers. Thus, Paul focuses everyone's attention back to the cross and its impact in the Judaizers' lives.

5:12 ὄφελον καὶ ἀποκόψονται
      I wish also   were cut off
οἱ   ἀναστατοῦντες ὑμᾶς.
those who   disturb   you!

I would they were even cut off which trouble you.

ὄφελον Aor. Act. Indicative
      1st. Pers. Sing. ὀφείλω Meaning =
      ought, would (to God), oh that!
ἀποκόψονται Fut. Mid. Indicative
      3rd. Pers. Plur. ἀποκόπτω Meaning
      = to amputate, cut off, cut loose
ἀναστατοῦντες Pres. Act. Indicative
      Nom. Masc. Plur. ἀναστατόω
      Meaning = to drive out of home, to disturb, trouble,
      turn upside down, make an uproar

Commentary Notes
   Paul wished to see the Judaizers cut off from the congregation of the Lord, that they by their own works would exclude themselves from these churches. It was not his desire for the Judaizers to continue in their fellowship with the Galatian churches. He did not wish the Judaizers to affect the Galatian churches in such a negative, infecting manner any more. He was tired of the spiritual confusion, the trouble, that they had caused the Galatians.

C. Called or consumed-5:13-16
5:13 Ὑμεῖς γὰρ ἐπ' ἐλευθερίᾳ
        you   For unto   liberty
ἐκλήθητε,   ἀδελφοί·
[you] have been called,   brethren:
μόνον   μὴ τὴν ἐλευθερίαν
only [use] not [the]   liberty

εἰς   ἀφορμὴν   τῇ   σαρκί,
as   an opportunity for the   flesh,
ἀλλὰ διὰ   τῆς ἀγάπης
 but through   [the] love
δουλεύετε   ἀλλήλοις.
serve [ye]   one another.

For, brethren, ye have been called unto liberty; only *use* not liberty for an occasion to the flesh, but by love serve one another.

ἐκλήθητε Aor. Pass. Indicative
       2nd. Pers. Plur. καλέω
       Meaning = bid, call
δουλεύετε Pres. Act. Imperative
       2nd. Pers. Plur. δουλεύω
       Meaning = to be a slave to,
       be in bondage, serve

Commentary Notes

   Paul now turns his focus on those that he led to Christ and uses an endearing term, brethren. He tells them that they have been called unto liberty. This is definitely an interesting verse. The word that is translated "liberty" here also means "freedom" in many senses of the word, but not in this context. The difference between freedom and liberty in the English language is that freedom is simply looked upon as just that, freedom. However, liberty is freedom plus responsibility. "Where the Spirit is there is liberty."

   The Holy Spirit is always concerned that a Christian seek to reflect Christ and be responsible for his own actions, his influence upon the weaker brethren, and his testimony before the lost. Paul wishes the Galatians to see that they are no longer slaves who have given up their rights, but that they are free to exercise their rights now as responsible Christians. Paul, just as many Christians today, did not want to see other Christians who had been freed from the Law, live in a lawless fashion. Paul did not approve of antinomianists (those who believe that when a person is in Christ, he is free from all responsibility to any law). No, Paul understood that when a person has been freed by Christ that he is set at liberty to be a responsible individual pointing men to Christ and not serving his own flesh.

Paul directs believers not to use liberty as an opportunity for the flesh. The word ἀφορμὴν, translated "opportunity," is a military term which has the idea of a site from which the enemy can attack and conquer an opposing army. It is the beginning point at which the carnal passions, the sinful nature of man, begin to control and manipulate the individual's life.

Paul also goes on to explain why guarding against such opportunities is so important by differentiating between the works of the flesh and the fruit of the Spirit. A Christian who is living lawlessly in the flesh can be guilty of any of the works of the flesh, and, therefore, cast a bad light on Christ. He would not be living a Christlike life. A Christlike life, the way that a mature Christian is to act (which was contrary to the way the Judaizers were acting) is to serve one another in true Christlike love. Love according to God's Word, just as Paul displays here, is always shown through an action. God so loved, that He sent. Christ loved and gave Himself. Christians should love by serving one another and not by making provision for their own flesh to control and wreak havoc in their lives.

> **5:14** ὁ γὰρ πᾶς νόμος ἐν ἑνὶ λόγῳ
> the For all law in one word
> πληροῦται, ἐν τῷ, ᾽Αγαπήσεις
> is fulfilled, in this, You shall love
> τὸν πλησίον σου ὡς ἑαυτόν.
> the neighbor of you as yourself.

For all the law is fulfilled in one word, *even* in this; Thou shalt love thy neighbour as thyself.

πληροῦται Pres. Mid. Indicative
    3rd. Pers. Sing. πληρόω Meaning = accomplish,
    finish, supply, execute, perfect, fill, fulfill
'Αγαπήσεις Fut. Act. Indicative
    2nd. Pers. Sing. ἀγαπάω
    Meaning = love

Grammatical Notes

The one difference between the two Greek texts that occurs in this verse is the ending of πληροῦται, which is declined as a present middle indicative third person singular meaning "it is fulfilling itself."[4] This is the meaning that our text drives toward and is implied in the surrounding grammar. The term that occurs in another text, πεπλήρωται, is a perfect middle/passive indicative third person singular, meaning "it has fulfilled itself"[5]; however, a perfect tense verb here does not fit grammatically with the latter portion of the verse in which the commandment is stated in a future tense. The present tense of the *Textus Receptus* fits perfectly, showing that the fulfilling of the law actually takes place at the same time when the believer "loves his neighbor as himself."

Commentary Notes

The apostle now takes liberty, defined as a Christian's choice to accept and fulfill his responsibilities in the body of Christ, to the place that God intends it to be: a loving, caring, responsible action from one to another, including both choosing to refrain from an action that might offend or not judging another for his choice. Paul says that all of the moral law is summed up in one word, an action, that of choosing to love (fulfill our moral obligation to) others as ourselves. It is a choice--not a feeling, emotion, or even a thought-and it is an action. Before a person trusts Christ as his personal Savior, it is as if he is strapped to the railroad track of God's law. This law is God's holiness which condemns the sinner guilty. Through salvation in Christ, however, he is freed from the rail and is now riding the train of God's love. As soon as this occurs in a person's life, he then is set at liberty to share with others what God has shared with him.

To reflect God's holiness (His purity), the Christian must love others without mixed motives. He does not display the love of God in an "I'll scratch your back if you'll scratch mine" attitude, expecting something in return. That is how the world loves, but not Christ. The world's love is a transaction love while Christ's love is a selfless love. Therefore, a Christian must choose to love his neighbor purely, because that is how God loves us. God's love is a train which always rides on the tracks of His holiness. Even so, love must have boundaries; without them it becomes lawlessness, or an opportunity for the flesh.

5:15 εἰ δὲ   ἀλλήλους δάκνετε καὶ
    if But one another ye bite and
κατεσθίετε,   βλέπετε μὴ ὑπὸ
[ye] devour,   beware lest by
  ἀλλήλων   ἀναλωθῆτε.
one another ye are consumed.

But if ye bite and devour one another, take heed that ye be not consumed one of another.

δάκνετε Pres. Act. Indicative
    2nd. Pers. Plur. δάκνω
    Meaning = bite, thwart
κατεσθίετε Pres. Act. Indicative
    2nd. Pers. Plur. κατεσθίω
    Meaning = devour, to eat down
βλέπετε Pres. Act. Imperative
    2nd. Pers. Plur. βλέπω Meaning =
    to look at, behold, beware, regard, take heed
ἀναλωθῆτε Aor. Pass. Subjunctive
    2nd. Pers. Plur. ἀναλίσκω Meaning
    = to use up, destroy, consume

Commentary Notes

It is as if Paul were writing to a group of Baptist churches today when he wrote this verse. He paints the opposite picture here from that in the previous verse. He moves from looking at the goal in verse 14 to reality in verse 15. He tells them that if they act like a couple of wild beasts that attack each other by biting and gnawing on one another, then they need to be aware of the consequences of their actions: they will mutually destroy each other. Some of the worst fights that I have heard stories of did not occur between boxers and wrestlers in a square ring, but between pastors and deacons.

5:16 Λέγω δέ, Πνεύματι
       I say   then,   in the Spirit
περιπατεῖτε, καὶ ἐπιθυμίαν
   walk [ye],   and   the desires
    σαρκὸς   οὐ μὴ
  of the flesh   by no means
    τελέσητε.
  you will perform.

This I say then, Walk in the Spirit, and ye shall not fulfil the lust of the flesh.

Λέγω Pres. Act. Indicative 1st. Pers.
     Sing. λέγω Meaning = say, bid, put forth,
     tell, utter, speak
περιπατεῖτε Pres. Act. Imperative
     2nd. Pers. Plur. περιπατέω Meaning = to tread all
     around, walk at large, to live, deport oneself, follow,
     go, be occupied with, walk (about)
τελέσητε Aor. Act. Subjunctive
     2nd. Pers. Plur. τελέω Meaning = accomplish,
     make an end, to end, complete, conclude, pay,
     discharge (a debt), expire, perform

Commentary Notes

In this verse Paul gives the Galatians directions on how to overcome the flesh, its lusts, and the strifes and turmoil that it causes. He tells them that to be victorious Christians they need to have a continual habit of living in the energizing power of the Holy Spirit on the enamored path that He has for them. This is the only way to have victory over the fleshly lusts and the fights that it produces. This is the only one hundred percent guarantee that a Christian has of living the victorious Christian life.

Illustration

A man who drank heavily was converted to Christ and lived victoriously for several weeks. One day as he passed the open door of a tavern, the pungent odor drifting out aroused his old appetite for liquor. Just then he saw this sign in the window of a nearby cafe: "All the buttermilk you can drink 25 cents!" Dashing inside, he ordered one glass, then another, and still another. After finishing the third he walked past the saloon and was no longer tempted. He was so full of buttermilk that he had no room for that which would be injurious to him. The lesson is clear: to be victorious over our evil desires, we must leave no opportunity for them to repossess us.

Dwight L. Moody once demonstrated the principle like this: "Tell me," he said to his audience, "how can I get the air out of the tumbler I have in my hand?" One man said, "Suck it out with a pump." But the evangelist replied, "That would create a vacuum and shatter it." Finally after many suggestions, Moody picked up a pitcher and quietly filled the glass with water. "There," he said, "all the air is now removed." He then explained that victory for the child of God does not come by working hard to eliminate sinful habits, but rather by allowing the Holy Spirit to take full possession.[6]

D. Contrary or crucified-5:17-26

5:17 ἡ γὰρ σὰρξ ἐπιθυμεῖ   κατὰ
the For flesh [it] lusts   against

τοῦ Πνεύματος, τὸ δὲ Πνεῦμα
the   Spirit,   the and   Spirit
κατὰ   τῆς σαρκός· ταῦτα δὲ
against the   flesh: these but
ἀντίκειται   ἀλλήλοις,   ἵνα
are opposite to one another, so that
μὴ   ἃ   ἂν   θέλητε,
not the things you delight in,
ταῦτα   ποιῆτε.
that   you perform.

For the flesh lusteth against the Spirit, and the Spirit against
the flesh: and these are contrary the one to the other: so that
ye cannot do the things that ye would.

ἐπιθυμεῖ Pres. Act. Indicative
    3rd. Pers. Sing. ἐπιθυμέω Meaning = to set the
    heart upon, long for, covet, desire, would fain,
    lust (after)
ἀντίκειται Pres. Mid. Indicative
    3rd. Pers. Sing. ἀντίκειμαι
    Meaning = to lie opposite,
    be adverse to, be contrary
θέλητε Pres. Act. Subjunctive
    2nd. Pers. Plur. θέλω Meaning = to determine, will,
    intend, desire, choose, prefer
ποιῆτε Pres. Act. Subjunctive 2nd. Pers. Plur. ποιέω
    Meaning = make, do, commit, execute, exercise

Commentary Notes

Within a Christian the battle rages, the flesh warring
against the Spirit of God, and the Spirit of God against the
flesh. These are contrary to each other. They are 180-degree
polar opposites of each other just like the North Pole and the
South Pole. There is such antagonism between the two, that a
person in the situation that the Galatian believers were in does
not want to continue doing the things that he was doing. The

Galatians were trying to add works to their faith to be saved, which is nothing more than pride. It appeals to a person's flesh to believe that he might be able to aid the God of the Universe in his salvation. However, if he is listening to the divine directions of the Spirit of God, then he will not live to gain salvation, but rather he will add works to his faith, as James states it, so that others may know he is a true believer.

5:18 εἰ δὲ Πνεύματι   ἄγεσθε,
　　if Now of the Spirit you are led,
οὐκ ἐστὲ ὑπὸ νόμον.
not you are under the law.

But if ye be led of the Spirit, ye are not under the law.

ἄγεσθε Pres. M/P Indicative 2nd. Pers.
　　Plur. ἄγω Meaning = to lead, bring,
　　drive, go, keep, lead away, be open
ἐστὲ Pres. Act. Indicative 2nd. Pers.
　　Sing. εἰμι Meaning = is

Commentary Notes

If a person is continually being directed by the Spirit of God from the inside, then he has no need of being directed down life's path by an external guardrail. Every Christian has the Divine Director of life, the Holy Spirit, living within him, and if he is hearkening (listening and obeying) to His voice, then he will automatically live by the rules. External laws are given for people who break the law. The moral law was given for people who live according to the flesh and not the Spirit. For this reason, man is to live just as morally pure in New Testament Christianity today as Israel was to live just after receiving the Law.

5:19 φανερὰ δέ   ἐστι τὰ
　　obvious And [they] are the

ἔργα τῆς σαρκός, ἅτινά ἐστι
works of the flesh, which are
μοιχεία, πορνεία, ἀκαθρσία,
adultery, fornication, uncleanness,
ἀσέλγεια,
filthiness,

Now the works of the flesh are manifest, which are *these;* Adultery, fornication, uncleanness, lasciviousness,

ἐστι   Pres. Act. Indicative 3rd. Pers.
    Sing. εἴμι   Meaning = is

Commentary Notes

Paul now describes in verses 19-21 what the works of the flesh are. This is to help the Galatians see why there is need for the moral law, because there are lawbreakers, flesh walkers. Paul makes a special point to note to the Galatians that all a person has to do is recognize these in a person's life, because they are obvious, plainly evident to all. They stand out in a person's life like a sore thumb, because they are blemishes that mar a person's character and taint his reputation.

Notice that the term *works of the flesh* is plural. Sin weaves a tight web of many strands around a person when he allows his flesh to direct his thoughts, intents, and his actions. Also note that the listed "works of the flesh" are a very intricate combination of bad conduct and lack of control in the mind, will, and emotions.

Paul begins the list of the works of the flesh here in verse 19. The first work of the flesh that he names is "μοιχεία," which is a term applied to married persons breaking their bond of sexual fidelity and purity (adultery). The second, "πορνεία," is an all-inclusive term applied to all kinds of sexual sin and perversion, including harlotry, homosexuality, lesbianism, etc., used with married and unmarried persons alike. The third is "ἀκαθρσία," which is moral impurity, moral defilement, or unnatural pollution, whether acted out by oneself or with another.[7] The fourth is "ἀσέλγεια," which is "lasciviousness, license, debauchery, sexual excess, absence of restraint, insatiable desire for pleasure."[8]

    5:20 εἰδωλολατρεία, φαρμακεία, ἔχθραι,
          Idolatry,   witchcraft, hatred,
   ἔρεις,   ζῆλοι, θυμοί, ἐριθεῖαι,
   contention, jealousies, wrath,   strife,
   διχοστασίαι, αἱρέσεις,
   division,   heresies,

Idolatry, witchcraft, hatred, variance, emulations, wrath, strife, seditions, heresies,

Commentary Notes
    Paul continues his list of the works of the flesh with "εἰδωλολατρεία," which is worship of or doing service to an idol. Next, Paul names "witchcraft," which is from the word φαρμακεία. The Greek term φαρμακεία means "the occult, sorcery, witchcraft, illicit pharmaceuticals, trance, and magical incantation with drugs."[9] Next, is "ἔχθραι," which simply means "hatred, hostility, or enmity." Following this is "ἔρεις," which is stirring up contention or strife. Next, is "ζῆλοι," which means zealously moved with envy. After this, is "θυμοί," which simply means a passionate and emotional indignation, wrath, or anger. After that, "ἐριθεῖαι" means "to inflict or attack." Next, the word "διχοστασίαι" means a separation or division. The last word in this verse, "αἱρέσεις," has the meaning of a form of religious worship, discipline, or opinion that comes from choosing or selecting out a certain idea and accepting it as truth even though it is not.

    5:21 φθόνοι,   φόνοι,   μέθαι,
        Envyings, murders, drunkenness,
   κῶμοι, καὶ τὰ ὅμοια   τούτοις·
   riotings, and of like manner   those;

ἃ   προλέγω   ὑμῖν, καθὼς
of which   I tell before to you, just as
καὶ   προεῖπον,   ὅτι
also I have previously told you, that
οἱ   τὰ τοιαῦτα
those who   such things
    πράσσοντες   βασιλείαν
habitually perform   the kingdom
Θεοῦ οὐ   κληρονομήσουσιν.
of God not   will inherit.

Envyings, murders, drunkenness, revellings, and such like: of
the which I tell you before, as I have also told *you* in time past,
that they which do such things shall not inherit the kingdom
of God.

προλέγω Pres. Act. Indicative
    1st. Pers. Sing. προλέγω
    Meaning = predict, to say beforehand,
    forewarn, tell before, foretell
προεῖπον 2Aor. Act. Indicative
    1st. Pers. Sing. προέπω
    Meaning = forewarn, say before,
    to say already, to predict
πράσσοντες Pres. Act. Participle Nom.
    Masc. Plur. πράσσω Meaning = do,
    practice, perform habitually, commit
κληρονομήσουσιν Fut. Act. Indicative
    3rd. Pers. Plur. κληρονομέω
    Meaning = be heir, inherit

Grammatical Notes
    The first difference that occurs in this verse between the
Textus Receptus and another Greek text is the word φόνοι,
which is completely absent in the other text. The word φόνοι
is important because it is an outward result of the wrong inward attitude toward someone, murder stemming from and

following after envy, as is in the right Greek text.

The second difference located here in this verse between the *Textus Receptus* and some Greek texts is that the last καὶ translated *also* is absent from the other text. This word is important because it emphasizes the fact that this is not the first time that the apostle is warning the Galatians about the works of the flesh. He is reminding them of the serious nature of this topic while also reminding them that he had previously covered it explicitly with them. With the word's absence is also the lack of intensity, which does not truly reflect the character and nature of this letter from Paul.

Commentary Notes

Within this verse is the completion of the list of the works of the flesh. The next one is "φθόνοι," which means "envyings." Following next is "φόνοι," which means "murder, but more particularly slaughter, slaying, or killing by the sword."[10] Next is "μέθαι," which means "drunkenness." Finishing the list up is "κῶμοι," which means "riotous conduct or revellings." This was generally festivities in which many gods were honored and which almost always included "drunkenness with impurity and obscenity of the grossest kind."[11] Paul finishes his list, which is representative and not exhaustive, by stating that there are other things just like those mentioned above, which are works of the flesh too that he has not named specifically.

Paul's reason for listing such things is so that the Galatian believers will be able to better recognize what the differences are between the saved and the unsaved. Paul has told them this before but he wants to remind them again, so that they can determine those who are habitually practicing these things and those that are not truly saved. Paul concludes his comments here by stating that those whose lives are habitually characterized by these things will not go to heaven, because they have not become a new creature in Christ.

5:22 ὁ   δὲ καρπὸς τοῦ Πνεύματός ἐστιν
         the But fruit of the   Spirit   is

ἀγάπη, χαρά, εἰρήνη, μακροθυμία,
  love,   joy,   peace, longsuffering,
χρηστότης, ἀγαθωσύνη, πίστις,
  kindness,   virtue,   faith,

But the fruit of the Spirit is love, joy, peace, longsuffering, gentleness, goodness, faith,

ἐστιν Pres. Act. Indicative 3rd. Pers.
   Sing. εἰμι Meaning = is

Commentary Notes

Notice that the fruit of the Spirit is a singular fruit with a total of nine different aspects which should be manifest together as part of one fruit. As the apostle lists the fruit of the Spirit, he begins with "ἀγάπη," true and tender agape love that can be received only from God. Next, is "χαρά," which is not simply happiness or contentment, but a special joy which is imparted only by the Holy Spirit. "Εἰρήνη" is next, and it is a state of being tranquil on the inside that is evident on the outside. The Greek term "μακροθυμία" follows "εἰρήνη," and means "forbearance, long- suffering, self-restraint before proceeding to action. The quality of a person who is able to avenge himself yet refrains from doing so."[12]

Next is the aspect of "χρηστότης," which is goodness, kindness, or gentleness. "It is the grace which pervades the whole nature, mellowing all which would be harsh and austere."[13] After this comes "ἀγαθωσύνη," which is "character energized, expressing itself in benevolence, active good. Goodness does not spare sharpness and rebuke to cause good in others. A person may display his 'goodness', his zeal for goodness and truth, in rebuking, correcting, or chastising."[14] Following "ἀγαθωσύνη" is "πίστις," which is the quality of a person that makes them faithful and sincere to his word and his responsibility.

5:23 πραότης, ἐγκράτεια· κατὰ
   Meekness, self-control: against

τῶν τοιούτων οὐκ ἔστι νόμος.
[the] such   no there is law.

Meekness, temperance: against such there is no law.

ἔστι Pres. Act. Indicative 3rd. Pers. Sing. εἰμι
      Meaning = is

Commentary Notes
    The eighth aspect of the fruit of the Spirit that is mentioned is "πραότης." The Greek term "πραότης" implies mildness and forbearance. "Primarily it does not denote outward expression of feeling, but an inward grace of the soul, calmness toward God in particular."[15] The last aspect of the fruit that the Spirit of God produces in a person is "ἐγκράτεια." The Greek word "ἐγκράτεια" means continence or temperance and is a restraint of natural human impulses, modesty of indulgences, and abstinence from intoxicating drinks. When Paul finishes the list of what is to characterize the life of a mature believer, he states that "against such there is no law." There is no need for a law to direct a man who is displaying such characteristics in his life. These virtues serve only to enhance a person's relationships with God and man, because they will cause him to do all the more right.

5:24 οἱ   δὲ   τοῦ Χριστοῦ, τὴν σάρκα
      those And of Christ, the flesh
ἐσταύρωσαν σὺν τοῖς
have crucified with its
παθήμασι καὶ ταῖς ἐπιθυμίαις.
affections and [its]   desires.

And they that are Christ's have crucified the flesh with the affections and lusts.

ἐσταύρωσαν   Aor. Act. Indicative
    3rd. Pers. Plur. σταυρόω
    Meaning = crucify

Commentary Notes
    Paul reminds the Galatians again of what has happened to the flesh of those who have accepted Jesus Christ as their Savior. Those who belong to Christ, because He purchased them with His own blood, have crucified the flesh. It is dead (Gal. 2:20). Not only has it been crucified, but its evil, inordinate affections and lustful desires have been crucified as well. The transaction was complete. Now the Christian must understand this truth and live with this in mind every day. Rom. 6:11 says that a Christian must "reckon [believe it to be so since it is] himself to be dead indeed unto sin, but alive unto God through our Lord Jesus Christ." If a Christian truly believes that he is victorious, then he will not give in daily to his fleshly desires and lusts since they have been crucified. He is dead to them and they are dead to him. These deaths took place when he trusted Christ, but he must appropriate this truth daily to the renewing and transformation of his mind.

     5:25 Εἰ   ζῶμεν   Πνεύματι,
        If   we live   in the Spirit,
    Πνεύματι   καὶ   στοιχῶμεν.
    in the Spirit also   let us walk orderly.

If we live in the Spirit, let us also walk in the Spirit.

ζῶμεν   Pres. Act. Indicative
    1st. Pers. Plur. ζάω
    Meaning = live
στοιχῶμεν   Pres. Act. Subjunctive
    1st. Pers. Plur. στοιχέω   Meaning = walk (orderly),
    to march in (military) rank (keep step),
    to conform to virtue and piety

Commentary Notes

Paul addresses the Galatian believers with an appeal to their hearts on the matter. Since they had received spiritual life in the quickening power of the Holy Spirit and He is the one that they claim to be following daily, they should be submitted in attitude and action to Him daily. They should be marching as a soldier in a platoon, to exactly the divine directions that He, their commanding Officer, gives them. It is only when a Christian is walking with God in this manner, that the Spirit of God can produce His fruit in his life.

5:26 μὴ   γινώμεθα   κενόδοξοι,
        not Let us be self-conceited,
    ἀλλήλους   προκαλούμενοι,
one another   provoking,
    ἀλλήλοις   φθονοῦντες.
one another   envying.

Let us not be desirous of vain glory, provoking one another, envying one another.

γινώμεθα Pres. M/P. Subjunctive
    1st. Pers. Plur. γίνομαι
    Meaning = be
προκαλούμενοι Pres. M/P. Participle
    Nom. Masc. Plur. προκαλέομαι
    Meaning = provoke, challenge, to irritate
φθονοῦντες Pres. Act. Participle Nom.
    Masc. Plur. φθονέω
    Meaning = to be jealous of, envy

Commentary Notes

Paul knew the people that he was writing to, and he knew the problems in their churches too. He knew that the problems in the churches were the people. "Where there are people, there are problems." Paul took a peek behind the curtain of Galatian "flesh" and diagnosed their personal problems all in one verse. He then spends the majority of the next chapter prescribing the correct doses of what spiritual medicine they should take. The first problem that he points out is their self-conceitedness. He knew how they acted (remember, he had started their churches). The areas in which the Galatians were becoming conceited are the same areas men struggle with pride in today when they feel they have a seeming advantage: faults, freights, finances, and flesh. Paul also warns them about provoking each other in these areas in which they have felt superior to the others. The ground is level at the foot of the cross and all are on the same level. While there were those who felt superior and disdained others, there were also those who felt inferior and envied others. The Galatians were having a problem with focusing on each other and their life situations and not on Christ their Savior.

[1] Parsons, *Bible Illustrator.*
[2] Robertson, 760.
[3] Stott, *Only One Way: The Message of Galatians,* 134.
[4] Machen, 58.
[5] Ibid., 183.
[6] Parsons, *Bible Illustrator.*
[7] Zodhiates, *The Complete Word Study Dictionary New Testament,* 108.
[8] Ibid., 270.
[9] Ibid., 1438.
[10] Ibid., 1451.
[11] Ibid., 903.
[12] Ibid., 939.
[13] Ibid., 1482.
[14] Ibid., 63.
[15] Zodhiates, 1208.

E. Condemning or considerate-6:1-6

6:1 Ἀδελφοί, ἐὰν καὶ προληφθῇ
  Brethren, if indeed is overtaken
ἄνθρωπος ἔν τινι παραπτώματι,
  a man   in any   trespass,
ὑμεῖς οἱ πνευματικοὶ καταρτίζετε
  you who are spiritual   restore
τὸν τοιοῦτον ἐν πνεύματι
  such a one in   a spirit
  πραότητος,   σκοπῶν   σεαυτὸν
of gentleness, considering yourself
  μὴ καὶ σὺ πειρασθῇς.
  lest also you might be tempted.

Brethren, if a man be overtaken in a fault, ye which are spiritual, restore such an one in the spirit of meekness; considering thyself, lest thou also be tempted.

προληφθη Aor. Pass. Subjunctive
    3rd. Pers. Sing. προλαμβάνω
    Meaning = to take in advance, eat before others
    have an opportunity, to anticipate, surprise,
    overtake, take before

καταρτίζετε Pres. Act. Imperative
2nd. Pers. Plur. κατατίζω
Meaning = repair, adjust, fit, frame, mend, restore
σκοπῶν Pres. Act. Participle Nom.
Masc. Sing. σκοπῶν Meaning =
consider, take heed, look at, regard
πειρασθῇς Aor. Pass. Subjunctive
2nd. Pers. Sing. πειράζω Meaning = test, tempt,
prove, assay, examine, endeavor, entice, scrutinize, try

Commentary Notes

Paul begins the last portion of his letter on a personal note when he states, "Brethren." He is talking now only to the true believers in the Galatian churches. What he has to say is very important because it deals with a Christian brother who has been surprised by temptation and been taken by a sin. Paul is not making provision for the church to assist a person out of sin who has willfully transgressed, planned and premeditated, but he does want the brother restored who has been overtaken, caught off guard, by sin and has given in to it. Paul knew that there were mature believers in the Galatian churches and there were immature believers, so he addresses the spiritual ones, the humble ones, the mature ones as those who are to restore the others. They were not restoring them back into the church, but they were restoring them back to the place of victory in their faith.

He gives specific instructions on how this restoration is to occur too. The ones overtaken are to be restored in a gentle, forbearing, kind, and forgiving spirit. Note that this is an aspect of the fruit of the Spirit. Probably the most important aspect here is that Paul tells them that they must keep themselves in mind, realizing that they are not above being overtaken themselves. All Christians need to realize their own weakness; it is like having a good healthy fear of God in our life. It will always help us to be on our guard against sin. God wants Christians in churches to be involved in restoring overtaken brethren, not overlooking their faults, nor being fault finders.

6:2 ἀλλήλων   τὰ βάρη
  one another's burdensome weights
βαστάζετε, καὶ οὕτως ἀναπληρώσατε
  Bear ye, and   so   accomplish
τὸν νόμον τοῦ Χριστοῦ.
  the law of   Christ.

Bear ye one another's burdens, and so fulfil the law of Christ.

βάρη from βάρος Meaning = Weight,
    burden, burdensome weight
βαστάζετε Pres. Act. Imperative
    2nd. Pers. Plur. βαστάζω Meaning
    = bear, carry, take up, lift, sustain
ἀναπληρώσατε Aor. Act. Indicative
    2nd. Pers. Plur. ἀναπληρόω
    Meaning = to complete, fill up, fulfill,
    supply, accomplish

Commentary Notes

Paul moves on from dealing with faults to now dealing with spiritual freights or burdens. He gives direction to the Christians in the imperative, which means that he is giving them an order, a direct order. He says, "Bear ye one another's burdensome weights." He did not ask them to consider it, he told them to do it. Exactly what kind of weight is Paul talking about? He is not talking about responsibilities that an individual has toward his family such as providing food and shelter for them. He is talking about the kind of burdens that a person receives that tend to weigh him down as he goes through life, things that he must continually be in prayer about.

For instance, a man is at work and gets a telephone call that his parents were in a critical accident. His heart feels overwhelmed. He tells the boss that he needs time off to go to the hospital because of something important. His boss just happens to be a Christian and recognizes the urgency of the situation and the burdensome weight that all of a sudden has been placed on this man. So the boss takes a few moments away from his work and sits down and prays with the man and says to him as he leaves, "I will be praying for you and your parents." What has that boss just done? He has borne up the employee's burden. He has helped that man sense that he is not the only one who cares enough to be praying for his parents to live. He has fulfilled the law of Christ, which is summed up in, "Thou shalt love thy neighbor as thyself."

6:3 εἰ γὰρ δοκεῖ τις εἶναί
if For he thinks anyone to be
τι, μηδὲν ὤν,
something, nothing he is,
ἑαυτὸν φρεναπατᾷ.
himself he deludes.

For if a man think himself to be something, when he is nothing, he deceiveth himself.

δοκεῖ Pres. Act. Indicative 3rd. Pers.
Sing. δοκέω Meaning = think, seem,
be of reputation, suppose
εἶναί Pres. Act. Infinitive εἴμι
Meaning = to be
φρεναπατᾷ Pres. Act. Indicative
3rd. Pers. Sing. φρεναπατάω
Meaning = deceive, delude, to be a mind-misleader

Commentary Notes
Someone who thinks much of himself in an area when he is nothing is simply lying to himself. The real problem with this individual is not that he has lied to himself, but that he truly believes his lie. The next question is whether or not others believe him, generally not.

I illustrated this truth for our ninth- and tenth-grade Bible class the other day by walking out of the classroom as the teacher, the one in authority who took charge. I walked back into the classroom as a student strutting, trying to look like a cool cat giving high-fives to different students, as though I owned the place and everyone must bow to me when I walk into a room. I pretended that another student owed me $10 and needed to pay up or I would "whip up" on him. He had it in his pocket and gave it to me (which shocked me, but made it all the more real). Then I walked back out of the classroom and walked back in giving directions to the students as if I were the instructor, the one with the delegated authority in the classroom at the time. They all sat up, faced the front and turned to the passage in their Bible that I told them to. This was natural for them and they fell into line easily. I asked them what they thought about me the first time that I walked into the room. I asked them if they thought that I was really cool. They got weird looks on their faces and said no. So I told them that this is what it looks like when someone thinks too highly of himself. He has lied to himself and believes it, but no one else does unless they have no reason not to.

6:4 τὸ δὲ ἔργον ἑαυτοῦ δοκιμαζέτω
the But work of himself let prove
ἕκαστος, καὶ τότε εἰς ἑαυτὸν
each man, and then in himself
μόνον τὸ καύχημα ἕξει,
alone rejoicing he will have,
καὶ οὐκ εἰς τὸν ἕτερον.
and not in [the] another.

But let every man prove his own work, and then shall he have rejoicing in himself alone, and not in another.

δοκιμαζέτω Pres. Act. Imperative
3rd. Pers. Sing. δοκιμάζω Meaning = test, approve, allow, discern, examine, prove, try

ἕξει Fut. Act. Indicative 3rd. Pers.
    Sing. ἔχω Meaning = have, hold

Commentary Notes

If each man will not focus his eyes on others and compare himself with others, then it will be easier for him to focus on himself as compared to Christ only (Prov. 14:14). The man will be able to judge himself more objectively, to see if his own work is approved unto God, while not concerning himself with whether or not others are approved. When he finds his works lining up with that which Christ would do, then he may truly rejoice, and his rejoicing would not be vanity. Scrutinizing his own works and testing them according to Christ will allow the man to be free from the error of comparing himself with others and thereby being unwise.

6:5 ἕκαστος   γὰρ   τὸ   ἴδιον
    every man   For the [his]   own
    φορτίον   βαστάσει.
responsibility shall take up his.

For every man shall bear his own burden.

φορτίον from φορτίον
    Meaning = burden, responsibility
βαστάσει Fut. Act. Indicative
    3rd. Pers. Sing. βαστάζω
    Meaning = lift, bear, carry, take up

Commentary Notes

The Bible speaks clearly when it says that a man is supposed to take up the load of his temporal or physical responsibilities. This verse clearly shows that every man is to shoulder his own responsibilities. The responsibility differs from that in verse 2 because the weight described in verse 2 is spiritual and is meant to be borne up by others. This type of burden is the type that is designated specifically for that individual. It is the type of burden that is cargo designated for a ship to carry overseas. It is freight that is designated for a specific train to carry across land. It is not a burdensome weight that is meant to be shouldered by other believers, but it is that specific person's responsibility which only he himself is to bear.

Once more, it is also worthy of noting that this is the type of burden that Christ delegates to those who come to Him. He stated in Matt. 11:30, "For my yoke is easy, and my burden is light." How great it is to know that the burden that God gives to each of us to carry on our own (in His strength) is light. We can have peace and rest while we labor in the section of the Master's vineyard that He gives to us!

6:6 Κοινωνείτω   δὲ   ὁ κατηχούμενος
    let him share And who is instructed
τὸν   λόγον   τῷ   κατηχοῦντι
in the Word   with him   teaches
ἐν πᾶσιν   ἀγαθοῖς.
in   all   good things.

Let him that is taught in the word communicate unto him that teacheth in all good things.

Κοινωνείτω Pres. Act. Imperative
    3rd. Pers. Sing. Κοινονέω Meaning = to share with others, communicate, be partakers, distribute
κατηχούμενος Pres. M/P. Participle
    Nom. Masc. Sing. κατηχέω Meaning
    = inform, teach, instruct, inform
    to indoctrinate, to sound in the ears
κατηχοῦντι Pres. Act. Participle Dat.
    Masc. Sing. κατηχέω Meaning = inform, teach, to sound in the ears, instruct, to indoctrinate

Commentary Notes

Paul has just reminded the Galatian believers that each of them is to bear his own burden, which is his own personal part of the overall responsibilities in general, but now he gets specific. He directs the Galatians to see that those who have been learning the truths in the Word of God are responsible to support those that have been teaching them. Just as it is the teacher's responsibility to know exactly where the learner is and teach him what he needs to hear to grow and become Christlike, so it is the responsibility of the learner to meet the financial needs of the teacher. It is like a support group. The teacher spends his time supporting, undergirding, if you will, the faith and spiritual growth of the learner; and in turn the learner helps support and meet the daily needs of the teacher. The learner must communicate, share, and enter into the fellowship of the teacher financially. Christians are expected to support in all good things (both physical and spiritual blessings) the ones God had directed to teach them. Now that is bearing specific responsibilities indeed. The pocketbook is one of the truest tests of spirituality and displays either the faith and obedience of the individual in God or lack thereof.

F. Corruption or crown-6:7-10

6:7 μὴ   πλανᾶσθε, Θεὸς οὐ
   not Be deceived; God   not
μυκτηρίζεται· ὃ   γὰρ ἐὰν
  is mocked; whatsoever   for
σπείρῃ ἄνθρωπος, τοῦτο καὶ   θερίσει.
  sows   a man,   that also he will reap.

Be not deceived; God is not mocked: for whatsoever a man soweth, that shall he also reap.

πλανᾶσθε Pres. M/P. Indicative
    2nd. Pers. Plur. πλανάω Meaning = to roam,
    deceive, go astray, seduce, wander, be out of the way

μυκτηρίζεται Pres. M/P. Indicative
    3rd. Pers. Sing. μυκτηρίζω Meaning
    = to make mouths at, ridicule, mock
σπείρῃ Pres. Act. Subjunctive 3rd. Pers.
    Sing. σπείρω Meaning = sow, scatter, recieve seed
θερίσει Fut. Act. Indicative 3rd. Pers.
    Sing. θερίζω Meaning = harvest, reap

Commentary Notes

Paul specifically warns those Galatians who were leading themselves to believe the lie that God can be insulted, ridiculed, or mocked successfully by them or their actions. He tells them, "Do not allow yourselves to be led astray into error; hypocrites do not get away with double-crossing God." The way that a man lives his life, his continual, habitual lifestyle, determines what the harvest of his life will be.

6:8 ὅτι   ὁ   σπείρων εἰς τὴν
    Since the one who   sows   to [the]
σάρκα ἑαυτοῦ,   ἐκ τῆς σαρκὸς
    flesh of himself, from the   flesh
θερίσει φθοράν·   ὁ   δὲ
    will reap corruption, the one who but
σπείρων εἰς τὸ Πνεῦμα, ἐκ τοῦ
    sows   to the Spirit, from the
Πνεύματος θερίσει ζωὴν αἰώνιον.
    Spirit   will reap life   everlasting.

For he that soweth to his flesh shall of the flesh reap corruption; but he that soweth to the Spirit shall of the Spirit reap life everlasting.

σπείρων Pres. Act. Participle Nom.
    Masc. Sing. σπείρω Meaning = sow, receive seed, scatter
θερίσει Fut. Act. Indicative 3rd. Pers.
    Sing. θερίζω Meaning = harvest, reap

φθοράν from φθορά
    Meaning = corruption, destruction
σπείρων Pres. Act. Participle Nom.
    Masc. Sing. σπείρω Meaning = sow,
    receive seed, scatter
θερίσει Fut. Act. Indicative 3rd. Pers.
    Sing. θερίζω Meaning = harvest, reap

Commentary Notes

Paul focuses now on the only two ways that a person can sow spiritually; both reap a harvest. He reminds the readers that the one who sows to his flesh (the corrupt, unregenerate, sinful nature that is battling with the Spirit of God within a Christian) shall reap corruption. This corruption is harvested in this life by way of a lack of virtue as a person is controlled by indulging in his fleshly, sensual appetites and reaps debasement, degradation, and defilement. However, the one who neglects himself and sows his life or submits his life to the Holy Spirit shall reap life everlasting. The man who chooses to remind himself daily that he is dead to the flesh because it was crucified with Christ, and takes up his cross daily to follow Christ in humble obedience to the divine guidance and desires of the Holy Spirit shall reap his crop of benefits for all eternity. His life will not end in dead, decaying corruption but life that is everlasting.

    6:9 τὸ   δὲ   καλὸν   ποιοῦντες   μὴ
       the   And   good   while doing   not
    ἐκκακῶμεν·   καιρῷ   γὰρ   ἰδίῳ
    let us grow weary, [in] season   for   due
    θερίσομεν,   μὴ   ἐκλυόμενοι.
    we shall reap   not   if we do give out.

And let us not be weary in well doing: for in due season we shall reap, if we faint not.

ποιοῦντες Pres. Act. Participle Nom.
    Masc. Plur. ποιέω Meaning = do,
    make, fulfill, exercise
ἐκκακῶμεν Pres. Act. Subjunctive
    1st. Pers. Plur. ἐκκακέω Meaning =
    to be weak, to fail (in heart), faint, be weary
θερίσομεν Fut. Act. Indicative
    1st. Pers. Plur. θερίζω
    Meaning = harvest, reap
ἐκλυόμενοι Pres. M/P. Participle Nom.
    Masc. Plur. ἐκλύω
    Meaning = relax, faint

Commentary Notes

Let us not allow ourselves to get discouraged and become tired of doing good as the Spirit of God leads us. Paul knows that those who are sticking to the truth are having to war against those who are believing and acting out a lie. He reminds them to keep fighting the good fight and not to give up, retreat, or tire out too soon and slacken their work. The field must be completely plowed and the life must be completely planted in the Spirit, for it to receive the due harvest. Paul reminds them that they will reap in the proper season--harvest time will come, but they must be patient and not let down their guard. They cannot get too tired and exhausted and stop weeding out the bad, watering the good, and waiting for their harvest. It will be there in the proper time.

6:10 ἄρα   οὖν   ὡς   καιρὸν
        then Therefore, as opportunity
ἔχομεν,   ἐργαζώμεθα τὸ ἀγαθὸν
we have,   let us do   the good
πρὸς πάντας, μάλιστα δὲ πρὸς τοὺς
 to   all,   especially and to those
    οἰκείους τῆς πίστεως.
of the household of the faith.

As we have therefore opportunity, let us do good unto all *men,* especially unto them who are of the household of faith.

ἔχομεν   Pres. Act. Indicative
     1st. Pers. Plur. ἔχω
     Meaning = have, able, hold
ἐργαζώμεθα   Pres. M/P. Subjunctive
     1st. Pers. Plur. ἐργαζομαι
     Meaning = commit, toil, effect, be engaged in or with, do, labor for, minister, work

Commentary Notes

We must be looking for opportunities to continue sowing to the Spirit. The way to accomplish this is to do good unto all we come in contact with, especially other believers. Doing good one to another is an outward sign of love. This is the fulfillment of the law in the truest sense as spoken of in Gal. 5:14. It follows Christ's supreme example of dying on the cross in place of all humanity so that we could spend eternity with Him in heaven and not in hell. Early Christians were well distinguished because of their love one for another shown through good deeds to each other. Christians need to be laboring for God in the Spirit, and their love will show through their acts toward each other.

V. A benediction for the brethren-6:11-18
A. Paul's large letter-6:11
     6:11 Ἴδετε πηλίκοις ὑμῖν
       Behold how large to you
   γράμμασιν   ἔγραψα
   a letter   I have written
   τῇ ἐμῇ   χειρί.
   with my own   hand.

Ye see how large a letter I have written unto you with mine own hand.

Ἴδετε 2nd. Aor.Act. Imperative
2nd.Pers.Plur. εἴδω Meaning = see, behold, be
aware, understand, to know, consider
πηλίκοις from πηλίκος
Meaning = how great, how large
γράμμασιν from γράμμα
Meaning = letter, epistle
ἔγραψα Aor. Act. Indicative 1st. Pers.
Sing. γράφω
Meaning = describe, write

Commentary Notes

Paul cared for the Galatians. He wanted them to see exactly how much he cared; therefore, he wrote this Epistle with his own hand. On many occasions he employed an amanuensis to write his letters and then added special notes and a benediction at the end. In this verse, however, he takes special care to draw their attention to the fact that he wrote this letter in his own handwriting. This follows the personal spirit of the letter from beginning to end. How impersonal it would have been for Paul to employ someone else to write such a stinging, emotional letter to the Galatians with the opening remarks that he made to them. As personal as the letter is from his heart, so it was on paper, from his own hand. As to the greatness of the letter, it is such a lengthy letter that a personal friend might not write so great a letter to another. Its length is probably to what its greatness is a reference.

B. The Judaizer's glorying in circumcision-6:12-13

6:12 ὅσοι   θέλουσιν
As many as intend
εὐπροσωπῆσαι   ἐν σαρκί,
to make a good display in the flesh,
οὗτοι ἀναγκάζουσιν ὑμᾶς
these   force   you
περιτέμνεσθαι, μόνον ἵνα μὴ
to be circumcised, only that not

τῷ   σταυρῷ τοῦ Χριστοῦ
[for] the cross   of Christ
    διώκωνται.
they will suffer persecution.

As many as desire to make a fair show in the flesh, they constrain you to be circumcised; only lest they should suffer persecution for the cross of Christ.

θέλουσιν Pres. Act. Indicative 3rd. Pers.
    Plur. θέλω Meaning = wish, desire,
    will, intend, determine, choose, prefer
εὐπροσωπῆσαι Aor. Act. Infinitive
εὐπροσωπηω Meaning = to be of good countenance, to
    make a display, make a fair show
ἀναγκάζουσιν Pres. Act. Indicative
    3rd. Pers. Plur. ἀναγκάζω Meaning =
    to necessitate, compel, constrain
περιτέμνεσθαι Pres. M/P. Infinitive
περιτέμνω Meaning = circumcise, to cut around
διώκωνται Pres. M/P. Subjunctive
    3rd. Pers. Plur. διώκω Meaning = ensue, follow,
    persecute, pursue, press forward

Commentary Notes

The apostle draws the lines of distinction one more time in the conclusion of his letter so that the Galatians will have it fresh in their mind concerning the truth of salvation by the cross alone without circumcision. He shows them one more time what the people pushing circumcision for salvation truly are like. They are hypocrites who like to look good in front of people. Since they desire popularity and prominence among the churches, they put on a fake facade before others so as not to lose face. He directs the Galatians to see that these are the people who are compelling them to be circumcised by prescribing it as absolutely necessary to salvation.

The legalists were not concerned about the cross of Christ.

They wanted no part of the persecution that was affiliated with it. They were concerned with their reputation in the churches and the community but not before God. The cross of Christ stood for suffering and shame. It was despised by the proud and haughty, because it meant that they must humbly bow before the King of the universe for salvation.

6:13 οὐδὲ   γὰρ   οἱ
    neither For the ones who
περιτεμνόμενοι   αὐτοὶ   νόμον
are circumcised   themselves the law
φυλάσσουσιν· ἀλλὰ θέλουσιν ὑμᾶς
    keep;   but   they desire you

    περιτεμνεσθαι, ἵνα ἐν τῇ
to be circumcised so that in [the]
ὑμετέρᾳ σαρκὶ καυχήσωνται.
of you   flesh   they may boast.

For neither they themselves who are circumcised keep the law; but desire to have you circumcised, that they may glory in your flesh.

περιτεμνόμενοι Pres. M/P. Participle
    Nom. Masc. Plur. περιτέμνω
    Meaning = circumcise, to cut around
φυλάσσουσιν Pres. Act. Indicative
    3rd. Pers. Plur. φυλάσσω Meaning =
    beware, keep, observe, save, to preserve, obey, avoid
θέλουσιν Pres. Act. Indicative 3rd. Pers.
    Plur. θέλω Meaning = wish, will, desire, choose,
    prefer
περιτεμνεσθαι Pres. M/P. Infinitive
    περιτέμνω Meaning = circumcise, to cut around
καυχήσωνται Aor. Mid. Subjunctive
    3rd. Pers. Plur. καυχάομαι
    Meaning = to vaunt, (make) boast, glory, joy, rejoice

Commentary Notes

Paul reminds the Galatians that the same men who despise the cross of Christ do not live up to their word in the area of obedience to the law for salvation. They may have gone through an outward rite and ritual of circumcision, but they cannot even keep the law that they are pressing so stringently on the Galatians. They are inconsistent in this and Paul wants the Galatians to see exactly who these people are that despise him and the cross of Christ that he preaches. Since they did not want to associate with the cross of Christ, they selfishly pressed the Galatians to be circumcised in the flesh, so that they would have something to brag vainly about. The Judaizers wanted to receive undo credit for proselytizing the Galatians to religious observance of their legalistic system of a works salvation, thus giving them boasting rights over the Galatians.

C. The Christian's glorying in the cross of Christ-6:14

6:14 ἐμοὶ   δὲ   μὴ γένοιτο
　　　　to me But   God forbid
καυχᾶσθαι   εἰ μὴ   ἐν τῷ   σταυρῷ
I should glory except in the   cross
τοῦ   Κυρίου   ἡμῶν   Ἰησοῦ   Χριστοῦ·
of [the] Lord   of us,   Jesus   Christ,
δι' οὗ   ἐμοὶ   κόσμῳ
by whom to me the world
ἐσταύρωται,   κἀγὼ   τῷ   κόσμῳ.
has been crucified,   I   to the world.

But God forbid that I should glory, save in the cross of our Lord Jesus Christ, by whom the world is crucified unto me, and I unto the world.

μὴ γένοιτο 2nd. Aor. Mid. Optative
　　　3rd. Pers. Sing. μὴ γένοιτο
　　　Meaning = God forbid

καυχᾶσθαι Pres. M/P. Infinitive
καυχάομαι Meaning = to vaunt, (make) boast, glory, joy,
    rejoice
ἐσταύρωται Perf. M/P. Indicative
    3rd. Pers. Sing. σταυρόω
    Meaning = crucify

Commentary Notes

After Paul directs the Galatians' attention toward the legalists and who they are one more time, he reminds them of the same message that he preached to them the first time he met them, the cross of Christ. He lifted the cross up as high as he could before their minds one more time as a reminder to them of how they were truly born again. He reminds them in this way that the only spiritual bragging that he ever wants God to allow him to do is in the cross of Jesus Christ. He does not want to be remembered for anything else, only boasting about Jesus!

He has already mentioned in Gal. 2:20 that he was crucified to his flesh. Now he heightens his commitment to the cross by proclaiming in writing that he is crucified to the world too and it to him. He declares himself dead to the present Satanic worldly system and all of its evil influences. He shares this double crucifixion in the perfect tense allowing the Galatians to see that it has already happened in the past!

D. The creature that avails in Christ-6:15

    6:15 ἐν γὰρ Χριστῷ Ἰησοῦ οὔτε
        in For Christ Jesus neither
περιτομή   τι   ἰσχύει,
circumcision anything   is able to do,
οὔτε ἀκροβυστία, ἀλλὰ καινὴ κτίσις.
nor uncircumcision, but a new creature.

For in Christ Jesus neither circumcision availeth any thing, nor uncircumcision, but a new creature.

ἰσχύει Pres. Act. Indicative 3rd. Pers.

Sing. ἰσχύω Meaning = to have (exercise) force, be able, avail, can do, might, prevail

Commentary Notes

When a person is placed in Christ Jesus at the new birth, the physical standing of a person's body does not matter whether it has undergone the surgical knife for circumcision or not. It does not place a person higher in prominence or lower him, nor does the lack thereof affect his spiritual standing. The only thing that makes a difference is whether or not a person has appropriated John 3:16 into his own heart and placed his faith in the Lord Jesus Christ. John 3:18 states it as thus, "He that believeth on him is not condemned: but he that believeth not is condemned already, because he hath not believed in the name of the only begotten Son of God." The only thing that matters in Christ is whether or not a person's faith is resting in Him and Him alone for salvation.

If you are reading this commentary and have never placed your faith and trust in Christ, all the good works you could do in the world would not get you to heaven because you are an old, dead creature. You are condemned already. Why not place your faith in Christ's finished work on the cross for your sins and accept Him as your personal Savior today? He is ready and willing to save you from the eternal condemnation of your sins right now if you will let Him.

E. Peace and mercy upon the Israel of God-6:16

6:16 καὶ   ὅσοι   τῷ   κανόνι
     And   as many as   to [the]   rule
τούτῳ   στοιχήσουσιν,   εἰρήνη
    this   conform to,   peace
ἐπ᾽   αὐτούς, καὶ   ἔλεος,   καὶ   ἐπὶ
upon   them,   and   mercy, and upon
τὸν   Ἰσραὴλ   τοῦ   Θεοῦ.
the   Israel   of [the]   God.

And as many as walk according to this rule, peace *be* on them, and mercy, and upon the Israel of God.

> στοιχήσουσιν Fut. Act. Indicative
>> 3rd. Pers. Plur. στοιχέω Meaning = walk (orderly), to march in (military) rank (keep step), to conform to virtue and piety

Commentary Notes

Paul places a special benediction here in this verse to those who live according to the truth of placing their faith in Christ's finished work on Calvary to save them. He desires for them to experience and enjoy peace and mercy from God in their walk with Him. The people who are true worshipers of God are the true Church of God. These are the Israel of God, not because they live after the flesh as many of the nation of Israel did, but because they live according to the Spirit of God.

F. The marks of Christ-6:17

> **6:17** Τοῦ   λοιποῦ,   κόπους μοι
> From henceforth   trouble   me
> μηδεὶς   παρεχέτω· ἐγὼ γὰρ τὰ
> no man   let cause,   I   for   the
> στίγματα   τοῦ Κυρίου   Ἰησοῦ
> marks   of the Lord   Jesus
> ἐν τῷ σώματί   μου   βαστάζω.
> in [the] body   of me   I bear.

From henceforth let no man trouble me: for I bear in my body the marks of the Lord Jesus.

> παρεχέτω Pres. Act. Imperative
>> 3rd. Pers. Sing. παρέχω Meaning = present trouble, afford trouble, exhibit trouble, bring trouble, do trouble, give trouble

βαστάζω Pres. Act. Indicative 1st. Pers.
  Sing. βαστάζω Meaning = lift, bear, carry, take up

Commentary Notes

Paul has completed the letter in full and has displayed the truth before the Galatians and revealed the error of the Judaizers. He is done answering the attack and now in a firm, imperative manner asks that no one exhibit trouble to him on these matters anymore. He has not only dedicated his heart to Christ, but his eternity, his life, and his body. He had been scourged and stoned and on one occasion left for dead. He had been scarred for life physically simply because he believed in Christ and told others about Him too. He was a faithful ambassador in the lifelong service of God and he bore the memories as physical reminders to him and others too.

When he visited the cities where these churches were located, the people of Lystra stoned him almost to death. Paul reminds them of this by reminding them of the scars that he had received from their city simply for propagating the gospel of Christ. It must have been a vivid picture that came to mind haunting some of those in the church to see the apostle stoned and dragged out of the city, left for dead. It must have been a sight not so easily forgotten. My, how he cared for their souls!

G. Grace with your spirit-6:18

6:18 Ἡ χάρις τοῦ Κυρίου ἡμῶν
  The grace of [the] Lord of us
’Ιησοῦ Χριστοῦ μετὰ τοῦ πνεύματος
Jesus Christ with the spirit
ὑμῶν, ἀδελφοί. ἀμήν.
of you, brethren. Amen.

Brethren, the grace of our Lord Jesus Christ *be* with your spirit. Amen.

Commentary Notes

Once more we find Paul extending out his arms through the written page to the Christians here in the Galatian churches as he calls them, "Brethren." He cared for them and it showed! He bids them the grace of the Lord Jesus Christ not in the physical realm but in the spiritual, to their spirit. He wrote the letter to combat the law and flesh as the means of salvation and he closes his letter with what he has emphasized as the only way for any to get to heaven, grace through Christ applied to man's spirit. "Grace, grace, God's grace, grace that will pardon and cleanse within. Grace, grace, God's grace, grace that is greater than all my sin."

APPENDIX A

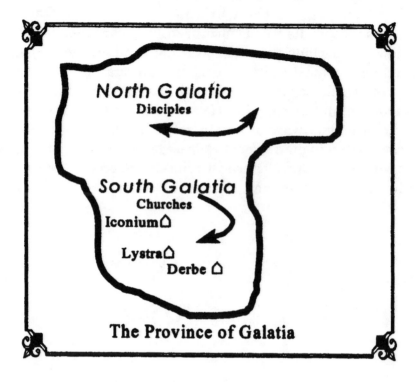

APPENDIX B

The Providential Preservation of Scripture

The original autographs are the beginning point of the history of the Greek text of the New Testament. This is where all copies of the New Testament originated whether in Greek, English, Latin, or any other language. Since the original autographs are not present today to guide scholars as to which Greek text is the faithful witness of them, it is necessary to study the evidence for each text and perceive from this which text has proven to be the most reliable. The two types of evidence to look at regarding the Greek text of the originals are Scriptural and empirical. The most important evidence is the Scriptural with the empirical (if observed properly) demonstrating the Scriptural evidence that God has promised to preserve His Word. This foundational truth must be the method of study when dealing with the Word of God. The most important view of the preservation of Scripture is God's view; therefore, the Bible must be consulted first. If there appears to be a conflict in testimony between the Scriptural and empirical evidence, then the Scriptural evidence must be the foundation from which to continue the study. Next is the evidence that has been passed down from the first generation of the New Testament text until now. If someone gets these views out of order, then he will not harmonize with the mind of God on this matter.

With this in mind, it is most important to know what God says pertaining to His Word and the preserving of it. The latter part of Ps. 138:2 states, ". . . for thou hast magnified thy word above all thy name." If God holds His Word in such a high regard, would He not then consider it of a high enough importance to preserve it? God has a very high view of His name and honors His name. Phil. 2:9 describes God the Son, Jesus Christ's name, as being "highly exalted" and as "a name which is above every name." This comparison gives a portrait of just how highly God esteems His Word above His name which is already highly exalted. If God's view of His Word is this weighty, then He definitely would not treat it as any other document set forth by man. Since God does not view His Word as any other manuscript written by man, neither should mankind, let alone Bible-believing Christians.

In Ps. 119:89 the Bible says, "Forever, O Lord, thy word is settled in heaven." This verse teaches that God's Word is established; it is firmly settled and unchangeable as well as set up in a place of authority forever. The following verse goes on to state, "Thy faithfulness is unto all generations: thou hast established the earth, and it abideth." The first verse reveals that God's Word is "settled and unchangeable far from the reach of men, in heaven."[1] The second verse reports that God is faithful to all generations concerning His Word.[2] The Psalmist gives a vivid illustration of how faithful God is in His Word to all generations. He says that God is just as faithful in His Word to all generations as He has been with establishing or setting in place the earth. "Both the Word and the world are secure in God's faithfulness unto all generations."[3] In the New Testament the Bible records the same words of Christ in Matt. 24:35, Mark 13:31, and Luke 21:33 which state, "Heaven and earth shall pass away, but my words shall not pass away." Christ draws the same analogy as the Psalmist does between God's Word and the world; however, He goes one step further. He says that eventually this universe will pass away, but His Word will still be established or settled and will not pass away. Edward F. Hills writes,

> When He was on earth Jesus constantly affirmed
> that His message was eternal, that the very words
> which He spoke had been given to Him by God the
> Father before the creation of the world.[4]

God's Word is eternal; therefore, the inerrant preservation of it is a must.

According to God's Word, He has promised to providentially preserve it faithfully to all generations. John W. Burgon writes,

> "... it has to do with a Book which is inspired, one whose
> true Author is God.[5]

There is no other book that God has claimed this for except the Bible. Since this is true, the Bible is automatically set apart from every other book when it comes to being preserved. Yes, human hands are necessary and have been used to preserve the text of Scripture from one generation to the next, but God Himself has promised to preserve His Word for every generation of people on this earth just as He has preserved His Word in heaven. In other words, the Bible is not just like any other book as some scholars would permit themselves to believe. Burgon uncovers this when he writes,

Aware that the New Testament is like no other book in its origin, its contents, its history, many critics of the present day nevertheless permit themselves to reason concerning its Text, as if they entertained no suspicion that the words and sentences of which it is composed were destined to experience an extraordinary fate also.[6]

Scriptural evidence will not allow for this assumption to be made about the Bible. The preservation of the Bible is in an altogether different class from any other book in history.

God was specific in preserving His Word just as He was specific in inspiring it. "Inspiration has to do with the recording of the truth."[7] In 2 Tim. 3:16 Paul gave the details of the inspiration of God's Word in these words, "All scripture is given by inspiration of God." The phrase *inspiration of God* comes from one Greek word, θεόπνευστος (*theopneustos*), which literally means, "God-breathed." John R. Rice says,

What God had Paul write down was really that "all Scripture is God-breathed." The Scripture does not simply claim that God   breathed on men and these inspired men wrote out the Bible. But God's claim is much stronger and more definite than that. What God says is that He breathed out the Scripture. God used men to write it down, of course, but the Scripture itself came directly from God.[8]

God was specific as to what degree He inspired His Word. He

did not simply inspire thoughts in the minds of the men used to pen the Bible. But rather, He inspired or breathed out the very words that these men wrote down. 2 Pet. 1:21 states, ". . but holy men of God spake as they were moved by the Holy Ghost." Peter was saying that these men of God were guided, borne along, directed, and led by the Holy Ghost as they spoke or wrote the Scripture. John R. Rice adds,

> Prophets who wrote the Old Testament did not them-selves make the decision that they would write the books they wrote. They did not decide what to write. The Word of God did not come 'by the will of man.' . . .The men used of God to write the Bible, both Old and New Testa-ments, wrote 'as they were moved by the Holy Ghost.' God then, working through human agents, wrote the Bible. It is God's Word, not man's.[9]

Both the Old and the New Testaments lay claim to the inspi-ration of God to every word of Scripture. Deut. 8:3 states, ". . . that he might make thee know that man doth not live by bread only, but by every word that proceedeth out of the mouth of the Lord doth man live." Christ confirmed this as well by claim-ing this same verse when He was being tempted by Satan. He quoted this verse in Matt. 4:4 which reads, "It is written, Man shall not live by bread alone, but by every word that proceedeth out of the mouth of God." On this John R. Rice comments,

> Whence came the Scriptures? Every word proceedeth out of the mouth of God, we are told! Jesus quoted that and Jesus believed that, and so must we.[10]

Through direction of the Holy Ghost, Paul distinguished the difference between a singular and a plural use of a word when he wrote in Gal. 3:16, "Now to Abraham and his seed were the promises made. He saith not, And to seeds, as of many; but as of one, And to thy seed, which is Christ." God was very careful in choosing every word of Scripture. He was concerned with even the distinctions of singular and plural. Christ tells us exactly how particular God was in this process when He states

Matt. 5:18: "For verily I say unto you, Till heaven and earth pass, one jot or one tittle shall in no wise pass from the law, till all be fulfilled." God was not only interested in making sure that the very words were there and that they were in the proper forms, but Christ informed his listeners that God was also concerned with the very spelling of each word in the Scriptures. A jot was the smallest of the letters in the Hebrew alphabet and the tittle was only a very minute portion of a letter similar to 1/2 of the small line in the crossing of a "t" in English. Albert Barnes notes,

> The Hebrew letters were written with small points or apices, as in the letter *Schin--ѿ--* or *Sin--ѿ--*which serve to distinguish one letter from another. To change a small point of one letter, therefore, might vary the meaning of a word, and destroy the sense.[11]

God was concerned with His Word down to the very letters in every word.

The Bible itself claims its inerrancy in inspiration. Under direction of the Holy Ghost, Paul wrote in 1 Cor. 2:13, "Which things also we speak, not in the words which man's wisdom teacheth, but which the Holy Ghost teacheth." The Holy Spirit guided the men not only as to which word or even the form of it but even down to the very spelling of each word. There were no mistakes made by these men as they wrote down what the Holy Spirit had guided them to write.

God chose to preserve His eternal Word "through the New Testament Scriptures and the God-guided usage of the Church."[12] God did not simply allow the Holy Spirit to breathe the very Word of God through the men He used to pen it and then simply leave the believers to fend for it themselves. Hills continues,

> The teachings of Christ and His Apostles were recorded in these Scriptures under the infallible inspiration of the Holy Spirit, and these sacred New Testament writings have been preserved down through the ages by God's special providence, operating not through a di-

vinely appointed order of priests and scribes (as in the Old Testament dispensation) but in a New Testament way through the universal priesthood of believers (1 Peter 2:9), through the leading of the Holy Spirit in the hearts of individual Christians of every walk of life.[13]

Since the Holy Spirit is the Divine Author of the Holy Scriptures, He would know which New Testament text represented the original manuscripts faithfully. Most scholars do not disagree with this fact when it comes to the recognition of the New Testament canon, yet when dealing with the text of the New Testament they set this truth aside before they even begin their research. Referring to the canon Hills responds,

> In the same manner also the Holy Spirit guided the early Christians to preserve the New Testament text by receiving the true readings and rejecting the false. Certainly, it would be strange if it had been otherwise.[14]

And Burgon continues,

> There exists no reason for supposing that the Divine Agent, who in the first instance thus gave to mankind the Scriptures of Truth, immediately abdicated His office and took no further care of His work; that He abandoned those precious writings.[15]

Hills and Burgon could both come to this conclusion Scripturally and logically. The Scriptural foundation for this is John 14:26 where Christ said, "But the Comforter, which is the Holy Ghost, whom the Father will send in my name, he shall teach you all things, and bring all things to your remembrance, whatsoever I have said unto you." The Holy Spirit was the Divine Agent that guided the New Testament Church in those first few centuries in discerning which writings were inspired and should be a part of the canon and which ones were not. God, in his Sovereignty, accomplished this "through the working of His preserving and governing providence."[16]

1 Edward E. Hindson and Woodrow Michael Kroll, *The KJV Parallel Bible Commentary* (Nashville, TN: Thomas Nelson Publishers, 1994), 1151.

2 Joel Mullenix, The History of the English Bible lecture, fall 1995, Pensacola Christian College.

3 Hindson and Kroll, 1151.

4 Edward F. Hills, *Believing Bible Study* (Des Moines, IA: Christian Research Press, 1991), 30.

5 John W. Burgon, Edward Miller, and Jay P. Green, *Unholy Hands on the Bible* (Lafayette, IN: Sovereign Grace Trust Fund, 1990), 1:5.

6 Ibid.

7 Henry Clarence Thiessen, *Introductory Lectures in Systematic Theology* (Grand Rapids, MI: Wm. B. Eerdmans Publishing Co., 1949), 105.

8 John R. Rice, *Our Perfect Book* (Murfreesboro, TN: Sword of the Lord Publishers, 1958), 4.

9 Ibid, 5-6.

10 Ibid., 13.

11 Albert Barnes, *Barnes' Notes on the New Testament* (Grand Rapids, MI: Kregel Publications, 1994), 22.

12 Hills, *Believing Bible Study*, 30.

13 Ibid.

14 Ibid., 33.

15 Burgon, Miller, and Green, 7.

16 Hills, *Believing Bible Study,* 36.

SELECTED BIBLIOGRAPHY

Abbott, T. K. *Essays Chiefly on the Original Texts of the Old and New Testaments.* London: Longmans, Green, and Co., 1891.

Allan, John A. *The Epistle of Paul the Apostle to the Galatians.* London: SCM Press, 1951.

Barclay, William. *The Letters to the Galatians and Ephesians.* Philadelphia, PA: Westminster Press, 1958.

Barnes, Albert. *Barnes' Notes on the New Testament.* Grand Rapids, MI: Kregel Publications, 1994.

Bartlett, C. Norman. *Galatians and You.* Chicago, IL: Moody Press, 1948.

Bere, Michael C. *Bible Doctrines for Today.* Book 1. Pensacola, FL: A Beka Book, 1987.

Betz, Hans Dieter. *Galatians: A Commentary on Paul's Letter to the Churches in Galatia.* Philadelphia, PA: Fortress Press, 1979.

Bible Illustrator [computer file]. Cedar Rapids, IA: Parsons Technology, 1991.

Blackwood, Andrew W., Jr. *Galatians.* Grand Rapids, MI: Baker Book House, 1962.

Blass, F. *Grammar of New Testament Greek.* Vol. 2. Aufl., Germany: n.p., 1902.

Bring, Ragnar. *Commentary on Galatians.* Translated by Eric Wahlstrom. Philadelphia, PA: Muhlenberg Press, 1961.

Broadus, John A. *On the Preparation and Delivery of Sermons.* 4th ed. Revised by Vernon L. Stanfield. San Francisco, CA: Harper & Row Publishers, 1979.

Brown, John. *An Exposition of the Epistle of Paul the Apostle to the Galatians.* Ann Arbor, MI: Cushing-Malloy, 1957.

Bruce, F. F. *The Epistle to the Galatians.* Grand Rapids, MI: William B. Eerdmans Publishing Co., 1982.

Burgon, John W., Edward Miller, and Jay P. Green. *Unholy Hands on the Bible.* Vol. 1. Lafayette, IN: Sovereign Grace Trust Fund, 1990.

Buttrick, George A. *Jesus Came Preaching.* New York, NY: Charles Scribner's Sons, 1931.

Caemmerer, Richard R. *Preaching for the Church.* St. Louis, MO: Concordian Publishing House, 1959.

Calvin, John. *Commentaries on the Epistles of Paul to the Galatians and Ephesians.* Translated by William Pringle. Grand Rapids, MI: Wm. B. Eerdmans Publishing Co., 1948.

Campbell, Ernest R. *Galatians.* Siverton, OR: Canyonview Press, 1981.

Carter, Cecil J. *The Oldest and the Best Manuscripts--How Good Are They?* Collingswood, NJ: Bible for Today Press, n.d.

Cole, Allan. *The Epistle of Paul to the Galatians.* Grand Rapids, MI: Wm. B. Eerdmans Publishing Co., 1965.

Colwell, E. C. *Hort Redivivus: A Plea and a Program. Studies in the Methodology in Textual Criticism of the New Testament.* Leiden, Netherlands: E. J. Brill, 1969.

_____. *What Is the Best New Testament?* Chicago, IL: University of Chicago Press, 1952.

Cousar, Charles B. *Galatians.* Atlanta, GA: John Knox Press, 1982.

Criswell, W. A. *Criswell's Guidebook for Pastors.* Nashville, TN: Broadman Press, 1980.

Dana, H. E. *An Introduction to the Critical Interpretation of the New Testament.* Fort Worth, TX: Taliaferro Printing Co., 1924.

Dana, H. E., and Mantey, Julius R. *A Manual Grammar of the Greek New Testament.* New York: MacMillan Co., 1927.

DeHaan, M. R. *Galatians.* Grand Rapids, MI: Zondervan Publishing House, 1969.

DeWolf, L. Harold. *Galatians: A Letter for Today.* Grand Rapids, MI: William B. Eerdmans Publishing Co., 1971.

Dyet, James T. *Galatians: Let My People Go!* Denver, CO: Accent-B/P Publications, 1971.

Epp, Theodore H. *Flesh and Spirit in Conflict: Practical Studies in Galatians.* Lincoln, NE: Good News Broadcasting Association, 1968.

Erdman, Charles R. *The Epistle of Paul to the Galatians.* Philadelphia, PA: Westminister Press, 1966.

Evans, William. *How to Prepare Sermons.* Chicago, IL: Moody Press, 1964.

Findlay, G. G. *The Epistle to the Galatians.* New York: A. C. Armstrong & Son, 1896.

Gingrich, F. Wilbur, and Frederick W. Danker. *Shorter Lexicon of the Greek New Testament.* 2d ed. Chicago, IL: University of Chicago Press, 1983.

Goodspeed, Edgar J. *An Introduction to the New Testament.* Chicago, IL: University of Chicago Press, 1937.

Greene, Oliver B. *The Epistle of Paul the Apostle to the Galatians.* Greenville, SC: Gospel Hour, 1962.

Greenlee, J. Harold. *An Introduction to New Testament Textual Criticism.* Grand Rapids, MI: William B. Eerdmans Publishing Co., 1964.

Gromacki, Robert G. *New Testament Survey.* Grand Rapids, MI: Baker Book House, 1974.

Guthrie, Donald. *Galatians.* London: Marshall, Morgan & Scott, 1977.

_____. *New Testament Introduction.* Downers Grove, IL: Inter-Varsity Press, 1970.

Gutzke, Manford George. *Plain Talk on Galatians.* Grand Rapids, MI: Zondervan Publishing House, 1972.

Hamilton, Floyd E. *The Epistle to the Galatians.* Grand Rapids, MI: Baker Book House, 1959.

Harrison, Everett F. *Introduction to the New Testament.* Grand Rapids, MI: Wm. B. Eerdmans Publishing Co., 1964.

Hendriksen, William. *Galatians and Ephesians.* Grand Rapids, MI: Baker Book House, 1979.

Herklots, H. G. G. *How Our Bible Came to Us.* New York: Oxford University Press, 1954.

Hills, Edward F. *Believing Bible Study.* Des Moines, IA: Christian Research Press, 1991.

_____. *The King James Version Defended.* Des Moines, IA: Christian Research Press, 1984.

Hindson, Edward E., and Woodrow Michael Kroll. *The KJV Parallel Bible Commentary.* Nashville, TN: Thomas Nelson Publishers, 1994.

Hort, A. F. *Life and Letters of Fenton John Anthony Hort.* 2 vols. London: Macmillan and Co., 1896.

Howard, George. *Paul: Crisis in Galatia.* Cambridge: Cambridge University Press, 1979.

Hunter, A. M. *Introducing the New Testament.* Philadelphia, PA: Westminster Press, 1946.

Ironside, H. A. *Expository Messages on the Epistle to the Galatians.* Neptune, NJ: Loizeaux Brothers, 1978.

Josephus, Flavius. *The Works of Josephus: New Updated Edition.* Peabody, MA: Hendrickson Publishers, 1991.

Kent, Homer A., Jr. *The Freedom of God's Sons: Studies in Galatians.* Grand Rapids, MI: Baker Book House, 1976.

Kenyon, Frederic. *Handbook to the Textual Criticism of the New Testament.* New York: Harper and Brothers, n.d.

_____. *Our Bible and the Ancient Manuscripts.* New York, NY: Harper and Brothers, 1951.

Knudsen, Ralph E. *Knowing the New Testament.* Philadelphia, PA: Judson Press, 1954.

Kroll, Woodrow Michael. *Prescription for Preaching.* Grand Rapids, MI: Baker Book House, 1991.

Kummel, Werner Georg. *Introduction to the New Testament.* Translated by Howard Clark Kee. Nashville, TN: Abingdon Press, 1975.

Lange, John Peter. *Lange's Commentary on the Holy Scriptures.* Vol. VII. Grand Rapids, MI: Zondervan Publishing House, 1960.

Lenehan, Arthur. "To Illustrate." *Leadership Journal* 18, no. 1, 14 January 1997 [journal on-line]. Available from http://www.christianity.net/leadership/features/illustrate.html. Internet. Accessed February 1997.

Lightfoot, J. B. *The Epistle of St. Paul to the Galatians.* Grand Rapids, MI: Zondervan Publishing House, 1974.

Logan, Samuel T., Jr. *The Preacher and Preaching.* Phillipsburg, NJ: Presbyterian and Reformed Publishing Co., 1986.

Luther, Martin. *A Commentary on St. Paul's Epistle to the Galatians.* London: J. Clark Publishing House, 1953.

Machen, J. Gresham. *New Testament Greek for Beginners.* New York: Macmillan Publishing House, 1923.

Mauro, Philip. *Our Liberty in Christ.* New York: Fleming H. Revell Co., 1900.

McGee, J. Vernon. *Galatians.* Pasadena, CA: Thru the Bible Books, 1977.

M'Clymont, J. A. *The New Testament and Its Writers.* New York: Fleming H. Revell Co., n.d.

McNeile, A. H. *An Introduction to the Study of the New Testament.* Oxford: Clarendon Press, 1953.

Metzger, Bruce M. *Chapters in the History of New Testament Textual Criticism.* Leiden, Netherlands: E. J. Brill, 1963.

Miller, Edward. *A Guide to the Textual Criticism of the New Testament.* New Jersey: Dean Burgon Society, 1979.

Miller, Kevin. "To Illustrate." *Leadership Journal* 15, no.1, 16 July 1996 [journal on-line]. Available from http://www.christianity.net/leadership/7L1/7L1022.html. Internet. Accessed July 1997.

Moorman, Jack. *Forever Settled.* Collingswood, NJ: Bible for Today Press, 1985.

Mullenix, Joel. Class notes for the course Galatians and Prison Epistles, Pensacola Christian College, 1994.

_____. The History of the English Bible lecture, fall 1995, Pensacola Christian College.

Neil, William. *The Letter of Paul to the Galatians.* Great Britain: Cambridge University Press, 1967.

Parsons Technology. Bible Illustrator. [Computer file]. Cedar Rapids, IA: Parsons, 1991.

Pattie, T. S. *Manuscripts of the Bible.* London: British Library, 1985.

Pickering, Wilbur N. *The Identity of the New Testament Text.* Nashville, TN: Thomas Nelson Publishers, 1980.

Rairdin, Craig, and Parsons Technology, Inc., QuickVerse for Windows, Version 3.0j, Computer Program. Cedar Rapids, IA: 1992-1994.

Ramm, Bernard L. *Hermeneutics.* Grand Rapids, MI: Baker Book House, 1967.

Ramsey, William M. *A Historical Commentary on St. Paul's Epistle to the Galatians.* Grand Rapids, MI: Baker Book House, 1979.

Rice, John R. *Our Perfect Book.* Murfreesboro, TN: Sword of the Lord Publishers, 1958.

Rice, John R. *The RICE Reference Bible.* Nashville, TN: Thomas Nelson Publishers, 1981.

Ridderbos, Herman N. *The Epistle of Paul to the Churches of Galatia.* Grand Rapids, MI: Wm. B. Eerdmans Publishing Co., 1953.

Robertson, A. T. *A Grammar of the Greek New Testament in the Light of Historical Research.* Nashville, TN: Broadman Press, 1934.

Robertson, A. T., and W. Hersey Davis, *A New Short Grammar of the Greek Testament.* Grand Rapids, MI: Baker Book House, 1977.

Robinson, Haddon W. *Biblical Preaching.* Grand Rapids, MI: Baker Book House, 1980.

Robinson, John A. T. *Redating the New Testament.* Philadelphia, PA: Westminster Press, 1976.

Roddy, Clarence Stonelynn, ed. *We Prepare and Preach.* Chicago, IL: Moody Press, 1959.

Rowlingson, Donald T. *Introduction to the New Testament Study.* New York: Macmillan Co., 1956.

Sangster, W. E. *The Craft of Sermon Construction.* USA: W. L. Jenkins, 1951.

Schaff, Philip. *A Companion to the Greek Testament and the English Version.* Franklin Square, NY: Harper & Brothers, 1885.

_____. Introduction to Westcott and Hort's *The New Testament in the Original Greek.* New York: Harper & Brothers, 1895.

Scrivener, Frederick Henry Ambrose. *A Plain Introduction to the Criticism of the New Testament.* 3d ed. Cambridge: University Press, 1883.

Seedmaster for Windows Ver. 3.1 Beta 6. White Harvest Software, Raleigh, NC: 1995.

Soden, Hermann Von. *The History of Early Christian Literature*. Translated by J. R. Wilkinson and edited by W. D. Morrison. New York, NY: G. P. Putman's Sons, 1906.

Souter, Alexander. *The Text and Canon of the New Testament*. London: Duckworth and Co., 1913.

Stevens, George B. *A Short Exposition of the Epistle to the Galatians*. Hartford, CT: Student Publishing Co., 1890.

Stott, John R. W. *Only One Way, The Message of Galatians*. Downers Grove, IL: InterVarsity Press, 1968.

Strauss, Lehman. *Devotional Studies in Galatians and Ephesians*. Neptune, NJ: Loizeaux Brothers, 1957.

Taylor, Vincent. *The Text of the New Testament*. Great Britain: St. Martin's Press, 1961.

Tenney, Merrill C. *Galatians: The Charter of Christian Liberty*. Grand Rapids, MI: Wm. B. Eerdmans Publishing Co., 1957.

_____. *The New Testament*. Grand Rapids, MI: Wm. B. Eerdmans Publishing Co., 1953.

Thiessen, H. C. *Introduction to the New Testament*. Grand Rapids, MI: Wm. B. Eerdmans Publishing Co.,1943.

_____. *Introductory Lectures in Systematic Theology*. Grand Rapids, MI: Wm. B. Eerdmans Publishing Co., 1949.

Trinitarian Bible Society, Preface to *The New Testament*. Avon: Bath Press, 1985.

United Bible Society, Preface to *The Greek New Testament*. Germany: United Bible Society, 1983.

Vines, Jerry. *A Practical Guide to Sermon Preparation*. Chicago, IL: Moody Press, 1985.

Vos, Howard F. *Galatians, A Call to Christian Liberty*. Chicago, IL: Moody Press, 1971.

Waite, D. A. *Defending the King James Bible*. Collingswood, NJ: Bible for Today Press, 1992.

Westcott, B. F., and F. J. A. Hort. *The New Testament in the Original Greek*. 2 vols. London: Macmillan and Co., 1881.

Whitesell, Faris Daniel. *The Art of Biblical Preaching*. Grand Rapids, MI: Zondervan Publishing House, 1950.

Wiersbe, Warren W. *Be Free*. Wheaton, IL: Victor Books, 1988.

Winer, G. B. *A Treatise on the Grammar of New Testament Greek*. Edinburgh, Germany: T. & T. Clark, 1882.

Wuest, Kenneth S. *Galatians in the Greek New Testament*. Grand Rapids, MI: Wm. B. Eerdmans Publishing Co., 1944.

Yoho, Walter Allen. Pneumatology class notes. Pensacola Christian College, 1995.

Zodhiates, Spiros. *The Complete Word Study Dictionary: New Testament*. Chattanooga, TN: AMG Publishers, 1993.

_____. *The Hebrew-Greek Key Study Bible*. Chattanooga, TN: AMG Publishers, 1991.

_____. *Lexical Aids to the New Testament*. Chattanooga, TN: AMG Publishers, 1991.

ABOUT THE AUTHOR

Dr. Stanley was named after his grandfather, Harry E. Stanley, who was saved early in life and called of God to pastor a church, and then into evangelism for some time in America. The last fifteen years of his life he was a missionary to Haiti. There he was used of God greatly. He loved to preach the Word and on one occasion held revival services with John R. Rice in Oklahoma. The Lord chose to take him home as he began to preach a revival service in an old fashioned campmeeting in the hills of Pennsylvania. One day in heaven Harry will meet his grandfather, who died before he was born, face to face for the first time.

Harry E. Stanley II was saved when he was thirteen and called of God to preach His Word at the age of sixteen. He graduated from Bible college with an Evangelism major and a minor in Biblical Languages. After finishing his masters degree, the Lord directed him to complete his doctorate at Pensacola Christian College. God has given him the opportunity to teach the Bible at both Bible college and Seminary graduate levels.

Prior to publishing this book, Dr. Stanley has also completed a basic guide to help Christians become better soul winners. He has been serving at Eagle Heights Baptist Church for the past four years as the Minister of Outreach with his father-in-law, Dr. Tom Sooter, who is the Pastor, and loves serving the Lord. He is continuing faithfully in ministry as Timothy was instructed, "But continue thou in the things which thou hast learned." (2 Timothy 3:14)

God has richly blessed Dr. Stanley's home through his beautiful wife, Gina, who also speaks to ladies' groups and four lovely children.